ALL BY MY SELVES

Walter, Peanut, Achmed, and Me

JEFF DUNHAM

NEW AMERICAN LIBRARY

New American Library
Published by New American Library, a division of
Penguin Group (USA) Inc., 375 Hudson Street,
New York, New York 10014, USA
Penguin Group (Canada), 90 Eglinton Avenue East, Suite 700, Toronto, Ontario M4P 2Y3, Canada (a division
of Pearson Penguin Canada Inc.); Penguin Books Ltd., 80 Strand, London WC2R 0RL, England; Penguin
Ireland, 25 St. Stephen's Green, Dublin 2, Ireland (a division of Penguin Books Ltd.); Penguin Group (Aus-
tralia), 250 Camberwell Road, Camberwell, Victoria 3124, Australia (a division of Pearson Australia Group
Pty. Ltd.); Penguin Books India Pvt. Ltd., 11 Community Centre, Panchsheel Park, New Delhi - 110 017,
India; Penguin Group (NZ), 67 Apollo Drive, Rosedale, Auckland 0632, New Zealand (a division of Pearson
New Zealand Ltd.); Penguin Books (South Africa) (Pty.) Ltd., 24 Sturdee Avenue, Rosebank, Johannesburg
2196, South Africa

Penguin Books Ltd., Registered Offices:
80 Strand, London WC2R 0RL, England

Published by New American Library, a division of Penguin Group (USA) Inc. Previously published in a
Dutton edition.

First New American Library Printing, September 2011
10 9 8 7 6 5 4 3 2 1

Illustrations by R. York Funston

Photo credits (numbers refer to photograph sequence):
Courtesy of the author: 1–5, 7–10, 12–15, 18, 20, 23–25, 27–32; courtesy ACTS Finals, 11; Carson Entertain-
ment Group, 16; Cleveland Improv, 17; Dick Clark Productions, Inc., 19; Steven Whitson, 21; NBC Universal
Photo Archive, 22; Fox Sports Net, Inc., 26; Gary Miller, 33

 REGISTERED TRADEMARK—MARCA REGISTRADA

New American Library Trade Paperback ISBN: 978-0-451-23469-8

The Library of Congress has cataloged the hardcover edition of this title as follows:

Dunham, Jeff, 1960–
    All by my selves: Walter, Peanut, Achmed, and me/Jeff Dunham
        p. cm
    ISBN 978-0-525-95141-4
    1. Dunham, Jeff, 1960–   2. Comedians—United States—Biography.   3. Ventriloquists—Biography.
4. Ventriloquism. I. Title.
    PN2287.D846D86   2010
    792.7'6028092—dc22
    [B]
    2009019368

Designed by Spring Hoteling

Printed in the United States of America

"Easily one of the funniest stand-up comics alive."
                                   —*The Dallas Morning News*

His YouTube videos have been viewed more than half a billion times. He has played to sold-out venues across North America, Europe, South Africa, and Australia. He has sold more than seven million DVDs, *Forbes* has ranked him in their Celebrity 100 list of the most powerful entertainers for two years running, and he has been the top touring comedian in the world for the past two years according to *Pollstar* magazine.

All by My Selves is the story of one pretty ordinary guy, one interesting hobby, one very understanding set of parents, and a long, winding road to becoming America's favorite comedian. With wit, honesty, and lots of great show business detail, Jeff Dunham shares for his legion of fans how he took what many considered an outdated art form and made it cool again.

"Dunham is the most successful comedian working in America."
                                   —*The New York Times Magazine*

For my parents. Why? Keep reading.

CONTENTS

INTRODUCTION

....

The Possibility of Crazy

I was never one of the cool kids. On the other hand, I don't think I was one of the particularly weird ones either. I was just more interested in doing things that the others weren't. It wasn't a conscious decision—I simply liked driving off the pavement every so often. If you get that, then you'll understand why I consider my everyday life these days to be pretty great.

I make my living standing in front of thousands of folks, usually four or five nights a week, carrying on conversations with formerly inanimate characters that have come to life with my hand stuck up their backsides. There's a curmudgeonly old man, hewn of only the finest hardwoods and some fiberglass. There's a soft, fuzzy, purple mischief maker who acts like he's lingered a little too long at Starbucks. There's a reluctant, slow-paced, mustached Mexican jalapeño on a stick; a skeletal suicide-bombing dead terrorist; a beer-guzzling, NASCAR-loving, cross-eyed white-trash redneck; an African American pimp who doubles as my manager; and finally a two-and-a-half-foot tall, giant-nosed superhero who claims he stopped a speeding bullet . . . once. Their names are simple and seemingly innocent enough: Walter, Peanut, José, Achmed, Bubba J., Sweet Daddy Dee, and Melvin. But their words bring laughter, start personal arguments, and sometimes create big controversies.

This "suitcase posse" and I regularly crisscross North America by bus and plane to play well over a hundred gigs a year. Plus, we've been to Europe and Australia, performing in London, Dublin, Amsterdam, Stockholm, Copenhagen, Helsinki, Oslo, Sydney, and Melbourne to an average of seven thousand people at each show. Many mornings I wake up trying to remember where I am before I open my eyes. The schedule can be a little disorienting, and sometimes even dangerous. In fact, I can accurately state that I'm the only American to have been rescued *from* the U.S. military *by* a foreign terrorist.

Many people would call my life crazy. I say it's refreshingly unconventional. But whatever you call it, it's all thanks to a trunkful of dummies. I've been pursuing this career since my first performance as a ventriloquist at age eight. Before lunchtime on that particular school day in 1971, I knew exactly what I wanted as a career for the rest of my life.

The odds of succeeding in my chosen profession have always been terrible. There are probably three thousand stand-up comedians in this country, and less than half of them make enough money to live just by touring. But then the number of *ventriloquists* that make a full-time living would barely fill up a clown car. After forty years of being onstage, it has taken far longer than I imagined to achieve any of the goals I set for myself so long ago, but my childhood pursuit of this dream has never wavered . . . not once. On the other hand, when you need a puppet named Achmed the Dead Terrorist to save your ass from a bunch of U.S. Marines pointing M4 rifles at your head, you kind of get to thinking that yeah, maybe this *is* a little crazy.

Peanut: Do we get to talk in this book?

Walter: You mean *annoy* everyone?

Peanut: Hey!

Achmed: I will KEEL the readers who do not like this publication!

 Jeff: No, you won't . . .

 Bubba J.: Can I say something too?

 Jeff: Of course you can.

 Bubba J.: I like pie.

 Jeff: . . . Thank you, Bubba J.

 Walter: Idiot.

CHAPTER ONE

The Gift That Kept on Talking

Stand-up comedians aren't normal. As a rule, most of us had bad things happen to us as kids, or grew up in less-than-perfect circumstances. Adversity builds character, or so the adage goes. It also creates problems and eventually might send you to therapy. Many of the best comics are the most screwed-up folks on the planet. Some end up with guns in their mouths, or at the least don't function like "normal" folks. You've probably heard the stories. But life's trials fuel a comic's twisted mind, allowing him to look at the world a little differently and make observations that average folks don't piece together. Sometimes when I hear a great comedian I think, "Wow, he's funny. Wonder what screwed him up." This of course isn't true of every comic, but a lot of them, admittedly, could have had happier childhoods.

I don't envy the guys who grew up with a great deal of strife, but many of them have been able to mine their early years for comedy gold. Fortunately or unfortunately, that's not me. I've had to work really hard at being funny because pretty much everything for me as a kid was positive, uneventful, and almost boring. Sure, Lady Godiva and William the Conqueror are somewhere in the Dunham lineage, but I was adopted. That means wacky ancestors don't count, right?

My parents, Howard and Joyce Dunham, adopted me a few months after my birth in April 1962. I had a happy, drama-free youth, growing up in an upper-middle-class neighborhood in Dallas, Texas. The only thing that was slightly unusual compared to most of my friends was that I was an only child. . . . I don't think that's why my parents gave me a dummy—at least they've never copped to it.

Walter: If your parents only knew *then* what they know *now* . . .

Jeff: What's that supposed to mean?

Walter: Wonder if it's still too late to return you and get a refund.

My father was the sole proprietor of the oldest real estate appraisal firm in Dallas until he retired a few years ago. My mother is a housewife. They are solid churchgoing Christian folk, and my mother still gets upset when one of my characters uses bad language. I keep trying to tell her, "MOM, it's not ME!"

Not long ago when I told my parents that I would be writing this book, my mother turned to my father, and as if I weren't even sitting there, said, "I'm very worried about what he might say about us." To which my father replied, "I'm very worried he won't say *anything* about us."

Peanut: Your dad's like a comedian!

Achmed: Did he beat you as a child?

Jeff: NO!

Walter: That's too bad.

My mother and my father have always supported me. Now in their eighties, they actually clamber onto the tour bus with me once or twice a year so they can watch the performances and hear the crowds. Traveling with eighty-something-year-olds on a tour bus . . . There has to be some sort of reality show in *that*.

But even if my parents are cool with life on the road, no one will ever describe them as "hip." However, if it hadn't been for them, I may never have become a comedian. As I mentioned earlier, the seeds were sown very early in elementary school.

At eight, I was a fairly typical kid. I did well in school and had a few friends in our neighborhood. I rode my bike everywhere and would take off on all kinds of adventures, usually alone, to explore as far as I could pedal before dark. Rain or shine, freezing rain or searing heat, I would ride my bike to school every day. And sickness? I got the perfect attendance award every year from first through sixth grade.

I wasn't an athlete but my parents insisted I play on every base-ball, soccer, and basketball team possible. Of course, the only sport I really liked was football, but they wouldn't let me play that because, as the mother of an only child, my mom thought I'd get killed. The same group of elementary school boys from my grade was on every team and I was always the third worst player. If teams were being chosen at recess, I was one of the last three guys picked.

I was just beginning to see girls in a new light, and Cub Scouts was starting to lose its minimal appeal. I wasn't exactly looking for something new to do, but I certainly hadn't found anything I was particularly good at yet.

Just before Christmas in 1970, my mother and I were walking around in a store called Toy Fair, at the Northwood Hills shopping center. For my birthday that year I had picked out a purple Murray bicycle, a banana-seat two-wheeler from the same store. (I didn't have an older brother or a knowledgeable enough dad to tell me I should have pushed for the much cooler Schwinn Sting-Ray.) As we walked around the store, I begged my mom for stuff here and there. I kept saying, "It's *not* too close to Christmas! PLLEEEEEASE?" Of course, I now realize she had taken me there to get ideas for Santa and had no intention of buying anything that day.

After we rounded a corner, just above my head, I saw a small, vinyl, orange-haired, bucktoothed ventriloquist dummy. His name was Mortimer Snerd. I'd seen ventriloquists perform on television but had never seen a dummy in real life. He was a simple little guy, about two and a half feet tall with a cloth body, a fake straw hat, a little checkered suit, and a bow tie. Sticking out of the back of his neck was a string you could pull to make his mouth open and close.

I took Mortimer down and showed him to my mother. She seemed totally unimpressed. So back he went to his shelf as I went to hunt for other treasures. By the time we got home, I'd forgotten all about him.

 Peanut: Poor Mortimer.

 Jeff: Why?

 Peanut: Imagine how depressing it must be to be rejected by a nerd.

Like most kids, I woke up early on Christmas morning, long before my parents, and snuck quietly into our family room, where the tree and presents were piled, to get a peek at everything. Well, I'd *feel* more than *peek*—at five a.m. it was still too dark to see much of anything, and I was too scared to turn on a light for fear of getting caught.

This particular Christmas, one of the gifts was not easily identifiable. It was sitting on the couch, and it had a cloth body and a molded face of some kind. I was stumped. A couple of hours later, when I was allowed to run in for the "first" time with lights ablaze and the eight-millimeter movie camera rolling, I had my answer—it was Mortimer!

Life is a series of "what-ifs." What if I hadn't made that turn in the toy store and seen the ventriloquist dummy? What if my mom had thought it was a featherbrained idea and that boys shouldn't play with dolls? What would I be doing today?

Well, it's now forty years later, and I'm still at it.

Walter: And if you keep practicing, maybe one day it will work out for you. . . . But I doubt it.

Trust me when I say that it doesn't take much for an eight-year-old to learn to talk without moving his lips, throw his voice, and manipulate a dummy all at the same time. It's just a step-by-step process and one that I pursued relentlessly.

Not long after Christmas, my father took me to the Dallas Public Library's bookmobile, where we checked out a couple of books on ventriloquism. I confess that I still have one of those books, and writing a check for that fine now just might require a five-digit number. And it did. More on that to come.

 Achmed: You know what happens if you're late returning a book in my country?

 Jeff: No.

 Achmed: Me neither. We don't have libraries.

 Bubba J.: I have a question.

 Jeff: What is it, Bubba J.?

 Bubba J.: How fast can a bookmobile get up to?

Not too much later, my mother and I went back to Toy Fair and purchased a record album called *Jimmy Nelson's Instant Ventriloquism*. If you don't recognize the name Jimmy Nelson, your parents might. Jimmy, who is now in his early eighties and has become a good friend, was a regular on Milton Berle's hugely popular television show, *Texaco Star Theater*, in the 1950s. He and his wooden partners Danny O'Day and Farfel did live commercials during the broadcast, both for Texaco and for Nesquik. Danny was a mouthy boy dummy, and Farfel was a talking, long-eared dog. Danny would sing: "N-E-S-T-L-E-S, Nestlé's makes the very best. . . ." And

Farfel would then finish the song—"Chawwww-klit!" and slam his jaw shut with a resounding *clomp*. During his heyday, Jimmy released two instructional record albums with Juro Novelty Company that taught ventriloquist lessons, and produced toy versions of Danny and Farfel.

The idea of making a dummy talk fascinated me, and I spent long hours in our "art room" listening to Jimmy's instructional LPs over and over and practicing the basics that any beginner must learn to perform ventriloquism. I can't exactly put my finger on why it appealed to me so much, only that it was unique and I figured it was a way to get myself out of my shell. I wasn't popular and I wasn't an athlete. Girls didn't pay attention to me, and with the other boys, I just kind of blended into the background. For an eight-year-old at that time, there was no such thing as stand-up comedy. . . . But somehow I figured that if I developed this skill of ventriloquism, I could make people laugh; I could finally *stand out*.

If you want to learn ventriloquism, or "vent," you can find a few courses online, or on DVD. You can even find CD copies of Jimmy's albums here and there. But the mechanics of learning to "throw your voice" are pretty simple. Anyone with a tongue, an upper palate, teeth, and a normal speaking voice can learn ventriloquism.

This isn't an instructional book, but I can give you the basics. The first thing to know is that a ventriloquist simply learns a different way of pronouncing words. Most sounds in the English language are produced without the use of lips, and are made inside the mouth and throat. Only a few sounds and letters utilize the lips. The only way a ventriloquist speaks differently is that he forgoes using his or her lips, and learns to reproduce sounds using the tongue, upper palate, and teeth only. Those "difficult" letters are B, F, M, P,

V, W, and Y. Every other letter in the alphabet can be pronounced without moving your lips: A, C, D, E, G, H, I, J, K, L, N, O, Q, R, S, T, U, X, and Z. Go ahead! Try it! Put your teeth lightly together, part your lips slightly, hold them still, and pronounce that long list of easy letters. If you watch in a mirror, you'll probably be impressed with yourself.

But now, try and pronounce the "difficult" letters without moving your lips. It can't be done . . . unless you use the ventriloquist's method: sound substitution.

Here is where I tip my hat to Jimmy Nelson and his record album *Instant Ventriloquism*. Recently Jimmy graciously granted me permission to share his method. This is the simplest way to learn vent: For the difficult letters, you say one letter, but THINK another. So for B, use the letter D. The word *boy* becomes *doy*. You can say *doy* without moving your lips, but it doesn't sound anything like *boy*. The trick is thinking the actual word and rehearsing. After you practice it over and over and over, the substitution sound starts to sound like the real sound, and eventually you will figure out for yourself how to make the sound as close to the real one as possible.

Here are a few more examples:

F becomes *Eth*
M becomes *N*
P is *T*
V is *The*
W is *Duddle-oo*
Y is *Oh-eye*

It all sounds ridiculous at first, but with many hours of practice, it can become very convincing. "Ny oh ny, tretty thunny stuth, don't oo think? Holy noly! Ethen ny nother can tronounce oords like ne!"

Walter: That explains it.

Jeff: Explains what?

Walter: Why I sound like an idiot most of the time.

After you master sound substitution, you have to learn to speak in a different voice from your own, manipulate the dummy, act, react, use proper microphone technique, et cetera. Oh, then there's that part about actually being funny. . . .

Walter: Did you tell them you're still working on that part?

Jeff: I'm always working on that part.

Walter: Seriously?

Back to the story at hand. Remember, I'm eight years old. I spent a lot of time listening to the record player in the art room, and sitting in my bathroom in front of the mirror for hours, practicing and practicing to make Mortimer come to life. I had the goal of impressing my classmates and making them laugh. After about a month of doing little else in my free time, I knew I was ready for my debut.

Peanut: And your parents knew it was time for a
therapist.

Jeff: Very funny.

Peanut: I think I would have left out the part about doing
little else in your free time.

Jeff: Why?

Peanut: Other than sounding pathetic? No reason.

Mortimer and I were going to give an oral book report on *Hansel
and Gretel*. I put my little buddy in his red-and-white-striped corru-
gated shipping box, strapped it on the book rack on the back of my
bike, and off I pedaled to Northwood Hills Elementary School for
our debut in Miss Bentley's third-grade class. Today, if I'm visiting
my parents, I still like to go by my old school after hours and look in
the window to where I first sat in front of the class. . . . I can see Mortimer on my knee, and me clutching him by his shoulder and pulling
the string on the back of his neck.

Bubba J.: My elementary school teacher was a nice lady.
Since I was having so much fun in the third grade, she
let me repeat it three times.

We did a two-minute presentation on the book and then launched into a ten-minute unscripted routine in which we poked fun at my classmates, our teacher, and the lunch ladies: So-and-so was pretty; so-and-so's feet smelled. I don't claim that Mortimer and I were terribly witty, but to third graders, it was pretty funny. Even Miss Bentley liked it. She gave me an A+.

It's clear to me that the dummies helped me through my early years at school. Miss Bentley didn't give me an A because I gave a good report. She gave me that good grade because there was something more to what I was doing. The shy, almost pudgy, fairly unremarkable kid with freckles and braces had found something that he might be good at. And it was something different. Miss Bentley and my parents were the first ones to really encourage me. My friends did too. I remember standing in line ready to file outside for recess after my book report. I asked a couple of friends, "Did it really sound like Mortimer was talking?" They all said yes, and that it was funny. Funny? Really? Me?

I was hooked. Any stage performer feeds off the emotions of his or her audience: There's a true synergy that takes place. I learned to love the laughs and the accolades. Also, performing let me say things through a dummy that *I* would never say. I would have been in a world of trouble if I, as just me, made any kind of fun of our incredibly stern and feared principal, Mr. Levine. But if Mortimer did it, everyone laughed.

I know that's one of the main reasons people laugh at my stuff today. These little guys get away with verbal heresy. And yes, it's the little guys, not ME! Truly. There's some sort of unwritten rule that allows my formerly inanimate characters to say things that humans could never get away with. I always just play the nice guy.

Today, Achmed is the best example of how far things can be

pushed. Here's a menacing little suicide-bomber terrorist, glaring out at the audience, and yelling, "I KEEL YOU!" and perfectly sane, God-fearing people laugh. Can you imagine if some other stand-up comic tried to do *that*? What if some guy dressed up like a terrorist and started yelling he was going to kill people? His life or at least his career would probably end quickly and dramatically.

I never set out to offend anyone with my material, and I have a line that I draw for myself that I won't cross, no matter where I am or what audience I'm playing for. A good portion of my act is just plain goofy. On the other hand, there are the parts that I try to keep as edgy as possible. Every good comic learns how to read an audience and feel just how far he or she can go. Another comedian of note once told me that if you're not offending a few folks here and there, you're not pushing the envelope enough. Experience and reading every audience is the key to figuring out how far you can go. I will admit that there's nothing better than hearing people laugh when they know they shouldn't, because they can't help it. If a couple of people here and there are offended or pissed, then I know I've done my job.

If characters like Peanut or Walter or Achmed say something I know they shouldn't, then I always look surprised or disappointed and protest what they just said. That's another reason I get away with those sorts of lines. I'm as stunned and as offended as the audience. So I end up onstage chastising myself for what I just made the characters say.

Achmed: So when I say I am going to keel you, that is actually you saying you are going to keel yourself?

Jeff: Well . . .

Bubba J.: My brain is hurting.

Wielding sharp-edged comedy can become an addiction. As a stage performer, you sometimes can't help yourself, and the audience can become completely engaged in the politically incorrectness of it all (if that's your act). However, you have to win over the crowd before you step into the controversial arenas. It's like a guy taking a woman for dinner and a night out: He has to gain her confidence and make her feel safe before making any moves on her. In the same way, an audience needs to feel comfortable before the comic starts running the bases. NOTE TO MY THREE DAUGHTERS: PLEASE READ THE ABOVE LAST FEW SENTENCES OVER AND OVER AGAIN AND TAKE NOTES. MOST GUYS BECOME MASTERS AT GAINING A WOMAN'S CONFIDENCE FOR ULTERIOR MOTIVES. BEWARE! YOU HAVE MY PERMISSION TO SMACK THE HECK OUT OF ANY GUY WHO TRIES ANYTHING ON YOU. AND IF YOU DON'T, I WILL. I PROMISE.

Walter: Seriously, how intimidating can you be to the guys your daughters are dating?

Jeff: What?

Walter: Sitting on your couch at home, surrounded by dolls. That's just sad.

On his album, Jimmy Nelson said that to become a good performer, you have to do as many shows as possible, here, there, and everywhere. After my debut with the book report, I did just that. I started by presenting more oral school reports with Mortimer. Almost immediately I noticed a shift in attention and acceptance from my fellow students as well as the teachers. After a couple of school talent shows and Cub Scout banquets, I realized that people outside my homeroom liked what I did as well. A good portion of the school would applaud and hoot when I was introduced. But then I began to wonder if the only way I could be accepted was with my dummies. I knew I wasn't cool, and I certainly wasn't one of the popular kids. Was the dummy some sort of personality crutch? But then again, was being accepted for being funny any different than being accepted for being good at something normal, like sports?

The summer after third grade, my mother signed me up for a week at a summer camp. It was a place called Sky Ranch, and was a nondenominational Christian camp near Denton, Texas. I figured that this would provide the perfect opportunity to see if I could make friends without using a dummy. I now had a little plastic Danny O'Day, and I took him to camp, but kept him hidden in my suitcase . . . for about a day and a half. When I learned there was going to be a talent show, I couldn't resist signing up. And even with a new crowd, I made 'em laugh.

When I got home from camp and started fourth grade, I looked for every opportunity to do shows and build my act. In the early years, when I was very young, my father would bring home store-bought magic tricks for me to try. My first one was the little red magic vase. It had a blue ball in it that any aspiring prestidigitator could make disappear and then reappear at will. AMAZING! My next trick had me demonstrate my mind-reading ability with a blue magic cube and box. Inside a small blue box was a cube with a different colored circle on each of the six sides. The magician would hand the box to the volunteer, and ask him or her to choose a color, and then put it face up in the box and put the lid back on, hiding the color choice from the magician. The box would be handed back to the magician, some hocus pocus words and motions would ensue, and then the magician would tell the dumbfounded patron what color had been chosen! FANTAS-TIC! I was good at this stuff! So, I added some magic into my vent act and thought maybe I could make some spending money.

I handwrote an ad for my new business on the top third of a sheet of typing paper. My dad then took me to his office, where I copied piles of these announcements:

NEED SOME ENTERTAINMENT?

VENTRILOQUISM, OR MAGIC, OR BOTH?

JEFF DUNHAM AND HIS FAMILY OF DUMMIES.

CALL 239-••••

FEE—$5.00

(I would have put the actual digits, but even forty years later, it's still my parents' phone number!)

Back at home, I took off on my purple bike and stuffed my flyer into as many mailboxes as I could pedal to. Then I waited. First day: No phone calls. Second day: No phone calls. Third: Same. Fourth: Nada.

What the heck? Didn't people want some ventriloquism? Or magic? Or *both*?

No one bit. Not one phone call. But by the fifth grade, after a few more Cub Scout banquets, church gigs, and talent shows, I started to get requests to entertain at younger kids' birthday parties . . . and get paid for them!

I can't recall much of what my act was back then, but most of the dialogue came from Jimmy Nelson's albums, with routines that he invited students to copy and perform. His bits were surefire, and perfect for a young entertainer.

Along with performing, I was now fascinated by every aspect of my craft: everything from the history of ventriloquism to all the different types of figures used. (*Figure* is the politically correct term for a dummy in the ventriloquist world.) I visited every library possible, and read everything I could find associated with vent. I kept coming across the name Edgar Bergen.

As I began to find from my research, Bergen, along with his characters Charlie McCarthy and Mortimer Snerd, had a hugely popular radio program from 1937 to 1956. My parents would tell me stories of many Sunday nights, sitting down with the rest of their families in front of the radio and listening to the hour-long broadcasts. Bergen was huge in his time. With a number one radio program, numerous films, and merchandise featuring his characters, Bergen made Charlie and Mortimer American icons. Edgar Bergen and Walt Disney were contemporaries as well as friends, and both were among the first in Hollywood to successfully and commercially exploit their fictitious characters, producing all sorts of merchandise. Like Disney memorabilia, Bergen's Charlie McCarthy and Mortimer Snerd items are highly collectible and sought-after even today.

Much of my act was and still is heavily influenced by Bergen. This is most obviously seen in Bubba J., who could easily be a distant cousin of Mortimer Snerd. More importantly, as a young performer, I was in awe of Bergen's success as a ventriloquist and thus by example tried to create characters of my own that were equally defined. I know I wouldn't be where I am today had I not been inspired by his genius.

 Bubba J.: You know what?

Jeff: What?

Bubba J.: I wouldn't be here today if I was still at home.

Jeff: That's good thinking, Bubba J.

Bubba J.: I know.

Bergen took a tired old vaudevillian sideshow amusement and turned it into a legitimate form of welcomed entertainment. I spent many hours listening to his old radio shows, starting and stopping the cassette tape player, and writing out his dialogues word for word. I wanted to know exactly what was making his audiences laugh.

Bergen didn't simply tell jokes like most ventriloquists did and still do today. This wasn't setup followed by a punch line. This was verbal situational comedy driven by characters and circumstances, much like any good sitcom. The banter between Bergen and the characters and with other guest stars were short sketches, but believable, and most importantly, *funny*.

Charlie McCarthy was a precocious, girl-crazy, wisecracking boy, with top hat, monocle, tux and tails. Someone once described him as "a child about town." His exchanges on the show with Bergen and guests like Al Jolson, Orson Welles, W. C. Fields, and Mae West had a real edge. It was sometimes salacious, sometimes political. Mae West was banned from the airwaves after a "steamy" exchange with Charlie. She appeared in two separate sketches on *The Chase and Sanborn Hour* with Bergen and McCarthy, which was the number-one-rated radio show at that time. Mae played herself, flirting very heavily with Charlie, utilizing her usual brand of wit and risqué sexual references. By today's standards it's very innocent, but it was naughty stuff back then:

> Mae: So, good-time Charlie's gonna play hard to get? Well, yuh can't kid me. You're afraid of women. Your Casanova stuff is just a front, a false front.

> Charlie: Not so loud, Mae, not so loud! All my girl-friends are listening.

> Mae: Oh, yeah! You're all wood and a yard long. . . .

> Charlie: Yeah.

> Mae: Yuh weren't so nervous and backward when yuh came up to see me at my apartment. In fact, yuh didn't need any encouragement to kiss me.

> Charlie: Did I do that?

> Mae: Why, yuh certainly did. I got marks to prove it. An' splinters, too. . . .

Pushing the limits even further, later in the broadcast in an Adam and Eve sketch with show emcee Don Ameche, Mae ad-libbed the line, "Get me a big one . . . I feel like doin' a big apple!"

In the following days, the *New York Sun* wrote: "On any other day of the week the skit would have justified the severest criticism from the standpoint of good taste, but on Sunday such a broadcast represents the all-time low in radio. The most charitable explanation is that the producers were mesmerized by the reputed glamour of the entertainer." NBC received letters calling the show "immoral" and "obscene." The FCC later called the broadcast "vulgar and indecent" and "far below even the minimum standard which should control in the selection and production of broadcast programs."

Six days after the broadcast, the general manager of the NBC station group banned any mention of Mae West's name and of the incident on the network. In effect, Mae West was gone, and wouldn't grace the airwaves again for twelve years.

 Walter: This has been my favorite part of the book so far.

Also, fictitious feuds between shows and stars were a big ratings ploy in the heyday of radio. W. C. Fields and Charlie McCarthy had one of the most notorious ones, with exchanges like:

> W. C. Fields: Well, if it isn't Charlie McCarthy, the woodpecker's pinup boy!

> Charlie: Well, if it isn't W. C. Fields, the man who keeps Seagram's in business!

My favorite was:

> W. C. Fields: Your father was a bootlegger's table!

> Charlie: Yeah, well your father was under it!

Mortimer Snerd, on the other hand, was somewhat the opposite of Charlie. He was simpleminded, and a true country bumpkin.

Bergen used to say, though, that "Mortimer is stupid, but he knows that he is stupid, so that almost makes him smart!" Here's a great example of Mortimer's special type of intellect:

> Bergen: I understand you had a cake at your birthday party?
>
> Mortimer: Duh, uh, yeah! Had cake, yup.
>
> Bergen: So, do you prefer vanilla or chocolate?
>
> Mortimer: Uh . . . chocolate. Yup. Chocolate.
>
> Bergen: Why is that?
>
> Mortimer: It don't show the dirt.

Both Charlie and Mortimer were alive in the consciousness of the American public. Because the material was so well written, and because Bergen was incredibly skilled with voices and characterization, many listeners didn't think it really was Bergen doing all the talking. Charlie would actually get more fan mail than Bergen, and purportedly, much of the radio audience actually believed he was a boy actor simply playing the role of a ventriloquist dummy.

In those days, the only forms of "instant" mass communication were the newspaper and radio. If you didn't make the news, you had to *invent* the news. And Bergen was also brilliant at PR. He went so far as to giving Charlie his own room in his Beverly Hills home with a bed, a closet full of monogrammed clothes, a desk, a West Point cadet's hat, a feathered Indian headdress, and a Dorothy Lamour pinup. In her autobiography, *Knock Wood*, Bergen's daughter, actress Candice Bergen, talks about the bedroom and how her father made her sit on his left knee and talk with her "brother," Charlie, who sat to the right. There are charming, albeit creepy, pictures of the Bergen family with Charlie and Mortimer posing as well. Was Bergen crazy, or simply creative with photo opportunities and press manipulation? I think he was simply greatly talented, and a sharp businessman.

Walter: I'm going with "crazy." And that goes for you too.

Jeff: I'm not nuts.

Walter: Ha, ha, ha . . . you are *such* a kidder.

What kept Bergen unparalleled by any other vent of his era was his ability to create well-defined and beloved *characters*. It took me many years to understand that this was Bergen's true talent. Sure, he and Charlie and Mortimer starred in a few movies in the thirties and for- ties, and he also made many guest television appearances up until his death in 1978. . . . But first and foremost Bergen was a *radio* star. Hang on. . . . A *ventriloquist* became a star on the *radio*. That's ridiculous.

At first consideration, I think most people would regard vent as a visual medium. No one says that you listen to a ventriloquist. Rather, you *watch* a ventriloquist. But is that the most important sense uti- lized when being entertained by a vent? As I got older and began to better understand why Bergen's studio audiences were laughing, I began to realize the significance of radio and the spoken word in his climb to superstardom. I actually don't think he would have been as successful if he had come along later, during the television era. Because his radio audience couldn't see him, they couldn't watch to see if he moved his lips. So, throw out of the equation the first thing people usually focus on when a ventriloquist is performing. The listening audience could only pay attention to what they could hear. His characters and material were so strong that Bergen became a huge star and famous ventriloquist solely by the spoken word, and the most important thing he did was make people *laugh*. This began to sink in to me very early on.

The favorite dummy I used in my elementary school years was the toy Danny O'Day, but I very much wanted to get a "real" ventriloquist dummy. These more expensive and serious versions didn't simply have a string in the back of the neck to move the mouth. Rather, the more advanced characters had hollow bodies and a "head stick" that was attached to the bottom of the head, and was thus inside the body of the dummy. Controls on the stick were accessed by reaching through a slit in the costume on the back of the figure, and into the body cavity. Mounted on the stick were levers that controlled various mechanisms on the dummy's face, such as the mouth and usually side-to-side moving eyes, raising eyebrows, et cetera. I had no idea where to find a figure maker or craftsman who made this type of figure, and none of the local toy or hobby stores I phoned in Dallas could help me either.

Halfway through the sixth grade, I found a book in the large branch of the Dallas Public Library called *Ventriloquism for Fun and Profit* by the famous ventriloquist and voice actor Paul Winchell (whose most popular dummy was Jerry Mahoney). This book offered step-by-step instructions on how to build your own professional ventriloquist dummy from a block of wood or papier-mâché. I figured if no one else could build it for me, I'd have to do it myself.

My parents helped out by purchasing a few basic tools from the local hardware store, including a drill motor and bits, some sandpaper, and an electric jigsaw. With a set of X-Acto knives and some big blocks of glued-together balsa wood, I whittled out a guy whom my dad and I named Filbert S. Nutt. Dad also helped here and there with the woodwork, but even he would agree that he is clueless when it comes to tools. Our father-son projects in Cub Scouts and Indian Guides left a bit to be desired. . . .

When I was in the second grade, my father and I signed up for Indian Guides. Sponsored by the YMCA, fathers and their sons joined the local "tribes" and gave themselves Native American names—back then we used the term *Indian*. Dad and I were Big Fire Ball and Little Fire Ball. Our friends Emil and Scott Pohli had pretty creative names as well. Scott was my age and a good athlete. His father, Emil, had contracted polio as a young man, and was confined to a wheelchair. I was always impressed by Mr. Pohli's strength, determination, and optimism, and his sense of humor. Their names were Little Running Feet and Big Rolling Seat.

During one of our monthly Indian Guides meetings, large rectangular blocks of pine were given to each father-son team. These blocks were about half the size of a mailbox, with a one-inch hole drilled in one end and a matching-sized dowel sticking out the other. These blocks were taken home and finished by each father-son team, and then at our meeting we assembled them one on top of the other to make our tribe's totem pole.

Anyway, at this early age, I hadn't yet figured out that not all dads know how to fix or build things. Our totem pole was our first real father-son construction project. We got the block of wood home and I couldn't wait to get started! By the time dad had gotten home from work the next day, I had already gathered every hand tool I could find from around the house and garage. All the tools Dad owned fit on three small shelves in our utility room, but I also found a big handsaw in the garage. The wooden handle was cracked and loose, but years ago my father had keenly fixed that problem with some masking tape.

Mom said dinner wouldn't be ready for a while, so after he changed out of his business suit, I pulled Dad out to the garage to get to work. He hesitated for a moment, then took a deep breath and looked suspiciously at the wood and tools. He slowly picked up the wood and the saw, and carried them to the backyard, where there was a two-foot-high brick wall surrounding our back porch. He put the block on the wall as a sort of workbench. I couldn't wait! Dad was gonna make the best totem pole head of everyone!

He turned the block around, looking at it from every angle possible. I knew he was devising ways to cut and sculpt and make something fantastic. He turned the block sideways, put the saw at an angle on one of the corners, and pushed and pulled the saw back and forth. There were a few slips and grumbles and a lot of sweat as the saw got stuck in the wood now and then, but that's how sawing works. And all saws are rusty, right? It never occurred to me that Dad's tools were rusted because he hadn't used them in two decades.

Eventually, the first cut was finished. He had sawed off the front top edge of one of the sides. He then proceeded to do the same thing on the lower portion of that side. "There," he said. "That makes the forehead and the bottom is the chin." Then he took one of the two triangular scraps and sawed it into three almost-equal smaller triangular pieces. Placing one on the front of the block and holding the other two on either side, he said, "This is the nose and these two are the ears. You can glue those on. There you go."

"Uh . . . that's it?" I asked.

"Sure," he responded.

"But . . . well . . . what about painting it?" I asked.

"I think we have a little can of something in the garage."

"DAAAAD."

He went inside. I'm not going to say I was devastated, but I certainly wasn't overjoyed. I got some Elmer's glue and did the best I could to put the pieces on the face. No sanding. No sculpting of wood. No true woodworking of any kind. I found the can of orange paint and an old dried-up brush. After slathering the whole thing, I dug around in my room and found some tiny jars of model paint to put on the details of eyes and war paint markings. Horrible.

At the next Indian Guides meeting, Scott Fuller showed up with an eagle head complete with wings and a high-gloss, multicolor finish. It looked like something you'd buy at a store. Most of the other heads were at least close to being that good. At every meeting from then on, my head of the totem pole always ended up on the very bottom.

Despite that sad story and a couple more like it, including the time my mother MADE my father dump an entire bucket of water on my unlaunched Estes rocket because she was convinced that it was going to explode and kill us all, I must thank both my parents. I am eternally grateful for those very few times in my childhood that I was disappointed or disheartened. Mainly because of Dad's lack of skills with building things or with any kind of tool, I learned self-reliance. As an only child, there was never anyone to discourage my conquests or divert a chosen course. I was left to a world of exploration and my own imagination and dreams. My parents gave me the gift of encouragement and *never* discouragement or disparagement. While Dad didn't know how to use hand tools much beyond the very basics, he always encouraged my efforts. My parents would compliment even my saddest attempts and then make suggestions on how to improve. If there were times when I was doing something they didn't understand, they would question and make observations but give me the room to fail. They gave me tools . . . both literally and figuratively. They did this in everything from oil paintings my mother helped me with in grade school, to terrible science projects where I never won a thing. In college, when I had secretively started building my own full-sized helicopter and taking flight lessons to get my pilot's license, they were scared to death when they found out. But, later, when I'd finished the long project and after a great deal of prayer, they both rode through the sky as passengers in my homebuilt helicopter, trusting their kid not to kill them.

When I was young, if my father had taken over and done all the work on school or Scout projects, building the best whatzit of any of the other kids, I never would have learned a thing, and I'm pretty sure Walter and Achmed wouldn't exist today. As for that first dummy I carved during my sixth-grade year, Filbert and I performed together for only a few months. He was nearly as big as I was and looked almost as sad as our totem pole head. Filbert is still in storage in Dallas, and I shudder whenever I open that trunk. He's just too scary-looking. Building ventriloquist dummies is a skill I learned over many years, but I know I never would have had the fortitude or patience to learn if Dad had simply created a Disney-quality totem pole by himself.

 Peanut: You're crafting skills have really gotten better. I mean, I was blown away when I saw how ugly you made Achmed.

 Achmed: Hey! I'm right here!

 Peanut: Yeah, I know.

Also during my sixth-grade year, the *Richardson Daily News* ran an article on my ventriloquial pursuits. When the reporter called to request an interview, I thought, "This is show business! This is the *big* time!"

Well . . . I'll never forget watching outside our dining room window and seeing this guy drive up in a complete beater. I was stunned. I thought: Shouldn't a reporter arrive in a limousine? This was, after all, showbiz!

Ironically, on the same day that article was printed, the *Dallas Morning News* ran a story about another local ventriloquist named Keith Singleton. He was just a few years older than I was, but as I read in the article and saw from his picture, he had a professional ventriloquist dummy.

My father did a little detective work, found Keith's phone number, had a quick conversation, and Keith graciously invited us over to have a look at Marty. I couldn't have been more excited to see the dummy. I had never seen a real ventriloquist figure in person—it had a head stick and *everything!*—and even better, Marty had been custom-built by a *real* figure maker.

Keith let me operate the controls on Marty, and he told me about Finis Robinson, the creator of this twenty-five-pound masterpiece. Finis was older than dirt and lived in Waterloo, Iowa. He had been building dummies since the days of vaudeville, and his business slogan was the ever-rosy "The End of Gloom." I sent away for Finis's catalog, which featured a sampling of his creations over the decades.

Finis customized his dummies to meet his clients' demands. At least, that's what the catalog said. In the packet was an order form that you could fill out to specify exactly what you wanted. What color eyes? What type of hair? Color of skin? Texture of paint? Did you want him painted for stage or television? Did you want clothes too? And then of course, you had to choose the movements. Besides a moving mouth, did you want raising eyebrows and a stick-out tongue? How about cross-eye movement? Cool!

Sometime in the 1970s, Finis and his wife of a lifetime, Annamay, moved to Zephyrhills, Florida, where he continued to build figures until he passed away on July 4, 2001, at the age of ninety-three.

I still have that catalog, which I still sometimes look at today and smile. It reminds me that Finis must have been a bit nuts. On one page, he has a "walking figure." These types of dummies were an interesting oddity in the early part of the twentieth century. Vents would stroll onto stage, "walking" a life-sized dummy while at the same time making it sing or talk. To make these almost-robotic monstrosities move forward, the vent would simply hold the dummy by one arm, tilting the character slightly left and right. The foot that was off the ground would swing forward thanks to springs and clocklike mechanics, thus taking another "step." The performer could then maneuver the figure around the stage. For about $600 in the 1970s, Finis claimed in his catalog that you could order a walking figure and it would show up just like any other dummy, in a big, well-packed, cardboard crate. The trouble was, the picture of the walking figure looked suspiciously like his thirty-something-year-old daughter, Mayann, posing, standing as stiffly as possible in "dummy pose." If you looked closely, you could see where someone had drawn in pen the vent dummy "slot jaw" lines on her chin as well as "joints" on her exposed elbows and knees. In later years, I always joked with fellow vents that we should pool together some money and order the dummy just to see if Mayann showed up in a crate.

Anyway, on my particular order form, I decided I wanted a 1970s variation of the Charlie McCarthy type. Since Bergen, almost every ventriloquist used something akin to the Charlie icon. It made sense for me too, because most of my material was inspired by Bergen and was written for just that type of character

After sending Finis $327.56 of hard-earned lawn-mowing money, my first professional vent figure—complete with moving mouth, side-to-side eyes, raising eyebrows, and winkers—showed up in a big box. I named him Monty Ballew in honor of two people. Monty Moncrief, who was the program director at Sky Ranch, and Peggy Ballew, who was also a counselor at Sky Ranch for a few summers and was incredibly hot. She was in high school, and I was almost in seventh grade when I met her. She was my first major crush. I have no idea whatever happened to Peggy, but maybe she'll read this and realize that naming a dummy after her was my twelve-year-old way of hitting on an older woman.

Getting Monty Ballew was a major stepping-stone. I remember very well working on new material for him. Monty arrived the summer Richard Nixon resigned, and even at that early age I was trying my best to craft political jokes about Tricky Dick and Watergate. Soon the audiences were getting bigger, and I was getting bolder. A few months into my seventh-grade year, in the fall of 1975, I found myself in front of seventy businessmen, making fun of one of my childhood heroes: a real-life, pro-football Captain America.

CHAPTER TWO

How to Get a Job While Still a Minor

Monty and I didn't exactly follow the Golden Rule. We didn't do unto others as we'd have them do unto us. Instead, when we finished our regular material, we then poked good-natured fun at people and our surroundings. Even at a young age, I figured making an entire audience laugh at one or two people's expense was some sort of universal trade-off. Though I didn't realize it at the time, I was developing my own little superpower: I could get away with making fun of people and things with a dummy on my knee.

In my seventh- and eighth-grade years, the board of directors at Sky Ranch put me to work to help raise money for their new camp. Because I had performed every week at the old facility during the previous few summers, the suits at Sky Ranch knew who I was, and I guess they figured my act was a good way to lighten up the mood before they asked the guests to pull out their checkbooks. They put me in front of big-dollar Dallas businessmen during Kiwanis Club lunch meetings, or any kind of business gathering where corporate donations could be found. I didn't pitch anything; I just did my show. In twenty minutes I did my regular act, plus a goofily twisted Bible story or two, and then I'd do the thing that I was quickly learning was the best way to get big laughs: Pick on the big shots.

I don't exactly know where or when I came up with this formula, but when I'd get to the gig, I would talk to someone who knew a lot about the gathering and the audience. I'd get five or six names of the most notable guys there, whether they were liked or not, plus a few facts about them that were either well-known or embarrassing tidbits that only a handful of folks would know. What was the guy's exact job title? Was he horrible at golf? Had he made any stupid business decisions? Who was the token bald guy?

While dessert was being served, I'd be introduced. Once behind the microphone, Monty and I would do the expected part of the routine, then we'd start down my list. It was a great gig: a thirteen-year-old kid with a dummy and a microphone and a handful of names of rich guys to pick on. The laughs could get really big when business competitors were in the same room getting needled by a wooden doll in the hands of a kid barely into puberty.

One of the greatest times for me was when one of my childhood heroes, Dallas Cowboys' star quarterback Roger Staubach, also known as Captain America, was in the crowd. As a senior at the U.S. Naval Academy in 1964, Staubach won the Heisman Trophy, but before joining the National Football League, he spent five years in military service, with some of that time in Vietnam. He made the roster of the Cowboys in 1969, and eventually led the team to four Super Bowl appearances and two victories. To this day, I honestly don't know what pushed me, but somehow I knew I needed to make fun of him. At the time of the show, the Cowboys were in the middle of an incredible run. Staubach was a superstar, revered in Dallas as royalty, and here I was at thirteen years old, making jokes about bad plays he made the Sunday before. How I got away with all that still leaves me dumbfounded. But of course, it was the dummy talking, not the thirteen-year-old.

Jeff: Monty, we have a very special guest here this afternoon: Cowboys quarterback Roger Staubach!

Monty: *The* Roger Staubach?

Jeff: Yes. Do you know him?

Monty: Not as well as the Steelers defense knows
him . . .

Peanut: I talked to Monty the other day.

Jeff: You did?

Peanut: Yeah. He keeps asking when you're going to use
him again. . . . Awkward!

I had great respect for Staubach as well as some of my other
prominent targets, but somewhere along the way I learned where
that oh-so-important line was, and when not to cross it. Of course,
I angered a few victims or their spouses here and there, but the
laughs were much more important to me. Even back then, I figured
that if ninety-eight percent of the room was laughing, I was doing
something right.

Still today I try and do localized and personalized humor, and it
always gets big laughs. Before a show at Whatever Stage, I'll find
out who the local celebrities are or if there's a notable event taking place in that particular city, or if the town is known for something or if they have a sports team that's good or horrible . . . and
we poke fun at it all. Those are usually the more memorable pieces
of the shows for both the audience and me. It changes the performance from night to night, and the crowd recognizes that it's special

just for them. It makes the live experience become just that much more *live*.

I'll tell some of my favorite ad-lib stories later in the book, but there's one from my early years that stands out.

Until I left for college in 1980, I grew up attending Highland Park Presbyterian Church. Just like school and anywhere else, I would do as many shows at church as possible. Sometimes I'd perform in Sunday school classes; sometimes on youth retreats; sometimes at Wednesday night dinners. I was always trying to get onstage.

During most of the years I was at Highland Park, Dr. Clayton Bell was our pastor. Another family that attended the church was the William Herbert Hunts. He and his brother, former billionaire Nelson Bunker Hunt, in the late seventies had tried but failed to corner the world silver market, and most of our church's congregation was familiar with the Hunts and their business dealings. A dinner event was planned in honor of Dr. Bell and his wife, who were celebrating their twenty-fifth anniversary of being with our church. It was just about Christmastime.

During my act, I had Monty say that we were happy that we were there as part of the entertainment that night, but apparently we were second choice. He said that Herbert Hunt had wanted to get up onstage, and in honor of the pastor and his wife and their anniversary and the holidays, he had wanted to sing for them, "Silver Bells . . . Silver Bells . . ." Get it? The Hunts and the silver market? The twenty-fifth anniversary is the *silver* anniversary; the Clayton BELLS; and it was Christmastime? That wasn't a double entendre, it was a quintuple entendre. It wasn't the greatest *joke* in the world, but as people put the five things together in their heads, the low level laugh started, then built, and went on and on as folks got it all, then explained it to each other. Like I said, not a huge laugh, but having come up with it as a teenager, I'm still kind of proud of myself for that one, and my dad still brings it up every once in a while.

Jeff: Walter, how did you celebrate your twenty-fifth anniversary?

Walter: *"Celebrate"*? You're assuming way too much.

Let's get back to junior high. At age thirteen, I met another ventriloquist, who was about to make a pretty big name for himself in the television world. A few years after I met him, Jay Johnson moved to Los Angeles and became famous as the slightly crazy ventriloquist from the 1970s sitcom *Soap*, in which he played Chuck and Bob Campbell throughout the show's entire run. Ironically, Jay and I both graduated from Richardson High School in Richardson, Texas. He was Class of 1968, and I was Class of 1980. In early 1975, my parents took me to see him at a venue in Fort Worth called Charlie's Place. I don't remember much about the show, except that it was a variety-type dinner show, and Jay was in it and he was great. His was the first live ventriloquist show I had ever seen.

At that time Jay worked with a dummy named Squeaky, a talking Mickey Mouse watch, and a talking houseplant named Phil O'Dendron. Obviously Jay did some really unique vent bits, coupled with perfect technique and a great imagination. What stuck with me most after meeting him was that he was a genuinely nice guy. Here I was, some goofy kid, and he took the time to talk with me after the show and even responded to my letters later. He gave me the addresses of a couple other ventriloquists, plus information about a national ventriloquists' organization that published a bimonthly newsletter.

Jay hooked me up with Maher Ventriloquist Studios in Littleton, Colorado. Run by Clinton and Adelia Detweiler, if you needed anything ventriloquist related, they had it. They also published a newsletter, "Newsy Vents," which was chock-full of news and pictures of ventriloquists from all over the world. Up until that point, I had NO idea there were so many vents. In fact, some part of me considered that there might not be any others. Even from the beginning, I knew this ventriloquist thing was peculiar.

Timing is everything, and it just so happened that the very first issue of "Newsy Vents" that I read had a big ad in it announcing the First Annual Vent Haven Ventriloquist Convention. From July 10–12, 1975, vents from all over the globe were scheduled to gather at the Rowntowner Motor Inn, in Fort Mitchell, Kentucky. (The Rowntowner would later become the Drawbridge Inn.) And yes, I know how disconcerting that sounds—a convention of *ventriloquists*? Oh, and it was in *Kentucky*. I'll explain that in a minute. . . .

 Bubba J.: Kentucky is one of my favorite towns.

 Jeff: It's a state.

 Bubba J.: Finally!

I was now thirteen years old and I planned trying to beg my parents into taking me to the convention. But it turned out I didn't have to. I remember mentioning wanting to go just a couple of times, and showing them the ad in "Newsy Vents." As always, my parents were supportive in every way, and they simply made our trip to Kentucky that year's family vacation. Being an only child has its good and bad points, and travel was always easy when it was just the three of us.

As for the convention, I don't think I had ever been more excited to go anywhere. My two idols, Edgar Bergen AND Jimmy Nelson, were both scheduled to be there, plus there were going to be contests to find the best junior and senior vents. Whoa. I couldn't stand the wait.

Fort Mitchell, Kentucky, might sound like the oddest, most random of choices to hold an international convention for anything, but that little town just a few miles across the river from Cincinnati, Ohio, is the world's Mecca for all ventriloquists. In Fort Mitchell is the Vent Haven Museum, which houses the world's largest collection of ventriloquial memorabilia. It was the brainchild of the late Cincinnati businessman William Shakespeare Berger, a collector and advocate for ventriloquists. For many years he was the president of the International Brotherhood of Ventriloquists, an organization that folded only when his health began to fail in December of 1960. The museum collection continues to grow, and currently includes more than seven hundred vent figures, numerous oddities such as talking walking canes, beer steins, boots, and the list goes on.

You see, not all vents use only dummies. In bygone eras, just about anything and any item you can name has at one time or another been turned into some sort of vent puppet. A lot of vents are pretty inventive, and usually this creativity happens in the spirit of *trying* to create a new act. The worst example I can give you? One year at the convention, a guy showed up with a talking toilet. I'm not kidding.

Vent Haven contains literally mounds of history. There's a huge library of books on ventriloquism, hundreds of vent playbills, and photos dating back to even before the Civil War. Some of the dummies are hundreds of years old as well, most with colorful pasts. Many vents who wanted a safe refuge for their now silent wooden partners have donated them to the museums. Early versions of Peanut and Walter and José are there already.

 Walter: A museum with seven hundred dummies . . . Oh no, that's not creepy *at all*.

The convention is sponsored every year by the museum. Since that first gathering in 1975, I've missed only one. Throughout the years, I learned a great deal from many of the attendees and lecturers. Also I've seen some of the best and the worst performers in our art. You think open mike night at a comedy club is funny? Try open mike night at a ventriloquist convention. It's funny, but not always in a *good* way. There are usually some surprises and delightful acts, but others are . . . well, yikes!

As a self-trained vent, I literally had no contemporaries to compare myself to other than the pros. There weren't any television shows that regularly featured ventriloquists then. I knew nothing other than the two basic rules for success—don't move your lips, and make your audience laugh. You had to be as funny as Bergen, and with technique as good as Nelson. Now here I was at a convention where I could watch and emulate whoever seemed best.

Contests were held for both senior and junior vents, and no limit was put on the number of performers that could enter. In that first year, somewhere around forty kids aged seventeen and younger entered the junior contest, and with each vent doing five or six minutes each, that night wore on seemingly forever. But when the dust settled and the judges tallied their scores, at age thirteen I won first place as Best Junior Vent. I received a giant trophy along with a big heap of bewilderment and excitement.

Shy as I was at this age, I still made a few acquaintances, and some of them would become friends for life. My mother *made* me say hi to Jimmy Nelson at the first large social gathering, which was poolside at the Rowntowner Motor Inn. He couldn't have been more gracious and even posed for a picture with Monty and me. Yes, I was carrying my dummy around talking to everyone, as was just about everyone else. This was the time for everyone to let the figures socialize as well. It wasn't until a few years later that I realized how truly strange this convention was, especially to the poor non-vent guests who happened to be staying at the Rowntowner at the same time.

Some of the vents would take the dummy thing way too far and enter the creepy zone: They would take the figures into the coffee shop and talk among themselves and to others, or sit in the lobby with the dummies and chat with passersby. Of course the press would eat it up. Almost every one of the print or broadcast stories would paint the convention as a gathering of the nuts, and I don't blame them. If you're having a grilled cheese with Dummy Dan on one knee, and your buddy across the table from you is enjoying a muffin while chatting with his stuffed monkey, you *need* to be labeled *oddball*.

There was one lady who was so bonkers that I wonder if she has been committed yet. It was a convention in the early 1980s, and the movie *Magic*, about a murderous psychotic ventriloquist, had been released a few years earlier. This woman, whom I will call Fran, had literally fallen in love with Fats, the scary dummy in the film. Fran had, in fact, liked the movie and the figure so much that she had commissioned someone to construct a full-sized replica of Fats. She brought him to the convention and carried him *everywhere*. She even claimed she had a kid's seat in her car that Fats rode around in, probably scaring the crap out of anyone who looked in her window. Fats had a grotesquely large head, slightly larger than human, but with a typical dummy-sized body. The hands were disproportionately large, and the thing would give just about anyone the shivers.

I became a bit leery of Fran after one incident. I was walking by her hotel room door, and she just happened to be walking out. The door opened, and I couldn't help but glance into the room. There in one of the double beds lay Fats, with the TV on and the covers pulled up to his chin. I stopped in my tracks, backed up a few steps, and looked in again. I turned to Fran, who was standing there smiling, and I said, "Fats is in bed?"

"He likes it there," she said. I quickly walked away, wondering how long it would be before she was running after me with a knife and a screaming dummy.

 Achmed: I bet later she went to another movie and fell in love with that Chucky doll. . . . Is he one of your homegrown terrorists?

 Jeff: I guess you could say that.

 Achmed: I liked his films. Very inspirational.

The 1975 convention was one of the highlights of my early life. There was, however, a ramification that came from attending the convention that made an indelible mark on me forever.

I started charging for my shows early on and by the time that first convention rolled around, I was making $60 a gig for a thirty-minute show. W-2s were being filed, and I had to pay taxes. My father handled all the bookkeeping for me of course, but that year he got a little too generous with deductions. He had deducted both his and Mom's travel costs, but apparently you were allowed to deduct the expenses of only one guardian, so when my taxes were filed that year, a red flag went up somewhere.

Every day I would head out the front door and get our mail out of the mailbox on the street. On this particular day, I opened the mailbox, only to find an official-looking letter addressed to me from the IRS. It said I was being audited! I didn't know *exactly* what that meant, but after hearing Dad gripe about the IRS somewhat regularly, I knew it was something not to be overjoyed about. It's funny to look back at now, but as a kid, it scared the living crap out of me. Years later, I delivered some kind of payback when the characters and I were in Washington, D.C., taping the Comedy Central special and DVD *Spark of Insanity*. Walter said he had been sightseeing that day. He said he enjoyed going to the IRS building. I asked, "You took a tour?" He said, "No . . . I just stood outside and flipped 'em off!"

Junior high was the typical awkward time in life. I wasn't popular and yet wasn't a total outcast either. Back in the 1970s, the three caste classifications we used to identify everyone with were the preppies, the freaks, and the nerds. I think I was somewhere in the middle of preppie and nerd. I kind of had my own category. I played the trombone in the school band, was on the tennis team (hated every minute of that), and had a decent number of friends. Some of my buddies were the popular preppie sort; others were not. I entered school talent shows, still did oral reports with the help of a dummy or two, and got up in front of everyone to perform as often as possible. I was soon known around my junior high, which had a lot more students than my elementary school.

Eighth grade was the year that my two friends Lon Kelly and Ross Sivertsen and I started hanging out together. They introduced me to a TV show that had been on the air for a few years at that point. It was something called *Star Trek*.

I couldn't help it then and I can't help it today. I love the original series and even *The Next Generation* . . . and now, of course, the latest film. As a joke, and with some sort of major geek pride, for years I have carried a *Star Trek* MasterCard, complete with the original USS *Enterprise* emblazoned across the face. It wasn't until I wandered into the middle of a *Star Trek* convention in Las Vegas a few years ago that I realized that maybe I should be more of a *closet* Trekkie.

I had been living in Los Angeles for a while and was working a week at the Vegas Improv, which at that time was located inside the Riviera Hotel and Casino. For those gigs we had our days completely free, and one day I opened the magazine of what was going on that week in town. Lo and behold, there was a Trek convention taking place just a couple of casinos away. Another performer at the club that week was also a Trek fan, so off we went to check out the gathering.

Oh my lord. It took literally ten seconds from when we stepped inside the main room of the convention for me to figure out that I'd better stop telling people I loved this stuff. We paid our entry fee, and were pointed to the main room, where they were showing a slide show. Yes, a *slide* show. Each slide was a random frame from a random episode from the original television series. Just as the slide would barely come into focus, the entire room of Trekkies would yell out the name of the episode. I stood there, dumbfounded for a few seconds, taking in the uniqueness of the situation and the people in attendance. And these folks were *focused* and *dedicated*. My friend and I literally backed out of the room, afraid to turn around, lest we be shot from behind by a Phaser set on something above stun.

We made our way to the Dealers Room, only to be greeted by a bunch of folks in full costume and makeup. A couple of guys were carrying on a full conversation in Klingon, and a skinny guy with rubber Spock ears told us to live long and prosper, and I knew that was our cue to transport the hell out or be assimilated.

Peanut: Those Trekkie gatherings make the ventriloquist convention look like a board meeting.

For years I have remained a faithful fan, but I'm never above firing a comedy shot at all things Trek. Seriously, if you're dressing up like a Starfleet officer and you can quote the Prime Directive, but you don't know our own secretary of state, you need to be made fun of. (I know both.) I was pretty happy when the newest in the long line of Trek movies did well in the early summer of 2009. My MasterCard doesn't feel so geeky anymore.

Okay, now back to junior high. As my little career started to grow in Dallas, word of mouth about my act took root, and the local press actually took note as well. First, the Dallas version of *PM Magazine* did a very nice piece on my characters and me, which eventually ran nationally. A more noteworthy story, however, was done on us by a somewhat unknown local field reporter who interviewed Monty and me in April of 1976. Obviously, this guy had drawn the short straw that morning to be assigned the story on the junior high boy who talked to dolls.

At that time, the new thing in sports and news reporting was a portable field camera that utilized a new format called videotape. COOL! Well, the lowly reporter and cameraman showed up, but to my disappointment, they brought the old-school FILM camera. What a drag.

Anyway, these guys showed up and proceeded to *film* their story on me. In the background, my mom took pictures with her Kodak Instamatic camera. It's sort of funny to look at those pictures now, because the only one who looked excited in the shots was *me*. I'm betting the poor camera guy wanted to shoot himself, and the reporter looks like he would be having more fun getting a root canal. He was a young guy with long hair, and he didn't exactly grill me with tough questions, but I guess he would learn that skill later in his own career. That lowly reporter at channel 8 in Dallas in 1976 was none other than Bill O'Reilly. (Take a look at the photo in the insert of this book!)

I was pretty serious about my career at a very early age, and I never stopped thinking about the next way to move it all forward. Not too long ago, my three daughters asked if they could see some of my old yearbooks. I couldn't resist, so out came the annuals from Northwood Junior High and Richardson High School. The girls quickly noticed something unusual in each of my individual class photos. I wasn't by myself: A ventriloquist dummy was sitting on my lap in *every* single picture, *every* single year.

"Oh my gawd, Dad!"

"That is SO EMBARRASSING!"

"WHY?"

I offered what I considered a logical explanation. "I needed professional-quality studio photos to help promote my act, but they were too expensive to have done. So I posed with my main character each year for my school pictures. The photographers usually thought it was funny. What's wrong with that?"

The girls just stared at me. Then they did the sweetest thing in the world: They went through my entire senior yearbook page by page and marked all the pictures of me and my partner Archie with sticky notes. As they got toward the back of the book, they opened it to a full-page shot of me with a girl.

"Whoa, Dad! Who's THAT?"

"Archie," I said.

"NO," they said. "The girl!"

Oh. In 1980, my high school classmates voted me and my friend since kindergarten, Christy Dutter, as Most Likely to Succeed. The yearbook picture recognizing that honor shows Christy and me sitting on the hood of a brand-new, awesomely cool Datsun 280ZX. Seated between us was my dummy of choice at the time, Archie Everett. "See," I said, "that's cool."

"You're a geek, Dad," Ashlyn, my middle daughter, said.

"Can I at least tell you about the car?" I asked.

"It looks old," Kenna replied.

"It wasn't back then. And it was my fifth one!" I blurted out.

"FIFTH?" Bree and Ashlyn yipped, almost in unison.

"Yes, that was my brown 280ZX, and it was the fifth Z I'd driven the wheels off of in less than a year without having paid one cent." That story comes later. . . .

Achmed: What a good father.

Jeff: Thanks.

Achmed: It's so sweet how you let your daughters speak freely and look at books.

When I graduated from Northwood Junior High in 1977, my vent pursuits were progressing nicely. Though I didn't realize it at the time, I was learning to entertain a fairly wide range of audience members. I was getting laughs from my peers as well as young adults and even older folks. More important, businessmen who had seen me at the Sky Ranch fund-raisers began to book me for their own parties, banquets, and corporate gatherings.

I returned to the Vent Convention in the summer of 1976 and won Best Junior Vent again. I don't know if I could have won the contest three summers in a row because the only convention I ever missed was 1977.

That summer my church's youth choir toured parts of Europe. I couldn't sing a single note, but I played a decent trombone and was part of the orchestra. I also took Monty overseas with me, and even did a couple of bits between songs with an interpreter. That's right: I was a ventriloquist with an interpreter. Of course it was a disaster every time. The choir director would say something, wait for the interpreter to repeat it, then he'd turn to me and ask me a question, then stick the mike in my face. All the while *the one* interpreter struggled to keep up with all three of us. The choir director kept talking while I would try and pause for the interpreter to catch up. Timing is everything in comedy, and that experience put the dread in my head about ever again performing for an audience whose native tongue was not English. That would bother me well into later years, until I once again tried to make a foreign audience laugh. The outcome was a bit different. More on *that* later too.

Upon returning to the convention in the summer of 1978, I was honored with a couple more awards that very much helped build my determination. I entered the junior contest, but didn't win a thing . . . because they decided to make me the winner of the senior contest instead. I also won the Bill DeMar Figure Manipulation Award.

Figure manipulation is what the vent does to make the dummy move and seem alive by doing more than simply moving the mouth. Bill DeMar was an incredible manipulator of dummies and puppets, and I was honored that he chose me for the trophy that year. Bill has since become a friend and he was truly one of the best acts I ever had the pleasure of watching at the convention. His timing and movements breathed life into his characters and made him stand out from everyone else. I have emulated much of what Bill did and taught during his lectures when it came to manipulation. Operating a "soft puppet" like Peanut, versus a "hard figure" like Walter, involves two completely different types of manipulation. So if you ever see Peanut move and come to life, much of that is thanks to Bill.

Peanut: I've been working out.

Jeff: So?

Peanut: I'm tired of being referred to as a "soft puppet." Go on, feel my abs. . . .

Jeff: No—

Peanut: FEEL THEM!

Also at the 1978 convention, I picked up a new main character who took the place of Monty. Each convention, a generous figure maker would watch the contests and then pick out the ventriloquist whom he thought had the most promise to put one of his dummies to good use. The award was called Most Deserving Vent. In 1978, Alan Semok, one of our great contemporary figure makers, selected me and presented me with one of his creations, which was a boy figure. I later named him Archie Everett.

Archie didn't become as famous as the current guys in my act, but he was my main character for a long time, including the four years we did regional Texas television commercials. This brings me back to those 280ZXs I had in high school.

If you watched television in Dallas in the 1970s and 1980s, you couldn't help but see the cheese-ball commercials for Carl Westcott Ford. In these seemingly "live" spots, Carl would appear on camera walking up and down his lot full of cars with giant prices stuck to their windshields. "Hurry out tonight," he'd say. "Your car is RIGHT HERE on our lot!"

"Geez," I thought, "I could do THAT! . . . and with a dummy!" So at age sixteen, I phoned the dealership and asked to speak with Mr. Westcott. Not surprisingly, I was put off over and over again. But I was persistent, making call after call, and one day, probably out of sheer frustration from his secretary telling him I was calling again, he finally heard me out.

"Mr. Westcott," I said. "I know I can sell your cars." He must have been having a slow day, because he agreed to let me come in and pitch him my ideas. A few days later, Archie and I showed up. I told him what I thought I could do and then Archie and I did a short bit for him. To this day, I don't know how I had the chutzpah to pitch myself like that. But I guess Mr. Westcott was impressed by my confidence, because he hired me. The first commercials were for his Datsun dealership in Richardson, Texas, Courtesy Datsun. Those commercials were horrendous thanks to my overconfidence, inexperience, and giant bundle of nerves. What made it worse was that we did them in the Dallas market, which wasn't exactly small potatoes. Everyone I knew saw them and saw how truly horrible they were. We shot them at the dealership, and I had never done any camera work like that before. I was timid and nervous and could barely get through it all. Westcott must have seen through the nerves, because he hired me for a much larger dealership, though in a smaller market—Courtesy Pontiac and Datsun was ninety miles to the east in Tyler, Texas.

Barely old enough to have a driver's license, I negotiated my own contract with the seasoned salesman. Apparently he thought my goofy antics and lame humor would actually work. In addition to getting paid pretty decent money, after a couple weeks of good commercials I bugged him enough that he finally agreed to let me "demo" almost any brand-new 280ZX on the lot. That meant that I could drive the vehicle for four thousand miles and give it back, only to pick out another one for another four thousand miles. During the four years I worked for Carl, I went through eight 280ZXs and one Pontiac Trans Am.

When shooting the commercials in Tyler, I was treated to the luxuries of showbiz a bit too early. At three p.m. every other Thursday, a big stretch limo would show up in front of Richardson High, and I would jump in the back with Archie in the suitcase. Carl's driver would then speed us off to East Texas.

At the dealership, Archie and I would utilize a different theme in these "live" commercials, where we would walk up and down the lines of new and used vehicles, extolling their virtues. For each of the taping days, I would come up with a different theme for the commercials. One week I'd dress Archie as a cowboy, or Superman, or whatever else I could think up to make people remember the commercials and the cars. We would shoot somewhere between fifteen and twenty commercials in the daylight, then wait for the sun to go down and do fifteen or twenty nighttime spots. The following is an example of how Archie and I did our thing, and for this one, I'd pieced together an outfit that looked, well, somewhat *Star Wars*–ish:

> Jeff: Good evening, folks. How are you this fine Friday evening?

Archie: Hi everybody! Its Archie Skywalker here, fighting Car Wars, and making the other EVIL car dealers fear the Force of Courtesy Pontiac and Datsun!

Jeff: Let's see what we have on the lot tonight, Archie! . . .

Then we'd walk up and down the lines of cars talking about their attributes. There was a commercial for Tuesday morning, one for Tuesday evening, one for Tuesday at midnight, et cetera. Then for the next two weeks, all the commercials would be shown in their appropriate time slots. It looked as though Archie and I lived at the dealership, doing commercials every single night and day, a few times every hour.

While the money and the demo Zs were seemingly the high points of the gig, there were other huge benefits to this job that I wouldn't recognize until much later in my career. This was the first time I had really performed on camera consistently, and I was practicing a skill and getting an education about television in a way that could never be understood from sitting in a classroom or studying books. After a few weeks of this work, I could do exactly 29.9 seconds of talking in my sleep. I could walk and talk and read and manipulate Archie and do ventriloquism and watch the director and listen for cues in my earpiece, all at the same time without missing a beat. This was invaluable experience. Many years later, when the little guys and I were on television shows like *The Tonight Show Starring Johnny Carson*, or when we shot the Comedy Central specials, I had a working knowledge of how things operated on both sides of the camera. Add to that my eventual Bachelor of Arts degree in Radio, TV, and Film, and it was as if I had the perfect little toolbox, ready to work on the career I was headed for.

Walter: You had a cool job and a cool car at that young age . . . impressive. Reminds me of me when I was that age.

 Jeff: Thanks, Walter.

 Walter: Except I had a girlfriend.

I did the car commercials well into my college years. When we finally ended the run, Carl gave me a decent deal on the latest model Datsun (which that year was changing over to the name Nissan), and it was a dark pewter 1984 300ZX. I ordered a Texas vanity plate that read DUMMY. And in 1984, I have to say, this was a pretty sweet vehicle to be driving around campus. It wasn't a Porsche or Mercedes, but I was very proud of the fact that I'd paid for it myself.

I still have that car, by the way. There are even receipts still in the glove box from dinners with one of my college girlfriends. Eventually I put 113,000 miles on it, driving all over the country doing shows. It was the first expensive thing the dummies paid for, so I could never let it go. It sat in my parents' back driveway in Dallas for almost twenty years, and I recently had it refurbished and rebuilt from the frame up, making it look and run almost exactly the way it did when it was brand-new.

Over the years, the speeding tickets I received driving that car helped a lot of officers in small towns between Dallas and Los Angeles meet their monthly quotas. My best ticket experience was late one Friday night, driving the hundred miles from Dallas to Waco. Around Hillsboro, I got nailed with a radar gun doing about 118 miles per hour . . . And I had just slowed down from 128. Why was I going that fast? Well . . . because!

The cops pulled me over and I was fully expecting to be hauled out of the car and off to the pokey. The guy sauntered up to my window, flashlight in my face.

"Hi," I said. "Any chance you could knock a few miles per hour off the ticket you're about to give me?" The guy chuckled. I spotted the other cop trying to stay in my blind spot near the back right rear of my car. I'm sure they were expecting me to be drunk or pissed off or both.

"Driver's license and proof of insurance?" he asked.

Both of them had their hands on their holsters as I reached into the glove box. I gave the officer the documents. A few minutes later I had a huge ticket. "Give the judge a call tomorrow. He's a good guy."

Well, the next day, I made the call. I talked to the actual judge himself. He was a good old boy like no other. In a full Central Texas drawl I heard, "Well, son, we get these big ones every once in a while. Looks like you like to go fast. Just pay the fine and go to traffic school. We'll wipe this one off for you." Holy crap! How did THAT happen? I honestly don't know what I did or said to deserve that treatment. Maybe it had something to do with my license plate.

My other favorite ticket incident happened somewhere along the Arizona-California border, when I tried to utilize my ventriloquial skills in an imaginative manner. In a fifty-five, I got pulled over for doing about ninety-five, and as the cop stood behind the car jotting down *Dummy* on his ticket pad, I grabbed one of my characters from the backseat and got out to try and do a little resourceful "tap dancing." The dummy was a goofy earlier version of Bubba J. As the cop looked up, the dummy said, "You got him at ninety? You shoulda seen us a while back. . . . We were doin' better than one hundred! Duh, huh, huh, huh!"

The cop laughed, and then he said, "Hold on, hold on! . . ." He went to the trunk of his car and got his camera. "Can I take a picture of you two? The guys back at the station aren't going to believe *this one*." I said, "Sure!" He took the photo, laughed again, and I headed back to the car, congratulating myself on having brilliantly avoided a very expensive speeding ticket. "Thanks, officer!" I yelled back.

"No, thank YOU, son!" he said as he returned to my car window and handed me the ticket with a $250 fine. Doh!

 Bubba J.: You shoulda said you were the designated driver.

 Jeff: I think he still would have given me the ticket.

 Bubba J.: Yeah, maybe you should get out of them the way my wife does.

 Jeff: How's that?

 Bubba J.: I don't know, 'cause she says it's a secret. But it must work 'cause the cops stop her a LOT.

When I started at Richardson High School, I was ready and in anticipation of this next "bigger pond." Once again, I immediately started looking for events and excuses and every opportunity to do my act in front of as many students as possible. But a tangent business I created gave me invaluable experience with sound, and music, and controlling an audience in an entirely different manner.

This was the late 1970s and disco was huge. I hated dancing and felt like a complete moron having no idea what I was doing on the dance floor. I was, however, becoming enamored with the emerging technology of high-quality portable sound equipment, plus I was really interested in how the mood of an entire crowd could be controlled simply by what they were listening to. So, to get myself off the dance floor, stay among my peers, plus at the same time make a little extra cash, I started my own deejaying business. Money from the vent shows paid for sound equipment, plus a huge collection of 45s. I also cobbled together some light stands with sound-controlled colored lights. I asked my friend Glenn Gaines to help me, and on weekends when I wasn't doing my vent act, we would pile the sound system, turntables, records, and lights into my first car, which was my parents' handed-down 1971 Mercury Marquis. Yeah, baby! A virtual boat (also known as a chick repeller)!

The business became pretty lucrative within a few months, and my father was always encouraging me to save my money. Instead, I would invest it right back into the business, getting bigger and better sound equipment. There was another guy at my high school who had superior speakers and amps, and even a van to haul his stuff around. Though he had superior gear, I'm pretty sure I could read the crowd better, and would play stuff that everyone liked to dance to more. It was much different from performing comedy, but this is when I began to realize that an audience is not simply a group of people in one place. It's more like a hive of bees. . . . It's an entity that the performer has to learn to understand and communicate with.

As my deejay business grew, I started paying attention to personality-driven radio, and in particular, Dallas radio station KVIL and their morning drive guy, Ron Chapman. Ron, like Carl Westcott, had been a Dallas staple for years. Chapman was number one in the mornings and he was loved by housewives and soccer moms and drive-time families. He was a master at morning radio and, while most of my friends were listening to either disco or rock stations, I was more fascinated with how Chapman could do what he did. He seemed like such a *great* guy. I was pretty young and naive and never considered for a minute that someone could be different in person than they were on the air. I was in for a big surprise.

A girl name Laura Mercer was in my high school class. We were acquaintances and spoke now and then, but it took some time before I realized that her father was Bill Mercer, the guy who did sports at KVIL during Ron's show. Anyway, Laura and I went on a couple of dates, and one night when I picked her up, I met her father. He and I talked a little bit, and I told him what a big fan I was of the Chapman morning show. "Well, then you should come by one morning and see how it works!" I jumped at the chance.

A few days later, I met Bill at his house at four thirty a.m. and we went to the hallowed radio studios just off of Central Expressway. I had never been this close to a celebrity, or even the studios at any place that was number one in a big market. "What a great guy Ron Chapman is!" I thought, "Everyone LOVES him!"

Bill walked me right into the studio and there I was, shaking hands and sheepishly saying hello to Mr. Chapman. Ron smiled forcefully and was a bit on the cool side, but he motioned me to a tall chair not far from the audio board. Keep in mind that even the best radio studios are usually not much larger than a good-sized bedroom.

Well, what I didn't know then about celebrity and performers is that genius is sometimes accompanied by personality eccentricities.

Ron ran a tight ship and that was one reason his show was so good. He demanded at the very least competency, and anything less was unacceptable. His ratings and the quality of his show reflected dedication, but God help the person who didn't meet his expectations. And apparently, things weren't going well that morning. But you'd never have known it on the air.

A song would end or a commercial break would finish, his mike would be live, and he was Ron Chapman! Morning show happy guy, the voice you loved to have wake you up in the morning. But apparently today, somebody hadn't made it someplace when Ron was expecting them, and when Ron was ready to do the phone-remote broadcast, the guy wasn't there. Remember, there were no cell phones in that day, so everything had to be done on landlines. Ron had a graying red mustache and goatee that came to a point at the bottom of his chin. His eyebrows were full, and he was starting to go a bit bald. He had piercing blue eyes that lit up when he was on the air, but became cold as ice when things started to go wrong. As a sixteen-year-old kid, I'd never seen a temper like this, nor a man turn into a devil so convincingly. The goatee and hair reminded me of Beelzebub himself, and I could swear horns were about to pop out of his head. Remember that I was raised in a very Christian home with no siblings. I had lived in a very conservative bubble most of my life, and cursing was for those headed to hell. I'd never seen a temper tantrum from an adult, much less from one that I held on so high a pedestal.

Whatever it was that went wrong I don't remember exactly. All I know is that a couple of sets of headphones became airborne, two telephones were almost slammed through the sound board, and I learned a string of curse words that could have peeled the chrome off a Harley-Davidson. The most amazing part of it all was that no one called him on it. They all looked as though they'd seen it all before. Bill just looked at me and shrugged, while I shrank into the wall, trying my best to appear as tiny and out of the way as possible. After a couple of hours, Ron opened the studio door like a doorman, and swept his hand in an arc to motion my exit. I got up and tiptoed out, a bit wobbly in the knees.

The rest of the morning was kind of a blur, but all I remember is Bill apologizing, saying, "Well, that happens every so often." I actually went back a couple more times after that, and the experiences were quite the opposite. But what I learned that day, both good and bad, would stay with me for a long time. I learned that people in the spotlight aren't always what you expect. They are humans just like the rest of us. But left unchecked, the ego and sense of entitlement and self-worth can soar far beyond anything acceptable to the rest of society. I was dumbfounded that morning, but as my career progressed, I've tried very hard to never become "that guy."

Earlier I referenced the movie *Magic*, in which Anthony Hopkins plays a rising star ventriloquist who happens to be a bit psychotic. In the story, his agent is from the William Morris Agency and is played by Burgess Meredith. As Anthony's character is speeding toward fame and fortune, his agent says to him one day, "Will you do me a favor, kid? Will you try not to turn shitty? It's almost an automatic once a guy makes it big."

All along this journey with every accomplishment and with every step up, I've done my best to not let it go to my head. You never know how long your fifteen minutes of fame are going to last, and I know it could all slow down at any time, for any number of reasons. I treat this job like a business, and I try to never take for granted how hard others around me have worked to further my career. And obviously, none of this would have happened without the fans. I know that if success is to continue, I must keep creating and working and giving the audience a great product. Just like a rock band, you play a few of the hits, but also give them something new every time they come to see you.

Walter: Oh, spare us. You're the biggest diva I know.

Jeff: Says who?

Peanut: Me.

Achmed: Me.

Melvin: Me.

José: Sí.

Bubba J.: I'm in!

My senior year in high school was probably my favorite of all school years. The Richardson High Class of 1980 had about 800 kids, out of the 2,800 kids in the school. I wrote a column in the school newspaper called "In a Dummy's Limelight," in which Archie and I would trade off writing the column, riffing on things I found funny—and just like my act now, it had no socially redeeming value whatsoever. For my junior year, I was an "Eagle Guard," an elected position that I won with no problem, because during the entire day of voting, I walked around handing out sticks of Fruit Stripe gum with labels that said, "VOTE FOR JEFF DUNHAM, EAGLE GUARD!" And then during my senior year when I was voted captain, all handouts during elections were banned. The big job of the Eagle Guards was to, well, guard the eagle at football games. We were the Golden Eagles, and we had a big painted metal bird mounted on a trailer along with a large bell and clanger. When our team would score, the five of us would run the trailer up and down the field like idiots, ringing the bell and blaring a police siren.

My two best friends in high school were Glenn Gaines and Steve Jones, and we were pretty tame, conservative guys who didn't drink or smoke or curse at our parents. I'm not going to say we were boring, because we were mischievous enough, but we didn't get into *real* trouble. Solid families and our religious beliefs supported by our group of friends who also went to Sky Ranch during the summers had a lot to do with that.

 Walter: "Mischievous"? Seriously? I think it was more like, "three friends with a nondrinking, nonpartying, virginlike ambience which repelled all other normal manner of cool teenagers."

 Peanut: Bingo! This is the first time Walter and I have ever agreed on anything.

 Jeff: All three of us have turned out very well, thank you.

 Peanut: Steve and Glenn talk to themselves too?

Besides the talent and variety shows at school, I sometimes used ventriloquism and voice tricks in extracurricular ways, without the assistance of a dummy. The most noteworthy example came during 'fifth period in upstairs B Hall during Government class. The teacher was a football coach who liked to take breaks during class while we read this or that, and one day while he was in the teachers' lounge smoking, I decided to try out my siren sound effect. I could belt out a disaster siren pretty darned loudly and really convincingly, so with a couple of buddies egging me on, I stuck my head out the classroom door, and let loose with the siren. To my astonishment, the entire upstairs B Hall, which consisted of about fourteen classrooms, began a fire drill. Classes were emptied and the kids began marching to their assigned positions outside. A few teachers caught on and sent everyone back to their classes, while I was led off to the assistant principal's office. I guess Mr. Clay thought it was funny, because he pretty much just looked at me and sent me back to class.

I did that same siren a couple of times in the school cafeteria too. It would usually silence the entire room of about two hundred kids, and then get a round of applause. One time after I did it, the young and cute Speech class teacher marched right up to where I was sitting and started to gripe me out, wagging her finger in my face. I have no idea what I was thinking, but she was close enough and in my face, so right in the middle of being griped out, I kissed her. She pulled back, completely astonished, and dashed out of the room to the sound of a big laugh from onlookers and applause. Once again, I have NO idea how I got away with THAT. Shame on my seventeen-year-old self.

Peanut: Nice story.

Jeff: What part?

Peanut: That you kissed the teacher and she ran away as opposed to some of today's teachers who would have started a relationship with you.

During senior year, my friend Bill Davidoff and I did the morning announcements. Every morning we were the voices of KRHS, the school's public address system. We would read the day's announcements, and then at the end, tell a joke of the day. One particular morning we had this one set up: I said, "Bill, it seems there was this young girl walking through the forest when she came upon a frog. The frog said, 'Young girl! Take me home tonight and when you go to sleep, put me in your bed and in the morning I will be a handsome prince!' Well, the young girl didn't believe the frog, but he protested over and over, imploring her to just give it a try. Finally after much arguing, she relented. Sure enough, when she woke up the next morning, there was a handsome prince in her bed!" Bill then said, "Jeff, I don't believe that story." And then I said, "Well . . . neither did her mother."

That afternoon, Vice Principal Gumm invited us into his office and said that he had received many complaints from teachers about our joke, and that we could still do the school announcements, but we could no longer tell a joke of the day. Dang it! That was my favorite part.

Well, I was a bit miffed by this censorship from teachers who clearly had no sense of humor, so the next morning at the end of announcements I said to the entire school, "Well, folks, it seems that yesterday's joke didn't go over well with some folks, so Mr. Gumm said we could no longer tell a joke for the day. So . . . if you have a bad day, don't blame us."

Well, Mr. Gumm busted into the little room where the PA was and hauled our asses right into his office. He was pissed, and justifiably so. I never told anyone exactly what Mr. Gumm said, but as he has since passed away, I guess I can now. He yelled, "YOU GUYS ARE DONE MAKING ANY ANNOUNCEMENTS AT RHS EVER AGAIN! I'M PULLING YOU OFF THIS JOB, BUT WHAT I *SHOULD* DO IS KICK YOUR TEETH IN!"

I don't blame him. But later, Bill and I laughed our heads off about it.

 Achmed: I had no idea.

Jeff: About what?

Achmed: That you were so "badass." You know, I could use an infidel like you.

I looked forward to the Senior Talent Show for a long time. I prepared and worked on it. I went to a guy who was the technical geek at my church and got some help with a wireless body mike. I then went to Toys "R" Us and bought a radio control unit for a model airplane that had four channels, meaning it could do four different things at once. Servos are the little electric motors that connect to the receiver and battery and move the various surfaces on the models. Well, I took Archie and rigged him up with the servos. Wirelessly he could now turn his head, move his eyes, and open and shut his mouth. I then took the transmitter (the controls) and disassembled it. Then I reinstalled it in pieces, sewing and duct-taping it inside my suit jacket. I then ran wires to three little micro controls that I would operate, hidden in my left hand. In my right hand, I had a mute switch for the wireless body microphone. I was ready.

During the talent show (keep in mind that this was 1979), Archie and I got into a big argument onstage. I got seemingly so angry that I left Archie in plain view of everyone, sitting on a stool by himself behind the microphone, while I stormed off the stage and into the middle of the two-thousand-seat auditorium, yelling at him from the crowd. I was using the mute switch in the palm of my hand, so I wasn't coming over the PA. It obviously looked like I was completely nuts. I would yell, "FINE! GO AHEAD! DO IT YOURSELF!" Suddenly, Archie's eyes snapped from left to right. There were a few gasps from the audience from those who saw it.

Again, remember when this was. Radio controlled stuff was not common, and the only real animatronics were at Disneyland. There was no Chuck E. Cheese's anywhere near where we lived in 1979. I yelled at him some more, and then Archie finally turned his head, moved his eyes back and forth again, and said over the sound system, "Are you throwing a fit?" Some people screamed, others gasped, and everyone else laughed. I don't remember much of the routine after that, but it was certainly something no one around there had ever seen before.

In those early years I was still experimenting with my act, trying to find my own niche. I never questioned what I wanted to do, but I knew I hadn't yet found *my* characters—the ones that would truly be unique to me and my show; the ones who would define me. I moved from character to character, new bit to new bit.

As the years went on, those closest to me never discouraged my desire to be a professional ventriloquist. The only person who really doubted me was, of all people, my ninth-grade school counselor. Ms. Lutz would call students into her office one by one to discuss life and where we thought we were headed, and one day I found myself at her desk, listening to a litany of queries as to what plans I had for myself in the somewhat distant future.

"So you've been having fun with your ventriloquist act, haven't you, Jeff?"

"Yes, ma'am," I replied.

"Well, I know that's fun. But I wanted to talk about your future a little today. Have you thought about what you might want to do for a living when you finish school?" she asked.

"Well, yeah," I said, a bit confused. "I'm going to keep doing my ventriloquism. . . ." I remember to this day honestly thinking that there was something wrong with her. She had these really thick, round, glass bottle–bottom glasses that made her look like a googly-eyed blinking fish. She took them off and put them on her desk, crossed her hands patiently, looking at me like I was the dumbest kid on the planet.

"Jeff," she said ever so softly, "let's be realistic. You really need to find something you can make a living with."

At that moment, I came to the harsh realization that there would actually be doubters along the way. She didn't get it. I had a vision and a focus. She either couldn't see it, or she didn't believe a kid should strive for greatness or the seemingly improbable. I didn't listen to her because I knew she was wrong. I had been taught to dream and make big plans and do the impossible. Ms. Lutz made me understand how important it is to encourage kids and let them follow their hearts.

Every summer and every week at Sky Ranch I did shows for the campers and staff. I was also assigned to do a few other tasks. Throughout my high school summers I was the archery instructor, the riflery instructor, a wrangler, a counselor, and a maintenance guy. But the summer of 1979, between my high school junior and senior years, was a significant one. It was my last summer at Sky Ranch, and that camp and staff had been very meaningful and significant to me. Second only to my parents, it had shaped my morals and core religious beliefs. It's also the place where I met my first, well . . . true love.

Karen was the swimming instructor at Sky Ranch in June of 1979. She had a brown one-piece swimsuit that just about killed me and a few other guys on work crew. She was three years older than me, but it didn't matter. We had fun. She was entering her junior year at Baylor University in Waco, Texas. I'd heard of the school, but had never paid much attention to it. I knew I was going to college, I just hadn't yet thought much about where. Of course you shouldn't pick a college based on where your girlfriend or boyfriend goes. You might as well use a Magic 8 Ball. But I did just that.

Baylor was a prestigious university with high academic standards, so to this day I have no idea how I was accepted. My SAT scores and grade point averages were good, but I really think all the extracurricular stuff I did outside of classes with the dummies and my ventriloquism got me in. (Not counting the fire drill, of course.)

I always knew I was going to go to college, and my parents had been saving for me to do just that for years. I didn't exactly need a college education to be a comedian, but I wanted to earn a degree. However, the real reason I knew I needed to go to college was that I wasn't ready to make it in the "big time." One day I wanted to go toe-to-toe with the big names in comedy, but I knew I had to be funny enough to do that . . . and that I wasn't, yet. Plus, there was Karen.

I graduated from Richardson High in May of 1980. A big summer was ahead of me with some important strides in store for my career and performing abilities, but I made a single goal for myself as I threw my graduation cap in the air that day—I said to myself that I wanted to be on *The Tonight Show Starring Johnny Carson* before my ten-year class reunion. Period. I knew I would need to accomplish a great deal to achieve that goal, but if I did, a lot would happen in the next decade to get me there, and a lot more would happen because of it.

Walter: I wish I hadn't gone to my last high school reunion.

Jeff: Why?

Walter: I liked everyone better on Facebook.

CHAPTER THREE

....

Three Radio Men and a Steek!

Before my freshman year at Baylor in 1980, I had a couple of summer gigs that felt like "real" show business. By this time Archie and I had been joined by two other characters in the act. The first was Little Dummy, who was a small toy vent doll from the 1950s that I reworked as a dummy for Archie. So, my dummy had a dummy! This was nothing new; it's actually a very old vent bit dating back several decades. In my particular version of it, I rigged a mechanism that enabled me to put the little dummy on Archie's lap, and then I could operate both figures from inside Archie's body. The bit, of course, was that Archie claimed he could do ventriloquism too, and hopefully, hilarity would ensue. I kept a version of this bit in my act for fifteen years, all the way through the early 1990s. On my first *Tonight Show* appearance, in fact, Peanut had his own dummy.

 Peanut: I still have a dummy.

 Jeff: Who is it?

 Peanut: He just asked "who is it?"

Timmy the Talking Tic Tac also joined the show. Writing today, I still cringe over that one. Timmy was supposedly one of the pieces of candy inside a box of orange Tic Tacs. He had a high little voice and would carry on a conversation with all of us. It was a corny bit, but it still got laughs and people remembered it.

In the spring of 1980, I auditioned for a summer job at Six Flags over Texas. It was a big step not to go to Sky Ranch, but I knew it was time to try to work on getting bigger and better jobs doing my act.

The audition for Six Flags went well, and I was invited to callbacks. The Six Flags parks these days are a little different than they were back then. From the 1960s through the 1980s, Six Flags had large and small production shows with singing and dancing and even variety acts placed here and there. It wasn't all just rides. Six Flags Show Productions was influential for up-and-coming performers, and it was a big deal for high school and even college-age performers to get a summer gig there. I knew Jay Johnson had worked there when he was in his teens, so I figured I could give it a shot too.

After callbacks, I was told that they liked me a great deal and that they could probably make a space for me somewhere. I was completely stoked. Many acts—some great, some horrible and sad—had auditioned that first day. Only a few of us made the second cut, and then I had to wait a few days when they figured out what to do with me. Up to this point in my career (such as it was), I had never experienced any real disappointment when it came to performing. For eight years it had all been Cub Scout banquets, camp shows, and a few corporate gigs here and there. The worst that had happened was that the laughs weren't as big as the last show. So I waited . . . fully expecting to get the gig. And I waited.

Days went by, then a couple of weeks passed. I was still confident that I would have a spot. I had no other plans that summer, and gigs for a seventeen-year-old kid doing a ventriloquist act were few and far between. Finally after a couple of weeks of waiting for the phone to ring, I decided I needed to call and see where I stood. I made it past a couple of receptionists and right to one of the guys who truly held my future in his hands. "Jeff, we love your act and think you're talented.

But all of our shows have now moved to strictly singing and dancing. They're all musicals. There's just no place in any of our parks for an act like yours right now."

I was dumbfounded. I had trusted them when they told me I had a spot. I guess they hadn't really promised me anything, but I was expecting *something*.

"But you guys told me . . ." It clicked in my head that I knew I shouldn't beg. Just like with the car man Carl Westcott, I needed to sell myself. Why not give *him* ideas? I started over. . . .

"I could perform outside, offstage. I've seen acts like that in the park before. What if we just found a spot, set up a sound system, and I did a few minutes a few times a day? I'm not looking for a lot of money either." There was hesitation on the line. "I know I can do this and people would love it," I said. This was one of those rare moments with one of those rare guys when I could actually feel the heart in the negotiations. I look back now and I know that if this had been simply business, he would have said, "Sorry" and hung up. Instead, this guy thought about it really hard.

"Okay," he said, "I can't promise you anything, but there's another person I want you to talk to. She saw you at the auditions too, and she books some of the stand-alone acts at the Texas park. Maybe she can help. Let me call you back."

A few days later I found myself walking around the Arlington Six Flags park with a woman named Mary looking at various spots where we could set up an area for me to perform. A sound system would need to be installed, and people would need to be able to sit or stand comfortably. We looked here and there, and each place was disappointing. There was nothing that looked like show business to me. Each area was either too noisy or too small or too out of the way.

We kept walking until we came to the Southern Palace, the park's main indoor, air-conditioned theater that seated a few hundred people and was the house of their big production musicals. There was a proscenium stage, the large audience area, a balcony for lights and sound and spotlights, a backstage, and even dressing rooms for the twelve or so cast members of singers and dancers. In my mind, that was REAL show business. This was where Jay Johnson and even John Denver had performed, early in their careers. We stood outside, looking up at the huge face of the building and the ten or so very wide steps that spanned its entire length. This is where a couple of hundred folks would stand, six times a day, waiting for the doors to open and let them into the theater. Even now, people were gathered, sitting and standing, talking quietly, eating hot dogs and drinking sodas.

"Hey!" I said. "This is it!" It was perfect. Here was a captive audience, doing nothing but waiting. It was a huge area, bigger than any we had looked at that day. The audience would be on the steps and then spill out farther below, and my stage was the front steps of the Southern Palace! Who'd care if I wasn't inside? I would have a guaranteed captive crowd that was there doing nothing anyway.

Mary stood there looking. It hadn't dawned on her that this could be a theater instead of just a waiting area. I pointed out that I would be at the very top, between the pillars. She then said, "It would be a pretty big undertaking to set up a sound system here. . . ." Wrong, I thought. Thanks to my deejay business I knew big, loud, portable sound systems pretty well. And I had all that stuff at home.

"I have all that," I said. "I have a couple of weatherproof Bose PA speakers and stands that would go perfectly next to those side columns. The amp is powerful enough for this area. I have a mixing board and microphones, and we can even play some music between *my* shows."

A few days after that, contracts were signed, and I went over my act with the powers that be to make sure everything was with okay them. Of course, "can I make fun of the park?" was one of my first questions. The only thing they wouldn't let me pick on was the food. Apparently that was a sensitive issue.

Bubba J.: Food has feelings too.

So there I was for the summer of 1980. Six shows a day, twenty minutes each. Temperatures would reach 100°F easily, and I would be standing in the sun, wearing a coat and tie and doing jokes about the Log Ride, Pink Things, and the goofballs in Iran. It wasn't the first time I ever delved into political humor, but Jimmy Carter was winding down his administration, the Iranian hostage crisis was ongoing, and Ronald Reagan was the forerunner for the Republicans. There was more than enough material. The rest of the routine was Little Dummy and Timmy Tic Tac yukking it up with Archie. I was becoming more seasoned as a performer, learning how to work audiences that were made up of people from every walk of life.

Day after day I did those shows—six times a day, six days a week. There couldn't have been better training. On a few of those hot and humid days, I considered it a performer's boot camp. Sure I liked it, but just like any job, there were the days and hours that I just didn't want to be there, or else it was incredibly hot, or the audiences weren't as great as the day before. But the point is, no matter what else was going on, it was my job to make those folks laugh.

 Achmed: If they didn't laugh, did you threaten to keel them?

 Jeff: No.

 Achmed: Works for me!

Not only did I become a better performer that summer, but I also had my first experience with an incredibly harsh and cruel critic. The timing of the event made it a truly noteworthy incident. Even to this day, thinking about how I was handled gives me a sick feeling but it taught me that not everyone would like my act.

One afternoon, I was closing one of my six shows, and was literally at the end of saying, "Thanks very much, and enjoy the rest of your day at Six Flags!" and as my voice echoed across the audience, a pigeon who had been hiding underneath the Palace's overhanging roof decided to give me his opinion of my act. And I mean RIGHT on cue. No, the poop didn't hit me on the top of my head or on my shoe . . . not my shoulder either. The aim was unparalleled. I had a mustache at the time. But it didn't just hit that. This shot was some sort of a trajectory that came down at an angle, went down in and through part of my hair and into my eyebrow. But it didn't stop there. It then splattered and left evidence across my nose, down my cheek, through my mustache, on my bottom lip, and finally onto my shirt and tie. I quickly turned, hoping no one had seen, wiping with anything I could find to quickly rid myself of this humiliation. To this day I don't know if anyone saw.

Walter: That was a historic day.

Jeff: Why?

Walter: A pigeon understood your jokes.

After a long hot summer day and all those shows, you'd think it would be time to go back to my parents' house and crash each night.

Well, word started to get around about my act and I got an invitation to perform at the one decent comedy club in Dallas at the time: The Comedy Corner. Not even legal drinking age, I went onstage at a couple of open mike nights and did a decent enough job to get booked as the act between the opener and headliner. Not many big names came out of that club, as opposed to a couple of the Houston establishments, but I made one good friend in Bill Engvall. By this time, Bill was chasing the big comedy dream doing corporate gigs and clubs. The Comedy Corner was one of Bill's home clubs and he really knew how to work a good ol' boy, drinking Texas audience. As for me, since I grew up having done all the family type gigs, not to mention the happy-happy ambience of working Six Flags, I wasn't ready for inside a seedy comedy club. I never saw the cocaine, and I'm sure Bill had very little to do with that as well, but in later years, other comics who were a good decade or more older than me would talk about how the coke flowed through that club. No one ever approached me, and I'm sure it had to do with the fact that I was barely old enough to drive. Plus, I was a ventriloquist, and I've never heard of a guy with dolls doing blow.

 Bubba J.: Doin' drugs is sad.

 Jeff: Yeah.

 Bubba J.: Beer is way cheaper.

This first comedy club experience was my introduction into an entirely new world. I realized that to be successful I couldn't do just clever material and cute vent routines. Nor could I simply tell dirty jokes either. The comedy club audience was a completely different animal. It was rude, impatient, demanding, judgmental, and even cruel at times. If you weren't funny within the first minute or so, you were quickly at the mercy of hecklers filled with pints of liquid courage. The overall mood of the crowd would determine the length of your grace period, which lasted anywhere from twenty seconds to two minutes.

Also in the mix was skill. I have never been impressed with "vent tricks" though I did a few myself. The multiple-voice thing I did always impressed people, but I knew deep down that doing that kind of thing had zero staying power. I have always believed that you can amaze an audience for a few minutes, but you can make them laugh for a lifetime. This insight was straight from the Bergen school that I had studied so intently. I hadn't mastered the funny yet, but I was working on it diligently.

Walter: Keeping working at it.

Jeff: At what?

Walter: "The funny." Who knows, maybe someday . . .

At the end of the summer, I headed off to Baylor for my freshman year, and I had no clue as to how much little Waco, Texas, was going to mean to me, or how much the time spent there would help build my career.

Baylor is a big Southern Baptist university, and I was very much influenced by the conservative nature of a very strict Christian environment. But I was a comedian at heart, and I had trouble not stirring things up a bit now and then. I didn't use questionable language or tell off-color jokes when I performed there . . . quite the contrary. I made sure that whatever I said was completely clean, but I liked to raise a few eyebrows and step on some toes here and there. One of my favorite targets was and will always be people who have no sense of humor. If you can't laugh at yourself, then sit back and Peanut or Walter will make sure everyone else does.

I went through my freshman year fairly quietly, but doing as many shows as possible here and there, just like in junior high and high school. But I didn't start having real fun until my junior year. We'll get to that in a bit. . . .

I performed a great deal at Baylor—parent weekends, talent shows, the Freshman Forum where they had a guest speaker twice a week, you name it. Of course I made fun of rival schools like the University of Texas and Texas A&M, but some of my biggest laughs came from picking on Baylor itself, and all things Baptist.

No one and nothing was immune. During my freshman year, I poked fun at then Baylor president Dr. Abner McCall. After a few of my shows and a few ribbings, his granddaughter told me that he thought I was funny and he loved the kidding. The next Baylor president, Dr. Herbert Reynolds, wasn't so easygoing. He was pretty stiff, and as far as I could tell, had zero sense of humor about himself and his job.

I can't remember the exact event, but it was a big Baylor function held in a spacious banquet room at the then Hilton in downtown Waco. I engaged in a little good-natured teasing of Dr. Reynolds, which consisted of nothing more than two or three pretty innocent jokes that got good laughs from the very conservative, mainly Baptist crowd. At the end of the evening I went up to Dr. Reynolds, shook his hand, and said, "I hope you didn't mind the kidding!"

He frowned and said, "You know I have children that are older than you."

"Yes, sir." I said, having no idea where he was going with the conversation.

"I'm the president of this university, and this office demands much more respect than what you are giving it." Without giving me even a second to respond, he turned on his heel and marched off.

I was bewildered. He was gone before I could even apologize, even though I wasn't sure if I wanted to. I had a pretty good sense of how far to go with jokes and subject matter and any particular audience, and at no point did any of the crowd that night respond in shock. The next day I was still bothered by the incident, and I went to talk about what had happened, discussing it with a couple of my professors. They told me not to worry. Even one of the deans, who had been at the show that night, told me that Dr. Reynolds was out of line, and I had neither done nor said anything inappropriate.

This became a pivotal moment for me. Very simply, I realized that a sense of humor affects almost every aspect of a person's personality. And as I began to perform across the country for varied groups and demographics, I found that the higher the person's rank, the larger and easier the target. And if they couldn't take a joke, well, that just made it more fun . . . for me *and* the audience!

By now Karen and I had gotten engaged, but a few months later I was treated to my first truly broken heart when she dumped me. I know my parents were actually relieved, because I was way too young to be getting married, plus from Karen's standpoint, I don't think show business had ever been her career of choice for a Prince Charming. Her father was a doctor and I, well . . . wasn't. She eventually got involved with a guy in the military and I got involved with a terrorist. It all evened out.

Achmed: WHAT?

Jeff: Don't worry, Achmed, it was a joke.

Achmed: No, I mean that you had a girlfriend!

After Karen, I went from girlfriend to girlfriend, or date to date, as it were.

Achmed: You were a whore!

During my junior year at Baylor, I was making some pretty decent money, doing shows not only in Texas, but a bunch of other states as well. Sometimes I would drive, other times I would jump on a commercial flight. It was not a typical college lifestyle. While most of my classmates spent their weekends on campus partying and going to Greek events and football games, I was usually out of town doing shows. Corporate gigs paid the best, and by mid-1983, I was usually getting between $600 and $1,500 a show, pulling in about $70,000 a year. Not bad for a full-time college student.

I honestly think that the only way I passed all my courses in college was because I had one of the first truly portable laptop computers that went everywhere with me. It was long before any type of portable Mac or laptop PC. I'll try and be non-geeky and quick with this: In 1983, Radio Shack (don't laugh) started selling the TRS-80 Model 100. It ran the DOS operating system and I did every bit of my homework on it sitting on commercial flights and in hotel rooms, and even kept track of jokes and new routines. It ran on four AA batteries, and businessmen would stop in the airplane aisles and ask me questions about it. (End of geek moment.)

Every show I did back then I tried to look at as a career builder, no matter where it was or who it was for. Experience in front of every type of audience possible was my real college. But no matter what the crowd, every one of the performances was another experience.

One of my least favorite gigs was for a huge gathering of high-powered Texas court judges at a hotel only three miles from my apartment in Waco. It was a somewhat typical corporate show, with a dinner, a couple of speeches, then entertainment. I'd brought with me the big heavy trunk that I carried Archie in. Since this show was only twenty minutes, I didn't prepare too much or worry about it at all. I had done these things a million times and with my set routine, and it always went just fine. I had a few names to make fun of, and before dinner, I had gone through my typical steps of simply setting the trunk and a stand for the dummy onstage before the show began. I'd done it so many times, I didn't even need to make sure Archie was ready. I'd just pull him out of the case and go. A few minutes after dinner, I was introduced.

I did a few jokes of solo stand-up, then got to the real part of my show.

"Now gentlemen, please help me welcome my partner, Archie Everett!" I opened the trunk and . . . EMPTY!

Peanut: Sounds like a good mystery. "This is the case of the empty case."

Jeff: I freaked out.

Peanut: Maybe Archie didn't feel you were paying him enough and he quit. I'm doing that tomorrow.

What the—? I stood there, dumbfounded and mouth open. Was it a joke? Had someone stolen him? I had been sitting not ten feet from the trunk the entire evening! Then I remembered. For a gig over the weekend, I had put Archie in a little suitcase, and NOT back in this regular trunk. I've always prided myself in being able to ad-lib pretty well. If something goes wrong in the audience or with one of the characters, I could usually come up with something pretty fast. . . . But a missing dummy? I had no goofy lines ready for this! Did I mention these guys were court *judges*?

Achmed: That's what happens when you do drugs.

Jeff: I wasn't taking drugs.

Walter: That's what happens when you're a moron. Why didn't you just use a sock?

 Jeff: It's not the same.

 Walter: Whatever.

A pause, then . . . "Gentlemen, I'm very sorry. It seems like someone has kidnapped my partner Archie." This got a nice chuckle, so I kept going . . . "If you wouldn't mind sitting here for a few minutes and talking amongst yourselves, I will go and try to find him." Another nice chuckle.

I bolted off the stage to a fair amount of laughter—they thought this was all part of the act. I ran out the front door, jumped into my car, and did some crazy-ass driving to my apartment. I figured if I got pulled over, later the judge would understand since he was probably back in that banquet room wondering, "What the—?" I made it back with Archie in twenty minutes. Twenty minutes!

I busted back into the banquet room, wondering if they had all departed. Instead of anyone having left, I found them all still sitting there, smoking cigars and shooting the breeze—apparently not caring much that their entertainment had flown the coop for almost half an hour! I told them the truth again about what had happened, then went on with the show, and it was fine. Afterward, the horror of opening that trunk haunted me for many days, but it finally started to fade until about a month later, when a friend of mine living in Fort Worth (a *hundred* miles away!) called and said, "I heard you left a room of judges in the dark for a while! HA HA HA HA." NOT funny.

I'm a great believer that we all have tiny pivotal moments and people who enter our lives that determine destiny in very large ways. As most of us do, I look back at my own life and career and know that if it weren't for three or four incidents, things might be very different for me right now.

One of those pivotal moments was during my junior year at Baylor with Wes Johnson, a former student at the university who now coordinated events and activities at the Student Union. I had performed in Baylor's annual talent show, the "Pigskin Revue," and Wes Johnson had been in charge of much of the production. He and I, along with another Baylor employee, Kathy Darden, had all become great friends and we went to lunch together almost every day. Once in a while, the head of the Student Union, Ruben Santos, who later became the mayor of Waco, would come with us. One day Wes got a simple trifold flyer in the mail from New Mexico State University that was advertising the "All American Collegiate Talent Search" (ACTS). It was very simple: The school was to submit a videotape of a student that they thought had some kind of talent, doing whatever it was he or she was good at. Would-be participants—singers, dancers, comedians, et cetera—were asked to show off their wares. The tapes would be viewed by a panel of qualified judges at NMSU, and the ten finalists would then be invited to Las Cruces, New Mexico, to perform in the big show at their indoor arena. A runner-up and winner would then be chosen and receive a plaque and some accolades. Wes asked me if I was interested.

"I don't have a recent tape of my act," I said.

"We'll set up a camera in the Union when no one's around, and you can just do a few minutes. That's all they want." Wes replied.

"With no audience?" I asked, concerned.

"What will it hurt?" was Wes's answer.

Okay, fine. I'll do my act in an empty room to a sad little video camera and Wes. This won't be awkward at ALL. Of course it turned into one of *those* times in life.

We sent in the tape and both Wes and I pretty much forgot about it until Wes got a phone call. There were ten acts chosen, and I was the alternate and they wanted me to perform. I actually placed in the contest. How did that happen?

 Walter: I know! Everyone else sucked?

A few weeks later, Wes and I were off to Las Cruces, and we had no idea what to expect. It was a huge venue, and I couldn't have been happier with the way my show went. Neither could one important stranger in the auditorium who had also been one of the judges: Dave Douds, a talent agent from the William Morris Agency, who approached me after the show.

"You were great," he said. "And we've all been arguing behind closed doors. We've concluded that you can't win because you're an alternate. I really fought for you, but there aren't enough of us who want to bend the rules. However, I think you should come back next year and win the whole thing the right way. And one other thing: Would you be interested in signing with the William Morris Agency? I think you have a great future ahead of you." Whoa! William freakin' Morris!

Dave had one condition. "I want you to finish college. Then when you're ready, come out to Los Angeles, and you can seek fame and fortune." Dave wasn't stupid. He was giving me a huge confidence boost, but I think he knew I wasn't quite ready for Los Angeles.

As flattered and overwhelmed as I was, I didn't sign with him immediately, and he didn't expect me to. I went back to Waco. I talked to Wes and Ruben and Kathy, and of course my father. Dad had tried to make it as a stunt man in LA back in the 1940s, so he knew the Hollywood dream. You can see him getting thrown around a little by Gene Kelly in the film *The Pirate*, from 1948. He even taught the famous actor-dancer a few moves for the film. So Dad understood my dream. I soon realized it would be stupid NOT to sign. Here was one of the biggest and best talent agencies in the world wanting to sign me and they would wait for me to finish school. For now I could stay in Waco, get my degree, stay a big fish in a small pond, continue to strengthen my act and, whenever possible, dip my toe into the comedy scenes in LA and New York. Perfect. It was a pivotal moment.

I continued with school, and soon I made some big adjustments to the act. I replaced the toy little dummy with another little dummy that Archie referred to as "UUUUGLY." I would pull him out and say, "He looks a little like me."

And Archie would say, "NAAAAAAHHHH . . . he looks a LOT like you!" I had constructed him to look as much like me as possible . . . how *much* did he look like me? Well, the clothes matched but I hadn't exactly gotten very good at sculpting. Mini-Jeff looked more like a mailbox with hair than he did me.

Peanut: A mailbox with hair?

Jeff: Yep.

Peanut: So it DID look like you.

I also dumped the Talking Tic Tac and replaced it with a tequila bottle, complete with a supposed talking worm inside. Believe it or not, this was a bit of a daring move for someone attending and performing at a conservative university with deep Southern Baptist roots. At that time, Baylor didn't even allow dancing on campus, much less talking liquor bottles. My favorite slightly off-color Baptist joke back then was, "Do you know why Baptists don't make love standing up? Because someone will think they're dancing." Bwwaa ha ha ha ha ha ha!

Because I was going to stay in school, I still had to worry about classes and my major . . . you know, the little stuff. I was planning on majoring in Business Broadcasting, but then I figured out I was no good in two of the areas necessary to fulfill that degree—math and foreign languages.

You'd think that someone who talked for a living could handle something as simple as Spanish or French. Oh sure, I could do the accents and make a funny-sounding French dummy, but conjugating verbs? Merde! (I had to look that up before I typed it.) So during the fall semester of my junior year, I stood in front of Dean Toland deep within the bowels of the Baylor administration building.

"Mr. Dunham, you have proven to Baylor University and a good portion of its faculty that you cannot pass a foreign language," he said.

"Yes, sir," I replied.

"This would usually mean that you couldn't get a degree and graduate. However, in light of all your service to this fine university"— he was talking about me doing shows and not cursing and then saying I went to Baylor—"we can waive this foreign language requirement and change the required hours to something you might find more useful." *Uh-oh, here goes.* "Our computer lab has recently purchased a good number of these new Apple computers, something called a *Macintosh*. I think two semesters of programming in Fortran, then a semester programming in Basic, plus a semester of Mythology should round out your degree requirements nicely."

"Uh . . . okay! Thank you, sir!" I blurted out. I understood the computer thing . . . but Mythology? Well, that worked out well since in the last twenty years I wrote one joke about Mercury and his hat.

Not long after that incident, Ruben became mayor of Waco. Ruben was a genuinely good guy; the kind of person who made you feel happy just to be around him. He had a warmth and laugh that were both contagious. With all that came a pretty good sense of humor too. I don't know what Ruben's exact ethnic background was, but he was very obviously Hispanic, and I used to poke good fun at him in inappropriate ways. He'd make white jokes right back at me.

One day we were walking in downtown Waco, going to meet Wes and Kathy for lunch. I thought it was cool that my friend, though a good bit older than me, was now the mayor, and I could still just hang with him. This happened to have been a hot day, and Ruben had taken off his typical coat and tie, and was now in rolled-up shirtsleeves, and I was in jeans and a T-shirt. We were walking down a fairly empty street when I saw an official-looking car slowing down as it got near us. It slowed more as it went by. On the side I read, "INS." Immigration.

"I hope you have your green card," I said to Ruben.

He laughed, but his eyes never left the car. "Uh-oh," he said, as the car rolled to a stop a few yards in front of us.

"Oh, this is awesome!" I said to Ruben.

"No, it's not," he said.

As the guy started to get out of the car, I started to laugh, and I couldn't stop. "Keep it down," Ruben whispered. The whole scene was even funnier in my head. A young white male and an older Hispanic guy with gray hair walking through downtown together . . . but the Hispanic guy was the mayor! Holy moly.

As the guy approached, he said, "Sir, I need to see your—" And as Ruben's face registered in the guy's head, I swear I almost fell on the ground, I was trying so hard not to laugh. "Sorry, Mr. Santos, I didn't mean—"

"No problem, son," was Ruben's reply.

"Yes, sir," the guy stammered. "Have a nice day." He was back in his car and gone in NO time. Ruben was amused, and a little miffed, all at the same time. We laughed about this one for a LONG time.

 José: That is a great story, Señor Heff.

 Jeff: Thanks, José. You want to hear more of the book?

 José: Zzzzzzzzzz . . .

During my junior year, some pretty important characters started showing up in my act. Before I had my own apartment, Ruben let me set up shop in the attic of the Student Union. Amid the dust and old furniture, I had a place to work and create. Here I taught myself how to build dummies. Between classes and sometimes late at night, I would be locked in the attic, molding, carving, welding, sanding, and painting away at figures that never saw the light of the stage.

Most of the basics of figure building I learned from Alan Semok (remember, he gave me Archie), who had become a close friend over the past few years. He would show me his techniques for building puppets, giving me tips on materials and procedures, and I would struggle along, trying to make usable dummies. I even made a few and sold them at the convention one year. They weren't the most beautiful things, but I was learning.

Peanut: Good for you on selling the dummies you made.

Jeff: Thanks.

Peanut: Must be a good feeling to get paid for something that was substandard. Good for you.

As a Radio-TV student, we worked with the local CBS affiliate, KWTX. This conglomerate had television studios, plus an AM and an FM station. To get experience, I auditioned for the morning drive-time spot as a personality at KWTX-FM, which was one of the highest-rated stations in Waco at that time. I got the job, but never considered even for a moment an actual career in radio. I just wanted to learn and have the experience. For eight months I got up at four a.m. so I could be at the station to do my shift from five a.m. to ten a.m.

One of the advertisers at the station was an entrepreneur named Roland Duty who was the sole proprietor of Poppa Rollo's Pizza, a well-established restaurant in Waco. Roland had used some creative advertising tactics in the past, and I don't know if he saw my act, or if someone at the station recommended him to me, but he and I got together to talk about doing some off-the-wall radio ads.

I pitched an idea to him that sounded fun to me. "What if we had a bunch of different voices for the different ingredients on top of a pizza?" I said. "There could be Trixie Tomato, the hot female voice. Then there's Pepe Pepperoni, the Italian voice. How about Otis Olive, a black olive? And then José Jalapeño, the Mexican jalapeño?" Soon I was doing thirty- and sixty-second commercial adventures with all these different voices running around on top of the pizza. Some of the commercials were lame, and others were pretty darned funny. I don't know if they sold any more pizza for Roland, but the characters certainly started me thinking.

 José: I miss Trixie Tomato.

 Jeff: Where is she now?

 José: Heinz.

Throughout college, I was constantly on a quest for those characters that would stand out from the trite and tired. Now in my head was a pizza . . . a pizza with multiethnic ingredients running around on top and telling jokes. I was convinced that this could be a new bit in my act.

I had moved into my own apartment by then and I was able to spread out. The most important area was my workbench. It was just a solid core door laid on top of two big wooden chairs. Many things were yet to be created there.

For the pizza I began by molding all four main ingredients out of Plastic Wood dough. The crust would be about three feet in diameter, made out of plywood and more Plastic Wood, and each character would pop up and a conversation would ensue. The first character I decided to put the movements into and paint was José Jalapeño. He was about ten inches tall from the top of his hat to the bottom of his chin. After painting him a nice jalapeño green, in order to let him dry, I put him on a small dowel rod and placed him in the window in the front of my apartment.

This was in 1983, and one of the recurring characters on *Late Night with David Letterman* was the bespectacled, aging, and pudgy Larry "Bud" Melman. One of Melman's bits revolved around offering servings of "toast on a stick." It was goofy as hell, and it made me laugh.

Not long after I'd put José in the window, one of the football jocks from the complex came by my open front door. He looked in the window and said, "Hey, look! A jalapeño on a stick!"

My expression never changed but my brain clicked. "Yep," I said. "Pretty funny, huh?"

"Heck yeah," the guy said, and he was on his way.

And there you have it. I put the tomato and olive and pepperoni in a storage box, and cut the dowel for José to the perfect length. I then glued and fiberglassed José to his stick and then onto a small desktop microphone stand, and there he stood.

 Peanut: You glued a stick up his butt?

 Jeff: Well . . .

 Peanut: And you call Achmed a terrorist!

Not every character I came up with was a success. Quite the contrary. For every José or Walter or Peanut, there were two or three that I categorize as, "What the hell was I thinking?" (My favorite disaster? Tony the Talking Meatball. And I'm not kidding.) But as with both Peanut and Walter, I had no idea where this simple little pepper on a stick would lead me and to what heights he would help my career ascend. José was the first of the trio that got me there, and numero uno was almost ready to start performing.

With most of my characters I first sort out the basic idea of who and what they are, then I think up a few jokes that might work, then I construct the first version of the character and try him out for a while. José was no exception, but the basic personality for him was already in place thanks to the Poppa Rollo's commercials. The inspiration for his slow demeanor was Slowpoke Rodríguez, Speedy Gonzales' cousin in the Warner Brothers' cartoons. The basic idea of a jalapeño on a stick was funny to me, and the idea that this poor guy was stuck where he was lent itself to some pretty silly humor. None of the jokes I came up with were very sophisticated, and I jumped on the "on a stick" thing right off the bat. Of course, with José's Mexican accent, the pronunciation changed to "On a steek," and I'm pretty sure that's where the hook for the audience was, just as it was for Achmed's "I KEEL YOU!" twenty-three years later. While José's catchphrase was never as popular as Achmed's, in the early 1990s, "on a steek" became a tag line all around the country, thanks to a bunch of appearances on numerous comedy shows. But back in the early 1980s, I had no idea how far and wide the laughs for José would travel, "on a *steek*!"

Jeff: Who are you?

José: My name José.

Peanut: José what?

José: José Jalapeño.

Jeff: I see.

José: . . . On a steek.

And even though José was Mexican, at times I would take liberty with his heritage simply for a good laugh:

Peanut: Are you Mexican?

José: No, señor; Mexicans are from Mexico. I am Cuban. I'm from Miami.

And then one of the biggest laughs in the original routine:

Jeff: Do you enjoy being in this country?

José: I'm afraid for my life.

Peanut: Why?

José: Taco Bell.

At first, I thought José might be a throwaway bit appearing for a few minutes in shows every now and then. But each time I brought him out, he was a hit . . . and I mean a BIG hit. He succeeded in front of every audience in Texas and Arizona, plus in Los Angeles where I would travel now and then trying out my act at the comedy clubs.

I wanted to see how I would do in the city where I knew I would eventually have to "make it" if I wanted to be a contender in the *real* showbiz world.

I think another key to José being such a success was that he was easily remembered. For years after putting him on TV and in front of crowds, if people saw my show, then years later if they had forgotten everything else, the one thing that would stay in their memories and that they would bring up to me would be, "Oh, you're THAT guy! . . . the jalapeño on a stick!"

Probably the most important club to me in those early days was the Comedy & Magic Club in Hermosa Beach, California. Another ventriloquist and friend, Dennis Alwood, who had been a friend of Edgar Bergen's, saw my act at the convention in Kentucky and insisted that I showcase for Mike Lacey, the owner of Comedy & Magic. Mike is another of those rare, really good guys who is truly interested in helping performers become everything they strive for. Alwood told Lacey about me and my act, and Mike was instantly supportive and encouraging. He booked me as a middle act (what they call the guy who performs between the opener and the headliner) and saw a lot of potential. Years later, it would be very much thanks to Mike Lacey that I was seen by the right guy who eventually put me on *The Tonight Show*. But this would be much, much later.

Right now it was still 1983, and I was in California for a weekend performing at the Comedy & Magic Club, when Dave Douds, my William Morris agent, came and saw the show with José. Once again, he was very pleased with what he saw. He called José "genius." (I'm really not sure it was genius . . . it was a talking vegetable on a dowel stick, after all.)

I always tried to make sure that whatever jokes I did with José were simply in character and didn't disparage Hispanics. I would do stick jokes and Mexican food jokes and jokes about anything that José might be dealing with on a daily basis. Yes, he spoke slowly and was very laid back, but he would usually one-up Peanut or me or both of us. Literally only two or three times in twenty years did someone get upset and think I was being racist using a character like José. Certainly there were a few jokes with him now and then that might have been a little too stereotypical, but just like I did with Sweet Daddy Dee, my African American character, many years later, I tried to go to the folks that it mattered to most and make sure I wasn't going beyond what was socially acceptable for the majority of people who were watching my act. And honestly, the only folks I ever spoke to who were upset about any type of racism that I was supposedly perpetuating were self-righteous, guilty white people. Not one time in all these years have I ever spoken to a Hispanic person who thought I was doing something in bad taste. In fact, at the Comedy & Magic Club those first few years, as well as at the Improvs in Dallas, Phoenix, and LA years later, the Mexican guys working at the clubs would stop what they were doing for the six or seven minutes José was onstage just to see "their" little guy! They would gather at the kitchen door and watch. Even some of the illegal guys who barely spoke a word of English would give me the thumbs-up after the shows and say, "José Jalapeño!"

With José in the act now, the routine onstage would crescendo with all the guys talking and arguing quickly, line by line. There was Archie, me, José, the Little Dummy of me, plus the tequila worm in the bottle. It was a five-way conversation that would make people laugh, but more important, they would remember it. Standing ovations would come after doing the very old vent bit of drinking while the dummy talked. In my case, it was "wine" (actually, it was cranberry juice, since I was at Baylor), poured from the bottle where the confused tequila worm resided. I say he was confused, because he was a tequila worm, yet he was in a Chianti bottle, which I used for years and years. It didn't make much sense, but when I first invented the bit, the first empty bottle I found was a Chianti with the typical straw basket. It looked good and the audience could see it easily, and I never bothered correcting the gaff, simply because it was what I started with, it worked, and it was funny. If it ain't broke, don't fix it.

Once again, there was good comedy leading up to this bit, but it was simply a "vent *bit*." Bergen entertained for a lifetime with jokes and character; not ventriloquist tricks. I still had a long way to go before my comedy would get bigger reactions than multiple voices and not choking on Chianti.

In the spring of 1983, I tried out for the All American Collegiate Talent Search again, and was chosen for the finals for a second year. I headed back to New Mexico State, and this time I won first place. It was a huge leap forward in my career, with unbelievable opportunities and experiences to follow that never would have happened otherwise. All credit goes to Barbara Hubbard, the executive director of ACTS. For many years, Bob Hope was a supporter of the program and would refer to Barbara as Mother Hubbard. There couldn't be a more appropriate nickname. For more than thirty years, Barbara has helped give birth to and nuture a big number of showbiz careers, mine included. Now at a spry eighty-three years young, she is still executive director, but because television shows like *Star Search* and *American Idol* have usurped the role ACTS once filled, the organization now focuses on providing scholarships to students entering the entertainment industry.

I probably wouldn't be where I am today if not for Barbara. She used her connections and relationships at university and college events nationwide, some of which ended up being once-in-a-lifetime experiences.

Walter: I love Barbara. Where would our career be without her?

Jeff: I'm not sure.

Walter: I have an idea, and it involves you wearing an orange apron from Home Depot.

The first big booking that Barbara got for me took place in the fall of 1983 at Miami University in Oxford, Ohio, during the school's Parents Weekend. I was slated as the opening act, and the headliner was the original Mr. Television himself, Milton Berle! I had no idea if I would be able to get even a glance at the legend before the show, but what I was treated to completely threw me for a loop.

I was introduced to Mr. Berle in his dressing room about an hour before the show, and as I was shaking his hand he said, "I heard a ventriloquist was opening for me. . . . So while I was sittin' on the plane today, I took the liberty of writing you some pieces of business. These are all great vent jokes." He handed me a sheet of notepad paper. I couldn't believe it. Here I was a college kid, and MILTON BERLE was giving me some handwritten jokes that he'd penned himself on the plane that day. It had to be one of the most surreal moments in my life. This was a guy who went all the way back to *vaudeville* as a comedian, and eventually became television's first superstar thanks to his role as host of *Texaco Star Theater* beginning in 1948. Of course as legend has it, not only did he know all the jokes in the world, but he'd also "lifted" most of them. I think the saying was, "Berle never met a joke he didn't steal." But I didn't care if some of the lines he'd given me seemed a little tired, because I could now say Milton Berle wrote me some jokes!

My performance that night went well, and three years later, Miami University invited me back for the same weekend, but this time Barbara had me opening for another legend: George Burns. This once again looked to be another great opportunity, but I came to within seconds of not doing the show that night at all. In fact, I almost never made it to the campus. . . .

My parents had always loved George Burns and they didn't want to miss this one, so the three of us purchased tickets together on an early-morning flight from Dallas to Cincinnati. Well, spring weather in Texas can be pretty unpredictable, and we ended up on the bad side of Mother Nature. After hours of flight delays in Dallas, plus an unscheduled plane change, we landed in Cincinnati forty-five minutes before curtain, but NO luggage showed up! This was before I learned not to check *all* my luggage, so guess what part of the act didn't make it to Ohio? Yup. Everything but me. I had no dummies! I had no act! I have since learned when flying commercial to carry on at *least* Walter's head, that way I have something to perform with. And yes, I have done shows without Walter's body, but that's another story for another time.

This time, here I was, ready to open for one of the biggest names in showbiz history, but all my partners were missing. What kind of luck is THAT? The airline said the delayed luggage wouldn't arrive until the next day. Holy crapola. Even worse, Oxford was a good thirty minutes from the airport!

My mother was about to cry; my father didn't know what to do, but I just stood there, looking at the baggage guy and shaking my head. "This sucks," I thought. "I'm so sorry, honey," my mom sniveled. "Maybe there will be another time."

"Come on," I said, "we have a car race to get to."

"What?" they both almost said in unison. They hadn't seen me make a couple calls in Dallas when I found out the landing in Cincinnati would be so late.

"Don should be waiting for us outside," I explained.

"Don who?" my dad asked.

"Don Millure. Dorothy's husband!" I replied with a sheepish grin on my face.

We started to run through the airport.

Don and Dorothy Millure were the curators of the Vent Haven Museum. The Cincinnati airport is actually located in Kentucky, just across the river from Cincy, and right in the middle between the airport and the big city is Fort Mitchell, the home of Vent Haven Museum. Though it was probably against some big rules, after Don raced us the eight miles from the airport to the museum, Dorothy and I quickly picked out the figures I had talked to her about over the phone. I knew the collection pretty well after having been there so many summers, and I wanted ones that would fit the act, be easy to operate, were reliable but not too delicate.

Racing down the road to the freeway, I said, "Don, we need to stop at a drugstore."

"For what? Are you sick?" my mom cried.

"No, Mom, I just need some supplies."

"Supplies?" my dad asked.

"Just trust me, Pop. And I'll need your artistic hand."

No one had any idea what I was talking about. Only fifteen minutes had passed since we'd stood at the baggage claim, realizing nothing was going to show up. So we still had thirty minutes to show time, with a thirty-minute drive ahead. The dash through the drugstore would have to be quick.

I told dad to get colored markers, scissors, and rubber bands. Mom was sent for masking tape, Scotch tape, and any kind of string, and I went for multiple colors of poster board and a toilet plunger. They thought I had lost it.

Back in the car, I started to draw. "Dad, I need you to sketch on this yellow poster board a Mexican sombrero about *this* big." Then I began to sketch an oversized José Jalapeño on the neon green piece of poster board. It was now fifteen minutes until show time.

Don was driving like hell, and my mom was doing her job of sitting in the backseat, praying.

In no time my father had penciled a beautiful sombrero, and I was cutting out cardboard José. I made eyes with the other pieces of poster board, then drew eyebrows, a big mustache, cheeks, and a nose. "How's he going to talk?" Don asked.

"No problem," I replied. As Dad filled in the hat and started to cut it out, I began to draw a wide mouth and thin lips. I then poked the scissors through the board and cut out the mouth. I used the rubber bands and tape plus a few more pieces of folded poster board to make a working mechanism to enable the mouth to slide open and closed. Then I took the dowel from the toilet plunger and taped José to his stick. I made a loop woven of masking tape for my finger to go through, and then tied the string to it, and the other end a few inches up the stick to the mouth mechanism. Voilà!

Mom's prayers must have been effective, because we hadn't died in a fiery car mishap, and now Don was driving like a maniac illegally through the Miami University campus, trying to get me as close to Millett Hall as possible without running over any aging parents or slow freshmen. It was now 8:05, and I was late. These things never start on time, so I knew I still had a shot. I bounded out of the car, leaving Don and my dazed parents in a car full of cutting scraps and art supplies.

"Can you believe it?" I heard a cellist say backstage. "Opening for *George Burns* and he didn't make it."

"I'm here!" I yelled, as I struggled down the hallway with three old suitcases and a cardboard contraption under my arm.

They'd held the show. Still in jeans, my leather jacket, and tennis shoes, I didn't look like anyone opening for an American legend. Usually in those days I dressed up. I should have looked a lot better than I did. Dressed in their black ties and tails, the two orchestra guys looked at me like I was a stray dog. Someone came running up to me and said, "Jeff Dunham?"

"Yeah, that's me," I said.

"You're on!" the guy blurted out.

Sure enough, word had already gotten to the right people that I was there and apparently ready to perform. Whether I was ready or not, I was heading for the stage, with not even a second to catch my breath. Sound check? Are you kidding? I was asking questions about the weekend and the president of the university and the opposing team, the campus and the cafeteria food, and the parking all the way to the stage so I could joke about all the stuff the students liked to gripe about. My parents made it in just in time to see me scramble onstage with my armful of stuff. There was one mike onstage, and I quickly asked for a folding chair. That was all the prep I had.

I'd been thinking about what I should do: Do the jokes and routines like I normally did? Then I thought, absolutely not. There's nothing funnier than the truth, so I gave them the whole day in a nutshell. I told them everything from the bad weather and delayed planes to stumbling onstage with the borrowed antique dummies from Vent Haven. It couldn't have gone over better. Somewhere around six thousand folks that night laughed at the stories and jokes and applauded my stand-ins.

Months later, even thinking about that day made me shudder. While all that mayhem was taking place, it would have been very easy to say, "This wasn't meant to be," but I simply wasn't willing to throw in the towel until it was absolutely certain that I couldn't get up on that stage. Plus, I really wanted to make Barbara look good and to keep getting those great bookings from her.

Any nagging doubts of whether I had really pulled off the show that night were put to rest a year later when Barbara and the school's concert board asked me to perform for the same weekend again a *third* time, and this time opening for Bob Hope! THIS go-round, however, I had all my characters, but the cherry on top of it all was when I was setting up for the show, and a student who had been there the year before came up and asked if I was ". . . going to do that bit where you pretend the airline lost all your dummies?" Good lord.

Walter: You never did ask *our* side of the story.

Jeff: You weren't even in existence yet.

Walter: I knew that.

José: It was the guys before you, señor.

Walter: Seriously, do I have to talk to the help?

I never met George Burns that night, nor did I even get to see him perform. I walked off stage and straight to a phone backstage to call the airline and track down my missing suitcases of dummies. (Working with borrowed figures can be very disconcerting.) A few years later, however, at the Hershey Arena in Hershey Park, Pennsylvania, I opened for Mr. Burns again, and it became another evening of note.

George Burns was of course pretty feeble in the last few of his hundred years. The only interaction I had with him was a quick introduction and a careful handshake. But there was still a great deal to learn by simply watching him perform.

Backstage that night in Hershey, I thought how cruel it was that this tiny and weak old man was being forced to work. Why was he there? Was he in debt? Why wasn't he retired? It was as if he could barely tell what was going on around him, and I thought I might break his hand if I shook it too hard. I thought even a good puff of wind might topple him over. How in the world was he supposed to get up onstage and entertain for five minutes, much less his scheduled hour? I felt sorry for him and almost didn't want to stick around to see the sad event that was about to unfold when he was led to the microphone and shown the audience. I wanted to remember him by the old films of him with Gracie Allen on their television shows, getting roars of laughter from the studio audience. I didn't want to see George Burns fail. I was in for a big surprise.

When George was introduced, he slowly shuffled to the mike, trademark cigar in his hand. The spotlight hit him, the audience went nuts, and it was as though someone had hit him with a defibrillator.

The old man came to life and he was transformed. Songs with the orchestra, jokes and stories and puffs on the cigar. His timing couldn't have been better and he never missed a line or a beat. When he came offstage to a standing ovation, he turned right back around and went back for the encore. Finally he came offstage to more thunderous applause, then the spotlight turned elsewhere, and there was the fragile little old man again, seemingly barely able to get to the car. He was a true showman and an old-time vaudevillian in every sense of the word.

The third big name Barbara hooked me up with was inarguably the biggest of the three. Unlike Milton Berle, Bob Hope never offered me any material, but I got to work with him at Miami University too, as well as at a Clemson University homecoming weekend, and a few other notable events across the country. One of my favorite times with him took place after our show together on October 17, 1987, also at Miami University.

Immediately following his performance, Mr. Hope and I and about twenty school dignitaries and guests were taken to the school's guesthouse on campus. We were treated to an after-hours hors d'oeuvres party, and everyone stood around making small talk. After a little while as the crowd slowly dwindled, I found myself alone in the living room on the couch with Bob Hope himself. He pointed to the remote and said, "Do you know how to work that thing?"

"Yes, sir," I replied, "I think I can figure it out."

"That Steve Martin guy is going to be hosting *Saturday Night Live*. I wanna see that," said Bob freakin' HOPE!

"Yes, sir," I stammered. I managed to get the TV on and to NBC, and sure enough, *SNL* was starting up and Steve Martin was the host. So there I sat, on the couch with Bob Hope watching *Saturday Night*

Live. How the hell did I get HERE? Bob kept pointing and saying, "Boy, he's funny. He's really funny."

An equally uncanny incident took place a couple of years later when Mr. Hope and I were in New Mexico performing at a national Lions Clubs convention. Backstage before the show began, I was introduced to him again, and he said, "So what are you doing after the show, kid?"

"Going back to my hotel, sir," I said.

"Why don't you get on the plane with Dolores and me and go home tonight? Back to Burbank."

I had moved to Los Angeles by then, so I stammered, "Uh . . . well, if that's not an inconvenience."

"Hell no! Jump in the car with us after the show."

"Yes, sir!" So once again, I found myself in a time and place that was so surrealistic, I didn't know what to think. There I sat on Bob Hope's private jet in the middle of the night. But to top it all, after Bob had nodded off to sleep, if I said it once, I must have said it four times during the flight: "No, but thank you, Mrs. Hope. I don't know how to play Gin Rummy."

 Walter: You could have played Gin Rummy with Bob Hope's wife?

 Jeff: Yep.

 Walter: And you DIDN'T?

Jeff: No.

Walter: You're an idiot. You should have changed the story a little bit and called it "Strip Poker with Dolores."

So during my college years, Barbara Hubbard got me work with Bob Hope, Milton Berle, and George Burns. . . . And a lot of this happened even before I could legally drink.

Bubba J.: What's that mean?

Jeff: What's what mean?

Bubba J.: Drink "legally" . . .

Jeff: Bubba J. . . .

Peanut: How cool, you got to work with all those famous old dudes.

Jeff: Yep.

Peanut: And now you're stuck with Walter.

 Walter: Someone hand me José so I can beat Peanut with his stick.

Also during my college years, I got a booking to be the entertainment at a huge corporate gathering for General Electric. It was an annual dinner for all their big brass, honoring the top salespeople and their spouses. Black tie, live band, five-course dinner, booze flowing, and at the fanciest hotel in Connecticut. They spared no expense and left nothing to question. You get the idea.

When I say they left nothing to question, that included my act. They made sure that the show would be absolutely squeaky clean and offensive in no way to anyone. I told them, "No problem." When I asked them for a few names and facts to personalize and use in the show, they had a list ready for me with some very mundane facts about the people listed. I said, "Okay, but what about the head guy? The CEO? Is he on this list?"

There were four men in well-pressed suits in charge of the evening and they all stood there looking at one another, seemingly not knowing how to answer me. I said, "What's wrong? I shouldn't make fun of him?"

Immediately and almost simultaneously they all said, "NO NO! You can't make fun of Mr. Welch!"

"Just a little?"

"No! He doesn't have a sense of humor . . . at *all*." So this was Jack Welch. THE Jack Welch. He was going to be there along with his wife.

COOL. Then I asked, "Well, can I at least acknowledge that he's there? Just say hi with the dummy?"

All four of these guys looked at one another, in fear for their jobs, and possibly their lives. "Well," one guy finally said, "just say hello to him with the dummy then move on. He's very well respected and doesn't like to be made light of in any type of forum."

"Of course," I reassured him. "No problem."

Whoa. THIS was awesome. I truly didn't want to get anyone into trouble, and I had all intentions of respecting their wishes and not making Jack Welch the butt of any jokes. Besides, I knew that if I did well here, there were probably more high-dollar gigs for me in the future with GE.

Well, cut to my show. Dinner had droned on, a few awards had been handed out, some dry speeches had been made, and now it was my turn. I got up and did a little stand-up, then introduced my main character, who at that time was Archie. I did a few jokes and then got to my list of names to poke fun at. There was the top sales guy in appliances here, the top regional sales guy there, et cetera. Finally Archie looks at me and says, "Who's the head guy of all this? Shouldn't we talk to him?"

There was dead silence in the room. Apparently the four guys in suits weren't the only ones who knew that Mr. Welch didn't like to be made fun of. I said, "Well, yes, he's here. Mr. Jack Welch."

Archie looked at me, waited a beat and said, "Jack Welch? THE Jack Welch? Top Cheese Mr. Welch? The 'No messy with Jackie,' Mr. Welch? THAT GUY?" Still a little uneasiness in the room, but a couple of chuckles.

"Yes, that's him" I replied.

"Where is he? Can I say hi?" Archie asked.

"Sure," I said. "He's right over there." Archie looked over at the head table and said, "Oh, uh . . . good . . . um . . . good evening, Mr.

Welch." Silence. Then from the table a low grumble, "GOOD EVE-
NING." I waited a pregnant beat, then Archie let out a huge breath
and said, "Okay, that enough. Let's not mess with *him*." Big laugh of
relief from the crowd, and a smile from the Welches.

Now you'd think that was the end of that. But it wasn't. Something inside of me clicked and I thought I just might have paved a
path for myself that had otherwise been hidden in the brambles of
fear and circumstance.

I went on to pick on a couple of other guys, including the number
one corporate sales guy for the past year. Everyone knew who he was,
and he was a big shot as well. Archie read his title off my sheet of paper to
the crowd in a slow and careful way. He then read the guy's job descrip-
tion out loud as well. He cocked his head at the paper, then looked back
out toward the guy and said, "You know, Bob, I've read the stuff about
you in the program, and I've talked about you to a few guys around
here, and no one is quite sure what you actually DO for GE." BIG laugh
from the crowd. I even saw Welch chortling at that one. Then Archie
asked, "What DO you do?" Another big laugh, and then we waited
for an answer. The guy had a sense of humor and apparently some big
cojones, because he responded with, "I don't know." Another big laugh.
Then he looked over toward Jack's table and said, "Mr. Welch, what
DO I do?" A HUGE laugh from the crowd. The guy was good. And
there it was. I couldn't pass it up. . . . When the laugh was dying away,
Archie fired back, "What are you asking JACK for? He doesn't know
what the hell HE does!" Now THAT laugh almost took the roof off the
place. And most important? Welch was laughing and banging on the
table.

Afterward I got to shake hands with Jack and his wife, with the
four suits standing around nervously. Jack assured me that the show
was great and that I had some good work ahead of me with his corpo-
ration. Throughout the next couple of years, I ended up doing a total

of eight well-paying corporate gigs with GE. All first-class events with unmatched accommodations and treatment.

In my college years I was booked on "Campus Comedy," a very early HBO comedy special hosted by *SNL* veteran Joe Piscopo. I shudder when I look back at that tape now, but in 1983, Joe was big news, and there I was, on national cable, doing the best I possibly could have done at the time.

In the early 1980s cable wasn't in a majority of U.S. households, but HBO was one of the most prestigious cable channels, and they were having success with some of their stand-up comedy specials. "Campus Comedy" was just what the title implied—college-aged stand-up comics doing their thing on a college campus. We taped it at Tufts University in Boston, and I wasn't nearly as nervous that night as I thought I was going to be. I think the main reason for this was because after meeting a few of the other performers, I realized I'd been doing stand-up a lot longer than almost everyone else. I guess it gave me a little confidence because I didn't feel intimidated like I had expected.

As for how it went, I didn't kill, but I did well; I wasn't the worst and I wasn't the best. But when the special aired a couple of months later, the editing that they had done to my set showed me how important timing was and how for television, you couldn't have any "fat" in the act. It had to *move*. In the editing bay they had removed every pause and breath that didn't add to the comedy.

On the negative side of things, I also realized that my act didn't make much of an impact on the audience. It wasn't memorable enough. The characters didn't have enough personality, and they weren't something people could identify with or that they felt affection for. The search for my own unique and defining characters would continue.

Peanut: Did you find anyone?

Jeff: I found you.

Peanut: I know. I just wanted to hear you say it, oh Jeff-fah-fah.

That summer at the 1983 Vent Haven Convention, I was honored with the Ventriloquist of the Year award, which at the time was an award voted on by all the vents attending that year. In the worlds of show business and comedy, it of course meant next to nothing, but to me, it meant everything. Even at age twenty-one, I had been working at my art for most of my life . . . thirteen years to be exact, and to be acknowledged as one who had "contributed most to the art of ventriloquism that year" was a true honor.

Don't get me wrong: Even then I knew what a quirky and looked-down-upon art form it was that I had chosen for my vocation. In the stand-up comedy world, vents were looked at as sad at best. Only a few decades earlier vents had been celebrated; now we were either made fun of or made to look like psychopaths who either murdered people with our dummies or who sat alone in dingy hotel rooms talking to ourselves, only *wishing* for social interaction. But I loved what I did. Laughs were an elixir and applause was social acceptance and approval. I could see no downside to what I was doing. There was none.

Fall of 1983, Dennis Alwood had heard that I was in the market for a McElroy figure. A McElroy is the Stradivarius of dummies, made by the McElroy brothers during the Great Depression.

These two young men were barely out of high school when, with very little training, they started making and selling these unbelievable dummies. Made not of carved wood, but molded out of Plastic Wood dough, the faces and mechanics on their figures showed just how far one can go with a dummy. The faces were wonderfully cartoonlike, and the mechanics were a marvel. Most dummies today have a moving mouth and possibly moving eyes and eyebrows—but the McElroys' little guys boasted as many as fifteen separate movements. The deluxe models had everything from a wiggling nose, to stick-out tongue and a fright wig. The brothers stopped production during World War II because of rationing of materials, and although the total number of figures they made has been debated for many years, I'm pretty sure they probably finished only about forty in total.

For years I had wished and hoped for a McElroy figure, but I never quite believed I could own one. Somehow Dennis had acquired Ezry, a character the brothers custom-made for the American singer and band leader Rudy Vallée back in the late 1930s. Ezry was supposed to have been a goofy, hayseed type character, but with a change of clothes and the right voice, I was pretty sure he would replace Archie and become my main sidekick.

Dennis wanted $7,500, which was a pretty high price for 1983, especially for a full-time college student. I had, however, saved enough from all the weekend shows, so I sent Dennis a check in full, and a few days later, Ezry arrived via American Eagle at the Waco Municipal Airport. I didn't love the dummy at first. In fact, his looks scared me a little. Though he had been repainted a few times, his face showed all of his nearly fifty years. And as for his mechanics, well, I had only seen pictures of the insides of a McElroy. Oh, man, was it a mechanical dream or nightmare, depending on your perspective. Ezry had sixteen movements all crammed inside the head. Here's the list:

1. Moving mouth (lower jaw)

2. Raising upper lip

3. Head movement via a cradle mechanism

4. A 360-degree eye movement operated by tilting the head the direction you wanted him to look (amazing and unparalleled in operation even by today's figure makers)

5. Cross-eyed movement

6. Raising eyebrows

7. Wiggling ears

8. Fright wig (tuft of hair in the front pops straight up)

9. Wiggling, sniffing nose

10. Stick-out tongue

11. Winking left eyelid

12. Sleepy eyelids taking both eyelids to half-mast

13. Light-up nose (a C battery inside the head powered a flashlight bulb inside the nose—the end of the nose was translucent and would glow red, achieving a drunk look)

14. Spitting (a rubber bulb inside the figure's body, previously filled with water, could be squeezed by the vent, and a stream of water would spray out a tiny hole between the figure's teeth at the audience)

15. Smoking (another rubber bulb would be squeezed by the vent inside the dummy's body cavity, then the vent

would place a lit cigarette between the figure's teeth and into a slightly larger tube receptacle inside the mouth. The bulb would then be slowly released and the smoke would be drawn into the tubing system and bulb. A flip of a valve inside the head, and squeezing the bulb would then push the smoke out small holes from the figure's ears)

16. And finally not a movement but a feature: One of the front teeth could be removed. When the vent pulled it out, the tooth even had slightly yellowed roots!

Walter: Wow. All I do is sit here looking like an a-hole, thanks a lot.

Bubba J.: I can pee myself. Want to see?

Jeff: No, we don't.

Bubba J.: Too late.

A good ventriloquist and puppeteer can entertain and bring the most simple of characters to life with a minimum of mechanics, but I wanted to see what I could do with one of these masterpieces. Would this guy be the defining main character I had been looking for? Whatever the case, I first had to do a little repair work.

Ezry had been created by a couple of geniuses and decades later, the mechanics were still mostly there, but were worn in places. I soon discovered that the tongue was completely missing too. I didn't really need a dummy with a working tongue, but I wanted the character to operate like he did originally, so many years before.

With no e-mail in the early 1980s, I exchanged snail mail with the brothers, who were now easily into their seventies. I told Glenn what was missing from Ezry, and he sent me some sketches of what I needed to construct. I had gotten pretty good at creating from wood and brass, solder and epoxy, so I constructed mechanics and a new tongue and went to work repairing the little guy. I got the tongue installed and working, and a few months later, showed the head to Glenn, who gave it his wholehearted approval.

I think what impressed the brothers more, though, was the fact that one of their creations was living onstage again. I renamed the character Ollie and made him the centerpiece of my show. I even did the dummy-on-dummy bit with him, and upgraded the toy little dummy to another little dummy that Ollie called "REEEAAALLY UGLY!" Of course, that dummy looked like me. I still had my mustache at the time and had done my best in creating a self-portrait in miniature dummy form. It wasn't perfect, but with matching clothes for whatever I was wearing onstage that particular night, the audience got the idea and it would get a pretty good laugh when I brought him out.

I worked with Ollie for a couple of years, and was pretty good with the complicated mechanics. Mastering the rows of keys under the head and inside the figure's body required a good deal of practice, but my goal from the beginning was to bring him to life using the movements sparingly, and relying on the humor and material to get laughs, and not the tricks. The very best compliment I ever received when working with Ollie was from George and Glenn, who said they'd never seen one of their creations manipulated better.

I was happy with what I would watch on videotape. But once again, I began to realize that there was nothing outstanding or truly memorable about Ollie. He was simple in character, complicated in usage, but like Archie, he was forgettable as a real personality. Was it the dummy, or was it the jokes and material that were lacking?

By the fall of 1984, I knew I wasn't going to graduate in four years. I didn't take many classes the semester I was on radio, plus I'd changed my degree so I was a few credits behind on graduation requirements. Oh, and that pesky foreign freakin' language thing . . . that had slowed things down a bit too. But soon an even bigger diversion came along very unexpectedly: the allure of a Broadway show. Wait . . . Broadway? You mean like the New York City kind of Broadway show? For who? A ventriloquist? Yeah, sure.

Bubba J.: How much older does *New York* have to be before it's *Used York*?

Walter: Bubba J., shut up.

Bubba J.: *Previously Owned York*?

Walter: Holy crap.

Bubba J.: Maybe if you combine it with New Jersey it's *Double Wide York.*

In the fall of 1984, some wacky, unpredicted planets had aligned and I found myself onstage at a comedy club in New York City auditioning for one of the producers of a Broadway show called *Sugar Babies.* From 1979 to 1982, the production had been a huge hit on Broadway. Mickey Rooney and Ann Miller were the leads, and in addition to the singing and dancing chorus line of girls, there were a few old men second bananas doing goofy burlesque sketches, plus there was a variety act. Juggler and comedian Michael Davis had been on Broadway with the show, but he had left, and now they were in the middle of the "bus and truck" version of the run, doing cities week by week, from coast to coast. They had gone through a few other variety acts after Michael, and were now looking for someone else to fill the spot. I went onstage and tried my best to fit the part of an old-time variety act, something I'd been desperately trying NOT to look like for quite a while.

I did a decent show and after a couple of introductions and hand-shakes, I was back at Baylor. I had a new girlfriend named Susan, and we were having loads of fun. Blond, blue-eyed, petite, and spunky, Susan was a sorority girl, and I couldn't have been more anti-Greek. My cousin Randy and I joked that our fraternity was called "Looney Ate a Pie."

Susan and I had been going out for a few weeks when I came back to my apartment to find a message on the answering machine asking me to call back about *Sugar Babies*. By then I had learned not to get excited about any gig, so I had almost forgotten about it. I called back and sure enough, they wanted me in the show. And in three days! They only needed me for the month of December, but still . . .

There was no turning *this* gig down. How long had it been, and how long would it be again before a ventriloquist was utilized in a Broadway show? And to be on the road with Mickey Rooney!? Was I nuts?

Sugar Babies was touring to one city per week in North America, and I started with them in Toronto. The gig couldn't have been simpler. We did seven shows a week, with two on Wednesdays and Sundays. I got paid $1,800 per week, plus a per diem for meals and hotel. That was a boatload of money for a college kid in 1984.

I had a twelve-minute spot between a sketch and a musical number where I did my regular act, but they let me customize it a bit and make jokes about whatever town we were in, plus yucks about Mickey Rooney. Mickey was *really* short, plus he was on his eighth marriage. So *that* made for some good jokes between the characters and me.

Up to this point, I had been living a fairly sheltered life in the middle of the Bible Belt, usually performing for Kiwanis Club banquets, talent shows, and Sunday school groups. The Real World of show business was about to hit me square in the face. Though a few of the cast and crew would eventually become like family to me, I hadn't seen or been a part of a group of folks like this . . . ever.

Where I was from, finding an innocent girl, or at least a not overtly promiscuous one to go out with, wasn't difficult. And homosexuality? At Baylor at that time, and in the late seventies at my high school, being gay was something that was fairly hush-hush. I was in for some eye-openers.

Most of the cast was made up of fifteen or so show girls (the Sugar Babies!), who wore skimpy outfits designed from the burlesque era, and they danced and sang and made the stage a beautiful and wonderful-smelling place.

Was I tempted to chase after these women? They were all tall and beautiful and in unbelievable shape! So?

Well, most of them scared me to death. Most of the girls were older than me, they smoked, drank, a few did drugs, and a couple of them admitted to having had *hundreds* of sexual partners. Conversely, here I was, twenty-two years old, a *ventriloquist*, I attended a big Baptist university, and I didn't drink. I was from Texas for God's sake, and I was in the middle of a serious relationship with a girl who was saving herself until marriage. I was the LAST guy any of them would have paid any attention to. So the answer is no, I didn't chase any of them. Instead, I made friends.

Two of the chorus guys, Dale and Gary, were an outwardly gay couple, something I had never been around. They were the nicest guys in the world, and Dale made me LAUGH. For no reason in the dressing room, he would belt out in a beautiful tenor voice in perfect pitch and tone, the first lines of some show tune or even "The Star Spangled Banner" . . . but he would purposefully hit the last note just flat enough to make one of your eyes squint shut and your teeth grind together . . . and he would do it just as loud and as proudly as could be. I would crack up every single time.

This was the middle eighties, when AIDS was scaring the hell out of everyone. My poor mother would send me article after article clipped from newspapers and magazines warning of the dangers of AIDS, convinced I was going to catch it from a toilet seat or simply by sitting too close to homosexuals. It was maddening, but sweet in a motherly way.

I made two really good friends in the show, Barry Woodruff and Susie Nelson. Later, Millene Michel would join us and we would be a great foursome touring the country and laughing our asses off for many months.

Walter: I don't know if going from talking about AIDS to being "a great foursome" was the best way to word the last few sentences.

Jeff: Not that kind of foursome.

Walter: Then just say "the four of us."

The most sobering moment of the run came, however, about four or five nights into my first week when Mickey summoned me into his dressing room. By then I had tweaked a few jokes and bits here and there to appeal to our older audience, so I was getting pretty good applause. I walked into Mickey's dressing room and he turned to look at me squarely, never losing eye contact. He was very short, so he had to look up at me, but he was not a small presence. He was truly a genius on the verge of insanity, and his energy and intensity were unmatched by any person I'd ever met before then or since. He pointed his finger at me and said, "You're getting some good laughs out there, but remember *one thing.*"

"Yes, sir?" I said.

Mickey Rooney replied, "The only reason you're here is so *I* can change *clothes.* Don't forget that."

"Yes, sir," twenty-two-year-old me said. As I walked out of his room, it took a minute or so to register exactly what the little legend had just growled to me. He had done his best to put me in my place. There was a fine line between sucking up to Mickey and simply playing ball with him, but I figured one dressing-down by the incredibly talented, legendary genius nutball was almost an honor.

As for the rest of the time, I quickly learned that Mickey had an opinion about everything. To carry on a "conversation" was to pretty much nod your head and agree with him because he never shut off. Was there wisdom in what he said? Maybe there were a few good tips here and there, but I really don't know, because everything came out so fast, I couldn't keep up.

I did my three weeks with the show and did pretty well. I went back to Baylor after Christmas break and started an entirely new set of classes. But I missed *Sugar Babies*.

One evening in the first days of January I tracked down Barry. He was at the hotel where the cast was housed for that week, and we talked about nothing for a bit, then I asked him who had taken my place. He told me no one had and that I was missed.

"Missed?" I said, "Well then why don't they put me back in?"

"From what I've heard, they thought you wanted to stay in school," Barry replied.

"What?" I exclaimed, "I can do that any time! I'd much rather be in the show and come back to college when the run is over!"

"Really?" he asked. "Then I'll tell them!"

And it was as simple as that. A quick conversation between friends, and I was back in the show. A week later I started one of the best years of my life. We traveled for twelve months, with very little time off, working a different town every week. It was work, work, work, and it was a blast. Barry and I became best friends and he helped me with my act immensely. He would give his opinion of what did or didn't work, and we would discuss pacing and timing and if I should blame the audience or myself for the success or a flop.

That year was also the year when I became more acquainted with Verna Finly, the woman who would eventually build Peanut. I had purchased a goofy monkey puppet from Verna at the convention a year earlier. Verna used soft materials such as cloth and foam, applying construction techniques similar to the Muppets. As Verna would explain to me many years later, it's difficult to find a puppet that both is constructed well from a practical standpoint, but also *looks* great. Verna could do both beautifully.

I will never forget picking up that monkey in the dealers room at the convention and it coming to life in my hands. The beauty of her work, plus whatever "thing" it was inside me that made a connection with that particular figure made some sort of magic happen. As wacky as it sounds, that's how it works: In the same way a guitarist has a feeling or "relationship" with his instrument, or a racecar driver feels his machine, that's the same kind of relationship a good ventriloquist has with the dummy. The only difference is, the dummy talks back, and then it starts to get creepy.

 Peanut: No, I think this whole thing started getting creepy on page two.

I know the dummies aren't alive, but they certainly live in my consciousness. And that's why I say, sometimes when I pick up a character, it speaks and lives more easily than others. I will walk around at the convention and experiment with dummies in the room. Some "speak to me," others do not. There's a weird synergy there, but ask a rock-and-roll guy about his bass or his guitar. . . . You'll get a similar answer.

The monkey became part of the act in *Sugar Babies*. Throughout the year, I was given freedom to experiment. Barry and I would
talk about ideas, and then I would call Verna and have her create
whatever harebrained puppet I had thought up. Some were good,
others horrible. I was simply trying to take the act to the next
level, and I was still searching for that defining, perfect main sidekick. I wanted to get giant laughs, big applause, and the best reviews
of anything or anyone else in the show. I wanted to compete with a
circus-act-death-defying juggler, and with Mickey Rooney.

Did I succeed? Of course not. I got good reviews in some cities,
and average ones in others. But the audiences were older, and Mickey
was their guy. With a jalapeño on a stick, in Tucson, Arizona, I killed.
In Westbury, New York, I died all seven shows. In New York, the
audiences were older and Jewish, and I was young and pure goyim.
Every night in New York when the curtain went down, I wondered if
I would be on a plane the next day, heading back to Texas.

What was the problem? This was true show business. The audience had paid good money to see a great show. I was still learning my
own style of comedy and how to write for myself, and I had not yet
garnered my own audience, nor did I have the main character that
would define my act and remain memorable.

I realized not long after the run that though I dropped out of
college for an entire year, 1985 on the road with *Sugar Babies* was the
best education, but for most of that year I wasn't truly happy with my
act. I knew it could be better and I knew the laughs could be bigger.
Struggle and the failures were my teachers. They made me want to be
my best, and I wasn't there yet.

CHAPTER FOUR

Birth of an Old Fart

At the end of 1985, *Sugar Babies* went dark for the holidays and I headed back to college to finish my degree. My goal was to graduate at the end of 1986 and it almost didn't happen. By the middle of the fall semester, I wasn't passing a single subject. I broke up with my girlfriend Susan, lost touch with many friends, and I'd lost a lot of weight. My parents had no idea what was going on. Was I doing too many shows? Was it depression? Women? Was I sick? On drugs? Addicted to porn?

None of the above. It was all about helicopters.

It had started six years before, in the summer of 1980, when I spotted a radio-controlled helicopter. In those days, radio-controlled airplanes were plentiful, and really serious hobbyists spent hundreds of hours and sometimes thousands of dollars building their little crafts. However, technology was just emerging for model rotorcraft. I'd never seen one before, and as the four-foot-long machine lifted off the parking lot and settled into a five-foot perfect hover, I was mesmerized. After watching it fly for a few minutes, I marched straight into the hobby store and spent about $1,000 on a kit, engine, radio, and everything else I needed to get started. Two weeks later, I'd built the thing and gone through multiple sets of blades and parts just trying to learn to hover. A few months later, and I could hover the $2,000 machine upside down, an inch off the pavement. Flash forward six years. In the spring of 1986, I was out in an open field not far from the Baylor campus, flying one of my model helicopters. A guy who was obviously not a Baylor student and who looked to be about my age stopped to watch the aerobatics. He was wearing a baseball cap that looked like it had been used to clean the counter at a Dairy Queen. His T-shirt and jeans were smeared with God knows what; and he drove an old blue Datsun pickup that was about as clean as his hat. He stood at a respectable distance until I landed and then walked over for a chat. People were always stopping to watch the flying and ask questions, so I tried to be as polite as possible but to also give off the air of not wanting to be bothered. The guy's name was Keith Jones. Turned out he'd been flying for a few months too. We chatted a little, and soon traded phone numbers and met a couple of times to fly together. Keith was a plumber and the son of a plumber. His parents were divorced and he lived on a couple of acres of land in a small farmhouse with his mom, sister, and sometimes girlfriend. We couldn't have been from more different backgrounds, but we soon became flying buddies and best friends.

One day when riding with him in the Datsun down a two-lane highway to lunch, some guy started tailgating Keith a little too aggressively. It went on that way for a mile or so, and Keith got a little miffed. I'd always wondered why he had a big foam cup filled with BBs on the floorboard, but I'd never asked what they were for. I was about to find out.

"That guy's an asshole," Keith said.

"Yep," I replied.

"Get the BBs," he said.

"For what?"

"See down there?" he pointed.

The rubber boot around the gearshift of the Datsun was gone, and you could see straight down through the floorboard to the pavement rushing past.

"Yeah," I answered.

"Pour that cup of BBs down the hole, slow at first, and then faster and faster in and we'll see how long it takes the turd to back off."

This was the funniest thing I'd heard in a LONG time. Keith continued driving and I started pouring the steel shot down the hole. Those balls of metal hit the highway at seventy miles per hour in a constant stream and in no time were peppering the other guy's truck. He must have had NO idea what was hitting his car or his windshield. The guy started to weave, then slow down, then swerve, then finally veered off into the ditch while we sped away, almost killing ourselves, we were laughing so hard.

Achmed: I love the BB story. Next time, try biological weapons—they work even better.

Jeff: Achmed!

Achmed: Just my two cents.

One day, Keith came to my apartment and told me that he'd found something really cool during a visit to the junkyard the day before. He told me there was an old but real, full-sized, two-seat helicopter that had been made from a *kit*, and it was sitting on a trailer. "A kit?" I asked. "For a *real* helicopter? One you can *sit* in? Let's GO!"

That was the first time I saw a very early version of a RotorWay helicopter. Keith recognized it first from their ads in *Popular Mechanics*. Sure enough, we bought a copy and there was a tiny little ad in the back: "PSSSST! FLY YOUR OWN HOMEBUILT HELICOPTER!" This couldn't have been any cooler.

Walter: Actually it could have been cooler.

Jeff: How?

Walter: It could have said, "Fly a Helicopter Built by a *Professional Helicopter Builder and Not You.*" You're a complete idiot.

That afternoon I ordered an information packet. A week later, and I found myself on a Southwest Airlines flight heading from Austin to Phoenix for a factory tour and demo ride. Two weeks after that, I got up the nerve to wire most of the money I'd saved from *Sugar Babies* to RotorWay. One of my goals had always been to own and fly a real helicopter, and now here I was taking the plunge. Sure I had to build the helicopter first, but their builder support and in-house flight training school were unparalleled.

A few weeks later, fourteen big crates showed up at Keith's house and we loaded them into his barn. Even the engine was in one of the boxes! I honestly had no idea if I could do this. There was welding and fiberglassing and assembling and construction and wiring and testing and tuning. At certain points the FAA had to come and inspect my work. Then I had to go for pilot training. It was a little stressful, but I kept telling myself, "This is just like the little ones, only bigger."

I spent the next seven months building the helicopter. My undivided attention was in that barn and with construction manuals, and NOT in my school's textbooks. That's when the GPA went south and my girlfriend moved north. But I built the aircraft, passed

RotorWay's flight school, and started flying all over central Texas in my homebuilt helicopter.

Walter: Could you be any more antisocial, playing with dolls *and* flying in a helicopter?

Bubba J.: I got in the mile-high club in a helicopter.

Jeff: Bubba J.!

Bubba J.: Okay, it was a ten-cent ride in front of the grocery store, but it still counts!

The only thing I didn't ignore during all this was my act. I was doing as many shows as I could book, and I was still planning on moving to LA to pursue my goals. Getting on *The Tonight Show Starring Johnny Carson* was still my top priority, but I now simply wasn't in as much of a hurry as I had been. After a few visits to Los Angeles and doing a few shows at a couple of the clubs, I realized that I wasn't quite ready to take on that town. I wasn't getting as many laughs or as big a laugh as the LA comics were in their hometown. This was an environment that was still very unfamiliar and somewhat frightening to me. Also, and just as important, I knew I was still missing that *edge*. What that edge was, I didn't know exactly. I just knew it wasn't there. I knew that experience plus a little maturity as a performer would help. So this helicopter business was a superb way to bide my time, but to also work on "the funny."

When I finally graduated in the fall of 1986, as my name was called and I crossed the stage to receive my degree, a familiar voice rose from the crowd and bellowed, "YEAAAAAAYYYYYY!" A public outburst like that from my father was unheard of up until that moment, but as he later told me, "When you graduated, I felt like I got a raise!" After six long years, he was finally done paying for college!

I finally had my Bachelor of Arts degree, but my parents had no illusions that I was ever going to try and find a normal job. There was only once in my life that I can remember either of them ever betraying even the slightest hint of doubt about my career choice. On one of my visits home from college, Mom and Pop and I were sitting at lunch at Luby's Cafeteria, where we ate almost every single Sunday after church. My dad said to me, "You know a lot of our friends talk about their kids and what they'll be doing soon. Fred Miller says his son John is going to be a neurophysicist, the Jacobs say Susie is going to be a criminal lawyer. We have to say, 'Well, Jeff is still doing his puppet show.'" To this day I'm still not quite sure if Pop was being funny or if he was trying to make a point. Even though the career choice might have seemed iffy at best, I always had gigs on the books, I was always making money, and each step was a new adventure for them as well as me.

Most important, *I* never questioned whether I would succeed. You could say I simply had confidence, but I didn't see it that way because I just never considered failure. There were no other choices because I left myself no other options. I didn't have a backup plan. I guess there's a little irony in the fact that one of my favorite inspirational lines in a movie was spoken by a puppet. . . . From *The Empire Strikes Back*, when Yoda was training Luke:

"Try not. Do, or do not. There is no try."

Walter: Good for you; you just quoted a midget in a rubber suit.

 Jeff: Wait a minute. . . .

 Walter: What a beautiful message.

 Jeff: I think so.

 Walter: "Quit trying." Yeah, that's nice.

After graduating, I stayed in Waco for almost two more years. I was having too much fun piloting the chopper. It wasn't unusual for me to simply take off from little McGregor Airport, and fly in any given direction with no destination in mind, simply seeing what I could find. I had a gas can strapped in the seat beside me, and if I was running low, I'd just land next to a gas station in the middle of nowhere, fill up, and be on my way. All I had was a paper map, a compass, and a lot of blue Texas skies.

Even though deep down I knew I wasn't ready for Los Angeles, at times it was easy to kid myself into thinking I was funnier than I was because I was playing for such easy and forgiving audiences at Baylor and at church shows or for small civic and corporate gatherings. I had a safe little act that made people laugh at those small performances and at the ventriloquist conventions. Some of those crowds were a little tough, but none of them were *the big time*. I'd only been out of my league on a few occasions during short visits to LA and New York, and even those were middle or guest spots where no one had purchased a ticket to see just me. There was really no pressure in shows like that. Being the middle act for a headliner is like an easy layup. No one expects you to be great. You just have to make the shot or get out of the game. But after the year of doing well in *Sugar Babies*, I thought I finally might have what it took to be on *The Tonight Show*.

On one of my excursions to LA in the spring of 1986, Mike Lacey got me an audition for one of *The Tonight Show*'s talent bookers, Jim McCawley. Comics either loved or hated Jim, and of course it was all based on if you got on the show or not. If he booked you, you loved him. If he didn't, well, guys used words to describe him like *stupid*, and *asshole*.

Lacey was convinced that I was right for *The Tonight Show* and convinced Jim to watch my act. McCawley was known to hit two and three clubs a night, hunting for fresh talent, and in those days, Carson was the only game on late night TV for comics. There were other talk shows that utilized stand-ups, but you really hadn't made it until you had done Johnny's show and done well.

That night at Comedy & Magic, I used Ollie and did my very best, most spectacular six minutes, which included José Jalapeño and the worm in the bottle and drinking while Ollie talked. I'd done the routine a million times and I thought I did really well. I was disappointed to find out after the show that McCawley left without a word. He was also there that night to watch Roseanne Barr, who was preparing for her third stand-up spot on Carson. This was very early in her skyrocketing ascension, much before her sitcom, and those first few times she destroyed on Carson with her stand-up. I've heard all the horror stories about Roseanne in later years, but that wasn't the woman I met that night. She couldn't have been more kind or encouraging. "Don't worry about it," she said. "He's a good guy, and you did great. I'm sure he'll call you. He probably just had something he had to get to."

I flew back to Texas the next day and expected a call from Jim any minute. Good news or bad, I just wanted to talk to him and hear what he thought. I called his secretary that morning and left every number possible. I told my parents that if he called their house, to please leave a message on my machine in Waco. Every hour I would call my answering machine no matter where I was to see if Jim had left a message. Even during the hundred-mile drive from Dallas to Waco, I stopped at a couple of gas stations just to call my apartment and check. For two days, nothing.

Finally at the end of the second day and after I had left multiple messages, his secretary must have talked him into picking up the phone, probably out of sheer frustration.

"You're pretty persistent," he stated.

"Yes, sir," I answered. I couldn't stand it any longer. "What did you think?" I asked.

This was six years into the ten that I'd given myself to make it to Carson, and the silence on the other end of the line was about to kill me. The clock ticked. I don't think there was a pause because he was annoyed. Maybe it wasn't even a real pause. It just felt like forever to me.

"Well, honestly, you're just not ready," Jim said.

Something inside me dropped and I suddenly felt incredibly stupid. How could I have even thought this was possible? Seriously. What were the odds? I was a ventriloquist. Deep down his answer hadn't really surprised me, but I had dreamed and imagined and hoped and prepared for so long for this moment.

"Was I close? What's not right?" I had to ask. There was silence on the line again. I could hear the hum in the wires, then some shuffling of papers, maybe a pen tapping.

"You're not ready," he said again.

"Okay, but what do you mean, exactly? What can I do to *be* ready?"

I pushed. I didn't want to let him go until I had *some* idea of what I needed to be doing to get on the show. Was there really a possibility?

Jim McCawley sat for a few more seconds, then he finally said, "Your skills are great and the bits are good, but it's just not funny enough. Johnny likes funny. You need *good jokes*. So when you've made it funnier, I'll come see you again."

"Really?" I asked.

"Of course," he replied.

All I wanted was hope and he'd just given that back to me.

McCawley was no asshole. He'd turned down hundreds of other comics many times, but most of the time he was talking to agents and managers and not some green, fresh-out-of-college kid. I think he heard the drive and hope in my voice and he knew how much I wanted to succeed. I hung up the phone dejected and depressed, but still with something to work toward. I had a lot of confidence from all those years of performing, but it didn't mean *anything* if I wasn't funny enough for Johnny Carson himself. How long would it be until I was ready to audition again? The most important thing I realized that day was that if it was to happen, it wasn't going to be nearly as easy as I thought.

Someone once told me that they didn't think a comic could write any meaningful material until at least their late twenties because a person hasn't lived long enough and been through enough crap to have a deep enough well to draw from. I understood and believed that. It wasn't simply fear holding me back from moving to Los Angeles. I'd already had practical experience with LA audiences, and I knew what I was in for. But I was only twenty-four, and as I said before, I knew my act still didn't have the kind of "edge" required. Also, I still needed that signature character that could show audiences that vent really could be mainstream again. I wanted characters that were different and memorable, comedy that was cutting edge, and an act that was as popular as any stand-up comic of modern day. But I hadn't figured out anything beyond Archie or Ollie. José Jalapeño was good, but he wasn't a leading man.

I continued to bide my time. I kept flying my helicopter. In the spring of 1987, I was hired to fill the variety spot in the much-scaled-down Atlantic City version of *Sugar Babies* starring Carol Lawrence and Rip Taylor. Carol had originated the role of Maria in *West Side Story* some thirty years earlier. Rip, aka "The Prince of Pandemonium," was known for a wild stand-up act that featured throwing confetti into the air and had been a big hit on *The Brady Bunch Hour* and *The Gong Show*. No, this was certainly not the original version of *Sugar Babies*, but it was experience and a gig most guys in my position would kill for, so off to New Jersey I sped.

A few days into the gig and I met a cocktail waitress named Donna. She looked as Irish as could be with red hair, fair skin, and a smile that melted me. After going out with her a few weeks, I learned about New Jersey dating etiquette. One night when my 300ZX sat unguarded in the casino parking garage, Donna's ex-boyfriend proceeded to knock in the car's windshield with a baseball bat. We knew it was him because he bragged about it to her the next day. Being the tough guy that I was at the time, I retaliated as best I knew how: I didn't do anything. I wanted to think about it for a while, but apparently my inaction was more effective than any revenge I could plan. Donna told me later that the goofball was constantly terrified of what I was planning for him and the more time that went by, the jumpier and more scared he got. We laughed about that for weeks.

 Bubba J.: Did her ex-boyfriend want to play baseball with you?

Jeff: I don't think so.

 Bubba J.: Maybe a baseball bat is what they go hunting with in New Jersey.

Back in Waco for a weekend break, I headed to my helicopter hangar. I hadn't flown in many weeks. I needed to get back in the air. Remember that at the time, I was an incredibly inexperienced student pilot, having logged only forty hours in the air. Inexperience combined with overconfidence is a dangerous thing in aviation. Welcome to my nightmare.

That day, I flew a few miles away from my hangar to practice autorotations. This was a good thing to master, because you never know if and when an engine just might quit. Odds are good against this happening, but a good pilot needs to have the instincts for what to do if and when it happens. During the autos, I was adding in 180- and 360-degree turns during descent. You spiral down pretty quickly in those turns, and it's darned exciting because in a really tight one, the ship is literally over on its side, heading down *fast*. On about my sixth one, I got turned around with my ground references and ended up at the end of the autorotation a few feet above the ground going *with* the wind. This was a BIG no-no in a helicopter this small with such light blades. I thought the wind was on my nose, when in fact it was right on my tail at fifteen miles per hour or faster. That's BAD for anyone, much less a novice pilot. Worse, I didn't recognize I was in trouble until it was way too late. When I pulled the nose up and asked the ship to slow down on ground speed, it didn't, and I ran out of rotor speed.

I tried to slide the helicopter in and cushion the touchdown, but there was no lift or speed left in the blades, and I was over a plowed cornfield. I hit once on the skids then twice, and now heading sideways at a pretty good clip, the right skid hit a furrow, folded under, and we hit and rolled at about twenty miles per hour. The world tumbled, the windshield broke, dirt and debris filled the cabin, and all I could do was hang on to the controls and wait for silence. The engine screamed, the blades plowed the dirt, a few parts flew, and then it was over. The beautiful ship ended up on her side and I was hanging from my harness.

The helicopter was a mess, but thanks to the good Lord, dumb luck, and a beautifully designed 4130 chrome alloy steel frame and roll cage, I was still alive. I trudged the three miles back to the hangar over fields, across creeks, and through a few brambles. I suffered only a mild bump on my head and a badly bruised ego.

When I got back to the hangar, I called Keith. He came out, and we got my trailer and headed for the field where my total wreck of a chopper was on its side, bleeding out fluids. It took us a couple of hours to haul the hulking mess onto the trailer and start heading back for Keith's barn. We were pulling a crashed helicopter, lying on its side. I had never been more depressed. Before pulling out onto the highway with mangled bird in tow, Keith scribbled out a sign on a piece of cardboard and hung it on the back of the trailer: SHIT HAPPENS. This was the first time I'd ever heard the expression. It's not exactly Socrates, Thoreau, or the Bible, but since then, saying those two simple words has comforted me a lot when I had no other answer.

 Walter: Sorry, Mrs. Dunham.

 Jeff: What are you doing?

Walter: I'm apologizing to your mother who's reading the book for your use of the S word.

Jeff: It's part of the story.

Walter: Well, I think we all could have gotten the point if you had said, "Stuff happens."

Jeff: I guess you're right.

Walter: Dumbshit.

Not long after that, *Sugar Babies* closed for good, and I went back to Waco, intent on doing nothing but aircraft repair. I was a firm believer in getting back on the proverbial horse, so I couldn't wait to get flying again and do a successful autorotation. Keith felt the same way, but with a slightly different twist: "You'd better fly it back to the crash site and do a bunch of autos to that same spot over and over. The odds of the same helicopter crashing in the exact place two times in a row are pretty low, so you'll be safe." That sounded like genius logic to me.

Three months later I did just that. I did an auto to the ground, and landed right on the spot where I'd crashed. I was wearing Ray-Ban Aviator sunglasses the day I crashed, and now I took them out of their case. I hadn't worn them since. They were bent pretty badly when I banged my head, and I very purposefully left them that way.

They also still had the dirt on them from where they'd landed on the ground when they flew off my head. I straightened them out, wiped off the dirt, put them back on, then took off again, and had a good day of flying.

Did I learn anything from that experience? Yeah, two things: Don't auto with the wind, and shit happens.

In the Harrah's *Sugar Babies*, I had tried replacing Ollie with a horse as a main character . . . yes, a horse. Verna made him, and he was a Clydesdale named Clyde. (I shudder even as I type these words.) I still did the little dummy thing and the worm in the bottle. . . . José Jalapeño was memorable and amusing, but I knew the whole show still wasn't as funny as it could be, nor were these the characters that were all-defining.

When I went to the 1987 ventriloquist convention that July, I was still searching. That year graphic artist Bill Nelson showed up with a frowning dummy, which looked very similar to Bergen's Frowning Charlie, a figure Bergen had made for the 1947 Disney film *Fun & Fancy Free*. A couple of years before, Nelson had illustrated a beautiful portrait of Frowning Charlie and sold print reproductions of the work. They were absolutely fantastic and I kick myself now for not having purchased one of the posters. But now, Nelson and figure maker Chuck Jackson had created their own version of a frowning figure and had named him Mr. Horowitz. I thought he looked great, but a *frowning* dummy? I remember overhearing people in the dealers' room at the convention talking in hushed sentences like:

"What in the world would you do with *that*?"

"You can't do comedy with it."

"He'll never sell."

I took those comments as a challenge, wondering what *I* could do with him. During conventions, dealers had the opportunity to get in front of the crowd and show or demonstrate their wares. Bill never wanted to perform. I thought to myself, "If I'm actually any good at this, I should be able to make that frowning Mr. Horowitz work."

"Could I demonstrate this one for you?" I asked Bill.

"Sure," he said. "I'm not going up there."

Within ten seconds of taking the dummy onstage, I realized I could easily connect with this type of character. I started to ad-lib.

"What do you do for a living?" I asked Mr. Horowitz.

"I'm an inventor."

"What have you invented?"

"You know how when you go in the kitchen and you close one cabinet and the other opens up?" he asked.

"Yeah," I said.

"I did that."

After a few more jokes and some big laughs, I walked offstage wondering if that had been a fluke. My friend Dale Brown told me I should buy the little guy, and Bill quoted me a price that was above anything I could spend at the time. Remember, I had spent most of my money on the helicopter, crashed it, and then spent almost half of that amount again rebuilding the thing. I barely had enough in savings to get back and forth to the convention that year.

"Bill, I really don't have that kind of money right now," I said. "Could you sell it for a little less? I'll make really good use of him."

He wouldn't bargain. I've since heard many versions of what happened that day. Some say Bill offered to sell the rights to the character to me and that I refused, but none of that is true. Back then, I wouldn't have even known what "selling the rights" meant.

I returned to Waco empty-handed, but I didn't forget about the laughs I got that day with the frowning dummy. After pondering for a while, I decided I could create my own version for about $50 in materials. I liked what Bill and Chuck had done, but I preferred Bergen's version, which had more of a pout to the lips and a more forced-looking frown. I was also thinking that an *old* man would be more interesting.

I took part of my inspiration for the character from Keith Jones's father, whose name was Walter, and who happened to be a cantankerous old fart. He wasn't a jerk, but more of a curmudgeon. You could tell that beneath that crusty surface was a guy with a sense of humor. He would grumble a lot but every so often you'd also catch a gleam in his eye after he'd said something that was ornery.

As I was contemplating basing my new character on Walter Jones, I then saw Bette Davis on Carson. This was a woman who had been everywhere and done everything. Carson asked her questions and she just spouted off her opinions on whatever she wanted to talk about. She didn't care if what she said was politically incorrect or offensive or outlandish. She didn't care what anybody thought and it was refreshing as hell. Carson laughed and spun around in his chair. Cool.

Walter Jones. Bette Davis. A frowning old-man dummy. I knew I was sitting on something that could be pretty funny but I didn't think an audience would like the negativity for more than five minutes. Boy, was I wrong.

 Walter: Boy, were you wrong.

 Jeff: I know.

 Walter: Turns out they couldn't take *you* for more than five minutes.

Jeff: That's not true.

Walter: Hey, shit happens.

I sat down at my workbench in my apartment late one night. Fueled by Dr Pepper, the same stuff that kept me going when building my helicopter, and with the television broadcasting Carson and then Letterman, I used a dinner knife and went to work on a big mound of plasticine clay that I'd purchased at an art store that day. The only other tool I used was a small broken mirror that I'd picked up next to the apartment complex Dumpster. After making the basic shape of the head, I then looked in the mirror with a frowning scowl and copied the lines of my face into the clay.

About four hours later, "The Star-Spangled Banner" came on TV, the station went off the air, and snow filled the screen. I looked at the clay. I'd never taken a sculpting class in my life nor had I read any books on the subject. But what I saw staring back at me was a face that made me laugh. If I made that scowl, it was me . . . just a few decades older and with a lot less hair.

Little did I know what that face was about to do for my career, and how many people he would make laugh throughout the next few decades.

The next day I made a two-piece plaster-of-Paris mold. I cast the head in Plastic Wood dough, making front and back head-shell pieces. I let the head harden for a couple of days and then installed a moving mouth and raising eyebrows. A "head stick" and controls were next. For the eyes, I found a local taxidermist and picked out some blue glass spheres and glued them inside the head, just barely visible through his squinted expression. I painted him a healthy flesh color, made a body with scrap plywood and pine, shaped the chest with bailing wire, and quickly molded and cast Plastic Wood hands as well. Arms and legs were stuffed athletic knee socks, and the feet were plywood. I went to Kmart for kids' clothes, trying to find things that looked as much like an old man's as possible. On a visit to Dallas a few days later, Dad let me have his thin red clip-on bow tie that he'd saved since his high school years. Done, and in only two weeks from start to finish.

 Walter: Lazy ass.

 Jeff: What?

 Walter: You were in such a rush to finish me, you forgot my hair.

I named the dummy Walter after Keith's dad, as well as after another Walter who had a welding shop not far down the street from my apartment complex. The two Walts knew each other, and both those guys were cut from the same cloth. It was a delight to see these two old grumps carry on a "conversation." What inspiration.

"Shut the hell up!" and "Who the hell cares?" were expressions that just spilled out of my Walter's mouth. Those words became his catchphrases and breaths of life.

Next I gave Walter a back story. At the time I made him a Korean War veteran (and twenty-five years later he's morphed into a Vietnam vet). He is also a retired welder, has been married forever, and is chronically pissed off at his wife. Well, at least he *says* he is. He's just a curmudgeon and actually loves his wife unendingly. He just wants to kill her half the time too.

I don't remember the first time I took him onstage. All I know is that he was a huge hit. What I mistakenly thought would be an extra few minutes in the show quickly became a monster success. Comedy works and characters succeed when an audience can identify with what's being said and who's saying it. Well, *everyone* knows someone like Walter. They're either married to him, or they work for him, or they're related to him. Whatever it is, we all *know* the guy. Walter and José were now numbers one and two of a soon-to-be threesome that would define and change my act and my life for good. They would help me accomplish goals and attain heights I had dreamed of and aspired to even as a young boy, but they would also be part of a bigger team in the distant future that would take me places I *never* dreamed I would perform . . . or where I ever thought I *could*.

As big a hit as Walter was, I didn't really think of him as ever being the main character. I thought of him as a great addition, and that I hadn't found the perfect main sidekick yet. So, the search continued.

 Walter: *Although the search continued for a main sidekick, I knew deep down in my heart that Walter was truly the one—*

 Jeff: Excuse me, what are you doing?

 Walter: I was typing the rest of the story for you.

Jeff: I'm writing this book.

Walter: Dammit.

It was now the spring of 1988, and all was well. I was still living single in my Waco apartment, flying my newly rebuilt helicopter as much as possible, and hanging out with friends in the newsroom at KWTX. Jordan Cox, Kelly Grinnell, David Franks, Barry Ray, Robin Johnson, Dave Evans, Skeeter Williams, Archie Woodard, and Laura Emerson: These were all folks whose friendships I cherished. I was the only one without a real job, but a lot of us had been at Baylor together and had remained friends, so they tolerated me hanging around. Every once in a while they would use the characters and me on air in the Baylor homecoming parades, or during the local segments of the Jerry Lewis telethons, or for pretty horrible local television commercials. My favorites were for the Central Texas Wild Animal Park. I would take a character or two out to the preserve and we would set up the camera with me standing next to or holding one of the live animals. Then I would try and ad-lib a thirty- or sixty-second spot getting in as much information as possible before either I or the puppet were pecked, poked, strangled, or chewed to death by the particular wild beast. Snooky the young chimp wins for using up the most tape for retakes. I used the gray monkey one day, and Snooky had NO idea what to think. Every time my ape would start to talk, Snooky would jump on my lap and either try to choke the ape, rip his head off, or bite his neck. And of course, the ape's neck and head were my arm and hand! The outtakes are something to behold.

As time went by and as I experimented with more and more

characters, including Walter and José, I realized that I really needed my main character to have a powerful personality without extreme personality traits that would pigeonhole him. In other words, he needed to be "broad." Think Mickey Mouse, Kermit the Frog, Bart Simpson, Bugs Bunny, or even Harry Potter. They aren't extreme caricatures such as Barney Gumble on *The Simpsons*, Cruella De Vil, or Yosemite Sam.

Achmed: When do we get to me?

Jeff: Later.

Achmed: I'm bored.

Bubba J.: Can I get this book on VHS?

I also knew that I wanted a main character to *move*. He needed to have energy to jolt the audience into attention. I'd seen the boring vent acts and I wanted to be different. I wanted some pop in my show and it had to come from the right character and the right puppet. I spent a lot of time alone in my hangar, tightening belts, checking torques, getting greasy, and putting duct tape on bloody cuts when I ran out of Band-Aids. All that time allowed my mind to wander to the problem of a main character. I will never forget after a long day at the hangar, standing in the middle of my apartment, and the image of Peanut just popping into my head. It all came together and made so much sense. Finally.

I called Verna, who had made a couple soft figures for me already, and started describing him to her in great detail. I told her, "I don't want him to be human, but at least humanoid. Not a monkey or an ape. He needs to be a unique creature unlike anything else, but certainly a mammal because mammals are warm and fuzzy. He needs to have appeal and be something that people would want to hug." I knew that if this was going to be my main guy, I wanted commercial potential.

One of my goals even as far back as high school was to have toy versions of my characters on the shelves of stores one day, and if one of these guys could be plush and huggable . . . well . . . all the better.

"I want skinny long arms and big hands so he can gesture easily. I don't want him to sit, so his legs need to be short enough so he can stand next to me, but not be too tall. I think he should have tan fur all over him, but his arms, legs, hands, and feet need more of a skin. His head should be that way too, and his belly." For the color of the skin . . . almost nothing made sense. If the skin was red, he'd look like a devil. Green, he'd look like an alien. Blue would be too Smurf-like. Yellow is too light for the bright lights; brown or gray, he'd look like a monkey. "So . . . purple? Not dark, but more of a lavender. I don't know of any popular characters who are purple." (This was pre–Barney the dinosaur.) "Give him a big tuft of green hair on top, green eyes, big lips. And make his nose removable."

"What?" Verna said. Purple skin didn't faze her, but a removable nose apparently got her attention. "I don't know," I said. "I just want to make sure he doesn't look *too* human, so maybe a nose I can take on or off. Can you put Velcro on the back of it?"

"Oh, well, yes," she replied.

After a few more conversations describing and showing what I wanted, plus sending some drawings back and forth with notes here and there, a few weeks later Peanut showed up. He was absolutely perfect.

I'd also asked her to give him *one* shoe. This would guarantee at least one good laugh with him in every show. My longtime friend and fellow vent David Erskine gave me the joke, and it dates back to vaudeville, from what I understand. I think it was the first joke Peanut ever told.

> Jeff: Peanut, you lost a shoe.

> Peanut: No, man, I FOUND one! (And then he would laugh hilariously at himself.)

One of the moves that I used very early on with Peanut was with his left hand swooshing over his head through his hair, and him yelling, "NNNNEEOOWWWW!" I used it to make fun of myself or someone in the front row for not understanding a joke. He did it his first performance ever, and he still does it today. It became a "catch" thing for him, just like José's "on a *steek*!"

Peanut: When I joined the act, everyone loved me.

José: I didn't.

Peanut: Everyone who didn't have a pole coming out of their butt . . .

Once I started working with him, all his mannerisms and his personality evolved very quickly. I named him Peanut because that was easy to remember and the name simply fit the character. It seems so simple now. As for his voice: Once again, it fits him. I tried to give him a back story that would give him an Earth origin, but something exotic that would be difficult to deny and easy to imagine. So it turns out he was from a race of people just like him who lived on the Micronesian Islands near Guam.

Another of Peanut's first jokes was corny as hell, but never failed to get a huge laugh:

Jeff: I understand you have some brothers.

Peanut: Yep: Eeny, Meeny, Miney, and Fred.

Jeff: Fred? What happened to Moe?

Peanut: Moe? Oh, my mama don't want no mo'!
(And once again, he would laugh his maniacal crazy laugh.)

Peanut debuted in Northern California at a firefighters fundraising event that was an outdoor show for the public. It was an all-ages, family crowd and the first show out, Peanut killed. On that same weekend, we headed back down to Los Angeles and did a guest spot at the Comedy & Magic Club in Hermosa Beach. Once again: gold. From that weekend forward, he was a hit in front of every imaginable crowd, blue collar and white collar, young and old, bikers and businessmen. The material was wacky and he was loud, obnoxious, and just plain crazy. He would make fun of me incessantly, telling me I was a loser for never having any dates, or he would pick on any poor soul in the front row, laughing at them and all his own jokes to boot.

Next I hit gold when I matched José and Peanut. Peanut was the perfect character to make fun of the slowpoke José, but José in turn would always one-up Peanut. Eventually I even got one of those cassette courses to teach myself some Spanish so the two could converse while leaving the bewildered me out of it all. Add to this mix Walter, who was almost the exact opposite style of comedy. Walter became my secret weapon when it came to winning over tired and soured audiences at corporate gatherings.

Walter and Peanut were perfect foils back then. Peanut almost always ended up being hero of the night when the audience was made up of fans. But any business crowd preferred Walter. Most of the businessmen at the end of a long evening of drinks, dinner, awards, and speeches certainly didn't want to have to sit through another painful forty-five minutes from a ventriloquist dummy. Well, Walter didn't want to be there either and was pissed he had to be there with *them*. Bringing Walter out and meeting these guys at their own level was an easy way to win them over.

Given the many soft and lovable characters Jim Henson had created, I was surprised that even the late Muppets creator liked Walter better than Peanut. At the tenth anniversary celebration for the Center for Puppetry Arts in Atlanta, Henson told me, "I just love Walter." He asked to see Walter up close and he complimented me on how much character I'd put into him. That was a huge moment for me. Later that evening between shows, I found myself alone backstage, and there lay Kermit the Frog, dead and on a table, like he'd been stepped on by Big Bird. I knew it was a major no-no, but I couldn't help myself: I went over and picked up Kermit and put him on my hand. COOL.

In the summer of 1988, my career clock began ticking. I was friends with a guy named John Williams, who was an old-time pilot with a hangar next to mine in Waco. He'd shared plenty of wisdom with me over the past couple of years. Once I came flying back to the hangar with summer storms flashing lightning all around the airport and winds gusting pretty high. I should have landed somewhere else to let the storms pass. After I landed and shut down that day, he came over to me and said, "Every pilot is given a certain amount of luck with his flying, and you've just used up a good portion of yours."

One day that summer, I was truly soul-searching, and I said to him, "I love just being here and flying, John. I'm making okay money, and I've never had more fun. I just wonder if it's time to move to Los Angeles and really chase after my dreams." John was in his seventies and was never happier than when he was flying, so I thought I had an ally when it came to staying in Waco and enjoying my helicopter. His answer surprised me. "Are you kidding me? Don't be crazy. Move to Los Angeles. Follow your dream. You can take up flying anytime, anywhere."

Not long after that, my friend Jordan Cox and I had a similar conversation. We were at his apartment and were killing ourselves laughing at some of the wacky jokes and bits I'd come up with for Peanut. Out of the blue and in the middle of the laughs he just stopped and looked at me and said, "What are you doing here?"

"What am I doing where?"

"In Waco."

"I don't know," I said.

"You're in *Waco*, man. You need to do what you need to do. It's time for you to *go*."

Here was another crossroads moment. I knew Jordan was right. College life was over. The helicopter could go with me.

I thought for a minute and said, "Yeah . . . I know."

Sometimes people who lived there would laugh at me when I said I loved Waco. But I did. It wasn't the town. It was the friends. Everyone's life would go on. Some of the closest relationships and friendships would remain, but most would be memories. It was time to pack up and head for Hollywood.

Peanut: Hollywood was beckoning.

Jeff: Right.

Peanut: It was time for us to ditch our real friends for a new set of phony ones.

A month later, in September of 1988, my friends in Waco threw a going away party for me. The next day I drove to Dallas, parked the 300ZX in the back driveway at my mom and dad's house, and hitched my forty-foot-long, loaded-down helicopter trailer to the back of my Nissan Pathfinder. As I pulled out of the driveway the next morning, my mom told me to stop. She ran inside the house. A minute later she came to my driver's-side window, and with tears in her eyes handed me a little bag of cookies.

I cried as I drove away from our house. I was my parents' only child and I had just left them in the driveway, waving a tearful good-bye.

But I knew it was time to move on and to move forward . . . to keep pursuing the dreams I'd had since childhood, and the Carson goal I'd set eight years before. I had three strong characters and the funny was growing. I had no more excuses. Here we go. . . .

CHAPTER FIVE

Better Five Years Late Than One Day Early

I'd made the long drive from Dallas to Los Angeles many times before, but this time I was pulling a forty-foot trailer with a two-seater helicopter sitting on it. I had about $6,000 to my name, and a truckful of dummies, tools, and dreams. I ended up in Redondo Beach, California, where Keith's aunt and uncle, Dave and Billie Bowen, rented me a room for $400 a month. That was a darned good deal even in 1988.

I was still signed with William Morris, and Mike Lacey booked me at Comedy & Magic regularly. He was still convinced that I was perfect for *The Tonight Show*, and even more so now. So I was living in Los Angeles, I had an agent, and the audiences laughed at what I did. Having never forgotten Jim McCawley's promise to see me again, I focused my efforts on getting on the show by making my act tighter and funnier. Lacey did some prodding and talked Jim into coming to see me again. I had been doing my six minutes everywhere I could as often as possible for the past six weeks. I knew I was ready.

It was now early December of 1988, barely two and a half months after actually moving to Los Angeles. That's a crazy short amount of time to have been in LA and to potentially be ready for Carson. There was a good reason for that, though. Unlike most comics who moved to LA to seek fame and fortune, I'd already been performing for eighteen years, and now I'd been working my butt off in LA, specifically honing my act with this one goal in mind.

It was a good show with a great audience that night in Hermosa Beach. I nailed it and McCawley saw it all. He met me in the Green Room afterward and congratulated me on my improvement. He loved Peanut, the little dummy of me, José Jalapeño, and the worm in the bottle. He said I'd done a great job making it just right for Johnny and *The Tonight Show* audience, and that he'd call me the next day and give me a date. I still have that old answering machine with the message from his assistant giving me the details. I was on the books for December 30, a Friday night, no less! I was stoked. It was finally going to happen. I almost couldn't believe it.

I flew back to Dallas for a week to visit my parents for the holidays. And when I told them I was finally going to be on *The Tonight Show*, they couldn't have been more excited. They literally told everyone they could, even strangers in line at Luby's. The three of us went to Neiman Marcus in Dallas, and Dad and Mom spent a little over $1,200 on my show outfit, which included an unbelievably nice Armani jacket. That was another important part of being on Carson, unlike the talk shows today. Back then, you dressed really well for the King of Late Night.

I flew back to Los Angeles a couple of days before the show. Jim and I had agreed that the night before I would run my set at the Comedy & Magic, and Jim would be there to make any last-minute notes.

That night the audience wasn't as good as they had been a few weeks before, but I still did okay. I was a little worried when I went back to the Green Room and McCawley wasn't there to give me his notes, but Lacey told me not to worry and to go home and get a good night's rest. He said it was going to be great. Taping was the next afternoon at four p.m., and I needed to be ready.

The next morning, I woke up early and I was an excited mess. My parents had phoned everyone, and people were calling to say they'd seen my name in *TV Guide*. At about nine a.m., when I knew McCawley usually arrived for work, I called his office. His assistant said he couldn't take the call, but he'd get back to me as soon as possible. An hour went by. I tried him again, and after being put on hold for what seemed like an eternity, he finally picked up.

"Any notes from last night?" I asked excitedly.

The long pause was deafening. He took a deep breath. "Jeff, I made a mistake. You're not ready."

Wait. What did he just say? I didn't want to hear the next sentence. My hopes and dreams and all that I'd worked for so long were now hanging in midair.

"But, it's in just a few hours . . . what?" I faltered.

Jim replied, "I've taken you off the show and I'm looking for another guest. I'm sorry."

I will never forget that moment. I had been on cloud nine. I was within hours of my goal, and now, as it all started to crumble, it was more than heartbreaking: It was devastating. There was nothing else in my life at that time that was as important as this one career goal and dream. I sat there on the phone, not wanting to hang up, hoping that somehow he was pulling a joke, or that he would change his mind.

He started talking again. "Look, this doesn't mean you can't ever be on. Right now, you're just not ready." And then he shared with me a piece of wisdom that I didn't want to accept but I understood fully. He said, "When you do stand-up for Johnny Carson, *it's better to be five years late than one day early.*" He encouraged me to "keep working" and then he hung up.

For a long time I stood there, staring at the wall in front of me with the dead phone still to my ear. I looked down at my desk and touched my father's electric pencil sharpener that he'd given me from his office a few years before. As I touched it, the knot in my stomach tightened even more. When I moved to Los Angeles and was setting up my desk, I plugged the sharpener into the wall and vowed to never empty the shavings until I had been a guest on *The Tonight Show*. Not hours before, I had looked at it, knowing I would be emptying it before midnight. I pushed it back a couple of inches. I hung up the phone.

I had to call my parents and as many friends back home as I could to let them know the show wasn't going to happen. To drive the knife even further into myself, I couldn't help but watch the broadcast that night. Johnny's monologue was great, the audience was hot, but the person that McCawley found to take my place was a girl named Merry Christmas. And that was the only reason she was on . . . because her name was the same as the greeting. Maybe I would have gotten on if I had a dummy named Happy Hanukkah.

After New Year's, I did what I'd always done and that was to keep working. The always passionate and committed Barbara Hubbard had booked me at a few more colleges in the past few years, and along the way I'd picked up an agent for the college circuit. This was a great arena for me, offering more experience and exposure with a younger audience. The money was good and I was traveling regularly now for the first time. The road isn't exactly easy, but I was slowly learning the tricks of travel when it came to getting through airports quickly, how much to carry on, what to do when flights are canceled, et cetera. In large towns and small, well-endowed schools and the less fortunate, I was also treated to the gamut of housing and sleeping arrangements. One night it would be an okay hotel or motel, the next night it could be someone's house or in a cold, drafty, unused dorm room. These were nights alone on the road, night after night, town after town.

Most of my money in 1989 came from colleges, small comedy clubs, and a few corporate gigs. The clubs were B rooms at best, and they booked me as a middle act. Headlining hadn't happened yet. Most important, though: All these gigs in all these different kinds of places with so many different types of audiences let me simply work on my act. My work ethic was pretty simple: If I was getting laughs, I was doing things right. If the crowd wasn't rocking, then I had to improve or lose whatever *wasn't* working. Both the college and club audiences were unforgiving and honest. If they liked you, they let you know. If not, for me anyway, they usually wouldn't boo or heckle, but they weren't generous with their response.

Dave Douds, the William Morris agent who signed me when I won the college competition, still tried to open doors for me as best he could. He was a senior agent, but I don't think many of his cohorts thought much of his new client. Think about it—William Morris was one of the biggest, most prestigious talent agencies in the world with clients like Bill Cosby, and now the state-fair agent signs the college-aged *ventriloquist*. Yikes. I don't think Dave was talking anyone at Morris into really taking me seriously.

In early 1989, Douds somehow got me onstage at the Melrose Improv to do a guest spot. I was given eight minutes to do my thing. Melrose at that time was what I considered a very dark but hip club. All the Hollywood elite would show up, including industry folks and the best of the best comics. It was *the* hangout, and I was *not* one of *the* guys.

Most people in the business looked down at me, and I could literally feel the internal groan when I walked onstage at Melrose. I was not hip or slick or cerebral. I was not a New York comic. I was a young guy wearing a tie and holding a dummy. But I got up there that night, and the audience just happened to dig what I did. In the crowd that evening was the ever watchful Budd Friedman, the man behind all the Improv clubs and the TV show *A&E's An Evening at the Improv*.

That night Budd walked up to me, stuck out his hand, and said, "Hi. Budd Friedman. Congratulations, kid, you got the show!"

"Thank you very much. And, nice to meet you." I said. I had no idea just how important Budd could be to me, nor did I know what a good relationship with him could do for a comic. I'd done so many of these guest spots around town for various clubs with Dave dragging me here, there, and everywhere that I didn't really know the significance of our handshake. I didn't even realize that evening was an audition for television! But that night was the beginning of a long and very important relationship.

Budd Friedman and the Improv Comedy Clubs were *the* chain to be in good with if you wanted consistent employment across the country. Just about every comedian wanted to be a regular in the Improv chain, but it was a difficult fraternity to be invited into. Anyone who wasn't a pure monologist wasn't considered a "real" comic. If you used any kind of prop, it was a crutch. So I was handicapped as a variety act. Guys felt like you were relying on something other than your wits and spoken words to get laughs. There were plenty of comics on the road who, without ever seeing my act, had concluded that ventriloquism was a tired and sad old vaudevillian art, pigeonholed in the same class as plate spinning and mime (my apologies to plate spinners and mimes), and that an act like mine could never be as hip or edgy as "pure" stand-up. Rarely did anyone have the balls to say anything directly to me, but throughout my eighteen years of working the club circuit, I found personal insults about my characters and me more than once on comedy club Green Room walls.

Peanut: Should we tell him?

Walter: Probably.

José: *Sí.*

Peanut: *We* did it!

Jeff: WHAT?

Peanut: He didn't understand; let's move on.

There were a couple of club owners and bookers who were as disdainful as some of the comics. While on the road one weekend doing college gigs, my agent set up an audition for me at Catch a Rising Star in the Big Apple. The Catch clubs weren't quite as prestigious or important as the Improvs, but they were a good stepping-stone.

Longtime friend and fellow ventriloquist Al Getler accompanied me to the club that night. We got there early in the evening, long before the show started so I could talk to the club manager and find out when I was to go on. This was a showcase night, which meant comic after comic would go on, each doing a fairly short bit.

When we found the club manager, I introduced myself, and reminded him that Dave had arranged the gig. He greeted me with a disagreeable smirk. Then, in a voice dripping with condescension, he said, "Oh, yes . . . hmmm . . . let me think. You're something I . . . *don't . . . like. . . .*" This was a first for me. I had no idea what he was talking about. Did he mean a Texan? Baylor graduate? Protestant? Then of course it hit me.

"I'm a ventriloquist," I said.

"Oh . . . yes," he replied nastily. "Well, you'll be on at about ten o'clock."

"Okay," I said. "How long will I have?"

"Six minutes. You'll get the light."

Nice. That was fine. Al and I waited. The show started at eight, so two hours passed. Then two more. Now it was midnight. Comic after comic kept going up, and another would be introduced. I found the manager again and asked him where I was on the list. "Don't worry; you'll get on." He grinned.

It was now after one a.m. Al had a wife and two little girls at home and plus I knew a fuck you when it was in the air.

"Ready to go?" I asked Al.

"Hell yes," he said. "You're better than this."

I always try to not let the ego get in the way of a good business decision, but this was no way to treat anyone, no matter what. We left, and Al and I have laughed about that guy ever since. Whenever I see Al I say, "YOU'RE SOMETHING I DON'T LIKE."

Walter: I think we found the title to your next book.

Jeff: Gee, thanks.

Walter: I wonder where that club manager is today.

Jeff: I'm not sure.

Walter: Probably still booking clubs . . . READ THIS AND WEEP, LOSER!!!

Jeff: Stop it.

Walter: Okay . . . LOSER!!

For every negative experience, there have been a bunch more good ones along the way. At least that's how I remember it. As cool as it was to meet Budd Friedman and to get the booking on *A&E's An Evening at the Improv*, more important was the small flurry of phone calls it caused in the next couple of days. Budd didn't book the talent in all the Improvs around the country, but soon he would want me to audition for the woman who did. Eventually I would be introduced to Debra Sartell, the Jim McCawley of the Improv chain. If Debra liked you, you had a *load* of work ahead of you. But . . . you had to prove yourself first. You had to go to comedy boot camp. Welcome to the nightmare gig in Las Vegas.

Not all Improvs and comedy clubs are made equal. There are the A rooms, and the B rooms, and the . . . well . . . shit holes. I'm not going to say the 1990s Vegas room was an exact shit hole, but it certainly made you realize really quickly if you had what it took to be a road comic.

Inside the Riviera Hotel and Casino was the Vegas Improv. It's where a comic got his or her chops. It's where you had to prove yourself. The crowds were tough, the guy who ran the room was a tyrant, you had to pay for your own drinks, and meals were with the hotel staff in the employee cafeteria. Mmmmmm . . . casino food! There was no ego allowed in this paradise.

Unlike other clubs around the country that usually had one show a night every day except Friday and Saturday (when there were two), this joint had the comics doing three shows a night, seven days a week. That was twenty-one shows a week! Twenty-one! (I still have a copy of my first check from Budd for those twenty-one shows—I made a total of $850 before taxes and commissions.)

The first week I was there, I was the middle act, and the headliner was Bill Engvall. I got along great with Bill and knew him from Texas. He even gave me a suggestion for Walter, and that was simply to use the word *dirtbag* as a punch line, because it was such a "Walter" word.

Jeff: Walter, what do you do for a living?

Walter: I write greeting cards.

Jeff: Could you give us some examples?

Walter: All right . . . how 'bout a get-well card?

Jeff: How does that go?

Walter: Sorry to hear you're sick . . . dirtbag.

Jeff: Anything a little kinder?

Walter: Belated birthday . . . sorry I missed your birthday . . . I thought you were dead.

Jeff: Do you have anything that's a little more romantic?

Walter: For someone you love?

Jeff: That would be good.

Walter: I love you as sunshine over oceans . . .

> I love you as moonlight over mountains. . . . They say
> love is forever. . . . I love you . . . dirtbag.

Another guy at that club was a big goombah by the name of Steve Schirripa. Besides being the director of entertainment at the Riviera, on a nightly basis Steve ran all three small showrooms located just off the main casino, at the top of the escalators. There was the Improv, La Cage, and Crazy Girls. Each room sat about two hundred people at best, and they all had self-serve bars in the back. Nice.

Steve would bark orders and intimidate employees left and right, and everyone jumped when he growled. Of formidable size and truly fitting the part, Steve was the epitome of a connected guy. Oh, and that's probably how you'd recognize him today: He was Bobby Bacala on *The Sopranos*. Now a celeb, back then Steve was just the scary guy that you knew would break your legs if you did something wrong, or at least that's what most everyone thought.

My first night at the Riviera, I met Steve in the showroom at the appointed time to set up. He gave me my little talk, which concluded with, sure enough, a threat to do me bodily harm if I went over my time. I told him no problem, but I wasn't quite sure there wasn't a little acting in his performance.

For the first few nights, I stayed within my allotted time for the most part, and maybe went thirty seconds over. I think I had to do something like fifteen minutes total. But on the Thursday night, it was an awesome crowd and I went two minutes over my time. Steve was in the back of the room shining and blinking the flashlight in my eyes. At three minutes overtime, I wrapped. By the time I reached the self-serve bar at the back of the room, Schirripa was in my face with his own mug and a big, fat, ringed finger.

"DO YOU KNOW WHAT FUCKIN' TIME IT IS!? DO YOU KNOW HOW FUCKIN' FAH YOU WENT OH-VU!? IF YOU

EVER, AND I MEAN FUCKIN' *EVER* DO THAT AGAIN, I WILL PERSONALLY *BREK* YOUR FUCKIN' *LEKKS! CAPISCE*?"

I stood there looking at him with a frown, not breaking eye contact. I'd seen other guys almost wet their pants at his dressing-down, but the drama just seemed a little cartoony to me. I had a feeling Steve was actually a good guy.

It just seemed a little over the top. So I took my chances, and in my best New York Italian mobster accent I said, "Yeh . . . I heah yuh. Yuh gonna *brek* my fookin' *leks*." He stood there for a few seconds, glaring at me. I then made a big, exaggerated grin, eyebrows raised, eyes wide open, and showing all my teeth. He was a good five inches taller than me, so he was looking down. I saw his jaw twitch, then he started to chew on the inside of his mouth. He was either going to smash my face in or—He broke into a big laugh, slapped me on the back, and said, "You're all right, kid. . . . Just try and stay in your time."

I've run into Steve now and then since, and he truly is a good guy. Just don't FOOK with him!

The Vegas Improv was of course the least glamorous of all the Improv clubs. The comics didn't even get a room at the Riviera. We had to stay at the most horrible of horrible dive motels on the strip, which was right *next door* to the Riviera. Peanut's joke was, "They remodeled our motel . . . they put new duct tape on the carpets."

One week while working Vegas, all three comics had our separate rooms broken into on the same night. It was obviously an inside job by someone who knew when we would be at the Riviera working. I had just purchased some really nice portable Bose speakers and a Sony CD Walkman. Remember those? They were all gone after the show.

I remember another time being woken in the middle of the night, jolted out of my sleep. I'd made it to the door, hand on the latch, turning the knob, almost bursting into the hallway to assail the attacker before I realized that the woman's screams weren't from terror, but from, well . . . *pleasure*. The sound through the wall wasn't even the slightest bit muffled.

Playing the road like this really wasn't any kind of glamorous life. It was grueling, it was lonely, and at times, sleazy. But if nothing else, after having lived a very nice upper-middle-class life back in Dallas and in Waco, it was a true motivator. I wanted to move up in the world.

With the exception of the Vegas Improv, while working almost all other clubs, the headliners got preferential treatment and much better accommodations than the lower acts. I shudder when I hear the words *comedy condo*. This is where the opener and middle (also called the feature) acts would stay. A club would purchase or rent a condo or apartment usually within walking distance of the club, and that's where you'd live for the week. Talk about sleazy: Road comics come from all walks of life, usually younger guys (and a few chicks) who were happy just to have a gig and a roof at night. You never knew who was sleeping in the bed the week before you, or what went on there before you arrived. It was much worse than even a sleazy motel because there usually wasn't a maid service. To further cut costs, the clubs usually made one of the lower-ranked managers or even a server head over on Monday mornings to "tidy up." Sometimes you'd arrive on a Tuesday, and the well-worn sheets would still be in the washer or dryer. Lord knows what stains those were on the carpets.

 Peanut: I'll tell you what was on the carpet—

 Jeff: Please don't.

Peanut: At the comedy condo, I was too happy to be sleeping in a trunk.

The final straw came in Minneapolis one winter when I was playing a club called Dave Wood's Ribtickler. Dave was a stand-up who I met working at the Comedy & Magic a few times, and he was part owner of this downtown Minnesota club. I'd never experienced *truly* cold temperatures, but this would be the week. Negative 40°F with a wind chill of −70°F. Holy mother. Southern Californians and Texans are not hearty folk when it comes to temperatures like *that*. But the cold wasn't the point. I got dropped off by the cab at the condo, and the front desk "guard" gave me my key. Oh, let me mention the cab: I'd heard this rumor before, but I had to confirm it. When the cabdriver picked me up at the airport, I asked him when the last time was that he'd turned off his engine. Two and a half weeks. Because of the cold, some of these guys would never turn the car off. They'd just let it idle, even when they were inside asleep for the night. Block heaters did no good at those temperatures, according to this guy. It was better for the engine to just keep chugging. It was too damn cold.

Anyway, I got to the condo and opened the door. It was like a bad movie. Stains on the walls, floors, and ceiling; discarded food containers scattered about; holes punched in the drywall; and a kitchen and bathroom that looked like something out of a bad *CSI* episode. But the final, *final* straw for me were the two or three crusty stains on the bedspread. I was disgusted and I'd had it. I also knew the only way out was to become a headliner in the A clubs.

Walter: Or get a real job!

After getting good reports back from the Vegas Improv, Budd finally set up a time for Debra Sartell to check me out. I was scheduled to do twenty minutes at the short-lived Sherman Oaks Improv, which was an ingloriously converted banquet room located inside the Marriott Hotel at the 101 and 405 freeway exchange. But unlike the jaded industry Hollywood folks from the Melrose club, this was certainly more my kind of crowd. This was a more typical audience for me. Afterward, one of the lower agents from Morris introduced me to Debra. "That was great," she said. "I'll start booking you right away as a middle." Whoa. Perfect. It was so simple a statement, yet such a huge career moment. The agent was almost as shocked as I was happy. Trust me on this: Next to *no one* expected a vent to be able to work the Improvs. And Debra was sticking her neck out to the club owners simply by booking me. But the proof had been the reaction by the crowd in front of Budd, as well as in the reports from the Vegas club. So now the *real* roadwork began.

There is nothing easier for a good comedian than being the middle act at a comedy club. There's very little pressure because no one is *expecting* you to be good. You don't have the responsibility of carrying the show. You just have to get up there, do your thing for twenty or so minutes, then get off. It's a layup. Well, I was just too darned competitive to be content with a layup. I *knew* I could headline. I sharpened my twenty minutes to a fine edge and it was becoming a very powerful set.

This was still 1989, and in addition to the Funny Bones and some other independents clubs, I started doing multiple weeks nationwide at Budd's other Improvs, courtesy of Debra Sartell. In addition to Melrose, the Improvs that existed back then were Dallas; Addison, Texas; Seattle; Washington, D.C.; Cleveland; Tempe, Arizona; Brea, California; Irvine, California; and San Diego. Shows were always Tuesday through Sunday nights, eight or nine shows a week. A couple of other names you might have heard of who were also middle acts at that time were David Spade and some guy named Adam Sandler. And pay? The three of us were getting top dollar for middles back then: $100 per show. So I was pulling in $700 a week. I was working probably forty-two weeks a year, so that's about $30,000 a year.

After one really strong week at the San Diego Improv, I called Debra and said, "I was wondering about headlining." She replied, "You what?" And I said, "Well, I really feel like there are people in the audience that are there just to see me." I could almost feel her roll her eyes over the phone.

"Don't tell me you think you're getting a *following*," she said.

"Yeah. I really think I am."

She took a deep breath and spoke a sentence that became the perfect challenge.

"You can move up from middle when the headliners can no longer follow you."

I replied, "Okay. Deal."

Peanut: This is my favorite part!

Jeff: What is?

Peanut: This is where I kick ass and take no prisoners and women fall at my feet!

Jeff: That's a little much.

Peanut: I can dial it back.

The tipping point happened at the Tempe Improv not too many weeks after that. In 1989, jalapeño peppers weren't exactly a popular food for most of the country, but in the Southwest, and especially Arizona, José Jalapeño's "on a steek" got a huge reaction. Then I topped his segment with the tequila-worm-in-the-bottle bit. I ended with the five-voice, fast-talking business. It was a killer set. It was made even bigger by the fact that no audience was expecting much more than average stand-up from the middle guy. Oftentimes I'd get standing ovations, and that's pretty rare for the middle guy. The best part? According to folks on the inside, I was making the headliners uncomfortable because I was tough to follow. I was soon given a trial run as headliner, at the . . . guess where . . . the *Dallas* Improv. That was my hometown, and I guess the powers that be wanted to give me the best chance at doing well.

José: I was so excited.

Peanut: You? How did you show it? By opening your eyes slightly wider?

The next big step was appearing on television in stand-up comedy shows as often as possible. It was 1989, and the then fledgling FOX network was having success with a show called *Comic Strip Live*. I performed on that show multiple times, as well as on more of *A&E's An Evening at the Improv*. Next was *Jonathan Winters and His Traveling Road Show* on Showtime, and a few others here and there.

For each television appearance, I had to pare a portion of the act down to a tight five or six minutes. I began to figure out by watching the stopwatch what would make a killer television comedy segment. The guys who did well in these stand-up shows or on Carson or Letterman did best if they got a good laugh within the first twenty seconds. And then, there was simple math: If the guy got a laugh every six to twelve seconds, the spot was killer. So that's five to ten laughs per minute. Conversely, if he or she was getting four laughs or less per minute, it simply didn't go well.

Also, the television audience is a different animal than the club audience. Usually they *want* the comic to do well, but they immediately start to get nervous if the comic is sweating, or if the laughs aren't there. At that point they begin to get quiet and it can all go south very quickly.

With each and every television appearance, *The Tonight Show* never left my mind. Between 1986 and the spring of 1990, I auditioned for Jim McCawley a total of eight times, and after each one, he turned me down. My ten-year high school reunion was scheduled for June of 1990 and I didn't feel any closer to achieving my goal than I had five years before. No matter how many shows I did on TV, or how many sold-out shows and standing ovations I got at clubs and colleges around the country, I wasn't happy with where I was. That elusive Carson goal was always seemingly just one audition away.

For as long as I could remember, my father had told me he wanted to go to Africa on a safari. He had grown up watching Johnny Weissmuller in Tarzan movies, and he had always dreamed of seeing the wilds of that continent. He was now sixty-three years old and he had finally made plans to go over there with a tour group on a two-week picture safari. My mother never wanted to go. She was delicate and fearful and knew she couldn't handle it. Dad was chomping at the bit.

"Who are you going with, Pop?" I asked.

"No one," he said.

"Dad, that's sad," I replied.

"I don't mind," he said. "It'll be fun."

I sat there thinking. I felt really nervous about leaving the country because I would be out of touch, with no one to answer the call if I got a big gig. But I also knew Dad wasn't getting any younger. He'd talked about this since I was a boy.

"I'll go, Pop," I said.

"What? Really? Are you sure?" he asked.

"Sure," I said. "It'll be fun!"

"THAT'S GREAT!"

We left a few weeks later and it was a once-in-a-lifetime adventure. Not only did we see every wild animal he'd ever talked about, but we took literally hundreds of pictures. We missed Mom, as neither one of us had ever gone that long without talking to her. To this day, I've never told Mom the secret of how much beer Dad drank that trip. I didn't even know he LIKED beer. Way to go, Pop!

Not long after we returned from Africa, my ninth audition for Jim McCawley and *The Tonight Show* took place. It was late March of 1990, at the Ice House in Pasadena, California.

It was just a guest spot, so afterward I was out in the parking lot putting the big trunk back into my car while the show was still going on. I was alone; the Morris agents had long since given up going with me or even scheduling these auditions. For the past few, it had simply been Lacey telling Jim to see me again at Comedy & Magic, or me calling McCawley at NBC and asking nicely.

I was a little depressed as I hefted the heavy case into the vehicle. The audience had responded well, but I didn't feel the six minutes was all that much different from the other eight times. I'd changed a few jokes here and there, updated characters, and tightened up the laughs a bit, but basically, it was the same stuff. I didn't know how to make it any better without starting from scratch. Jim walked out the club door and toward my car. I was ready for the same old, "Really good, but you're still not ready."

"Well . . . you got it," he stated with a smile.

"Got what?" I honestly didn't know what he meant.

"The show. You got the show. I'll call you tomorrow and we'll find a date."

My mouth hung open and I just stood there, blinking, not really comprehending what had just happened to me. Then his words took on meaning, and an honest-to-goodness joy swept over and through me.

I look back now and have to smile at what an innocent and simple time that was in my life. Completely self-absorbed in my own career with zero responsibilities other than to make sure I called my parents a couple of times a week just to say hi. That was it. I gave a little to charity here and there, rent was low, my health was good, no one was depending on me for anything, and my mom prayed for me every day. There was no war, no threat of terror, and the economy was good. All I had to do was get onstage every night and make sure that everyone who had paid good money for the show laughed a lot. And now a goal that I had set nine years and ten months before was about to finally be achieved, only two months before its due date.

I asked Jim later what the difference was that night, and he said it was confidence, timing, and better jokes. Well, that all made sense. I had practiced that bit over and over so many times that it had become second nature. But would it pay off when the *real* pressure was on?

Even though I'd done the bit a million times before, I rehearsed it over and over in front of the mirror and a video camera in my tiny room for the next few days. No fat. No unneeded pauses. Like I've said for many years: Ventriloquism is easy; comedy is hard.

Though I felt like it might be bordering on bad luck, I told all family and friends again. Mom and Dad once again called everyone that they could think of. This time I bought myself a designer silk suit for something like a thousand bucks. You could be on Carson for your *first* time only *once.*

Walter: A silk suit?

Jeff: That was the fashion at the time.

Walter: What, looking like a white pimp?

As a kid, my favorite fast-food restaurant hands down was Burger King. I decided that my LLBC (Last Lunch Before Carson) had to be a Whopper with cheese (no pickles), fries, and a chocolate shake. I had timed things just right so that I arrived at NBC in Burbank only a few minutes before I was supposed to. Once again, it was just me. No agent, no manager, no publicist, no family, and no girlfriend, which was okay since I didn't want any distractions anyway.

One of the guards told me where to drive and park, and it was unbelievably surreal. All the parking spots next to the main backstage entrance had name plates on them, clearly visible. There was a Corvette, spotless and beautiful. The name read JOHNNY CARSON. Holy crap.

I walked up the ramp and into the building. Huge painted images of Bob Hope, Johnny, and a few more of the historical NBC celebrities adorned the two-story walls. I was pointed to a hallway and led to my own dressing room. On the door was a blue card with *The*

Tonight Show logo plus my name printed on it. It was almost too cool to take in.

This was the Super Bowl for stand-up comics. I can only imagine what a football player feels like the first time he makes it to *that* Big Game. No matter what kind of preparation you've had, no matter how good you are, no matter how confident you are, it's still a *big deal*. The eyes of millions will be on you, and though most late-night shows are all taped and shown a few hours later, they're still very much live . . . just like that football game. There is pressure, excitement, nerves, and energy. Johnny Carson was the true American night-light. A huge chunk of America watched Carson every night.

Freddy de Cordova was Johnny's longtime executive producer, and he met me onstage for rehearsal to talk about what was going to happen in a couple of hours. He said I didn't have to run through my set line by line, but they at least wanted to see my setup and be shown the order of the act.

I went through everything with Peanut and the little guys. Then Freddy called me over to "The Desk" to chat a bit. This was *the* desk . . . and *the* couch. What countless stars had crossed this stage and sat right here, talking to Johnny? I felt like I was on hallowed ground.

Freddy said, "Jim tells me you have another dummy in your act that's pretty funny."

"Uh, yes, sir," I replied. "Walter. He's a cranky old guy."

"Well," Freddy said, "the odds of you getting to the couch on your first shot are pretty slim, but just in case Johnny feels like having you over, you should be ready. Could you use Walter for that?"

GULP. What the—? Almost never, and I mean almost *never* did a stand-up get called to the couch his first or even second time doing stand-up on Carson. You had to *earn* that call. Only on your third or fourth shot was it even thought about. Johnny had to really like you as a stand-up for you to have the honor of having any kind of one-on-one discussion with him. On your first few times, you'd do your set in front of the curtain, then hopefully get the "okay" finger-circle sign from Johnny from thirty feet away. Then the curtain would be pulled apart just so, and you'd exit the way you came. I had never even considered actually *talking* on air to Mr. Carson.

"Well, yeah, I have a few jokes that would work. I think Johnny would like Walter," I said.

"Perfect," replied Freddy. "Then can you preset Walter right here behind the couch and then reach over if Johnny wants to talk to him?"

"Yes, sir," I stammered. "He can sit on his own on the floor right there behind the couch."

Well, *that* was never going to happen. But of course with a live show, they had to be ready for anything.

There are times in all our lives when sometimes things just seem to fall into place, and other times when shit happens and there's no explanation. I look back on this first Carson appearance, and I know I couldn't have asked for a better setup. Friday night was *the* night in the Carson era. It always seemed to be his favorite night, and the audience was always a little more up. Well, here I was, booked on Friday, April 6, 1990. Not only that, but the host was Carson and the guests were none other than B. B. King and Bob Hope. How the hell did *that* fall into place?

When Doc Severinsen and the band started up, I felt like I was in the car of a roller coaster, strapped in, heading up to the top, with no way to stop or get out. This was IT. I was in my dressing room, watching it on a monitor. Next was Ed McMahon, and "Heeeeeeeeere's Johnny!" The crowd went nuts and out The Man himself walked. I hadn't met him or talked to him. I still hadn't seen him in person in the hallway or anywhere. But in a few minutes, he would be *introducing me*.

I watched and listened. The audience was awesome. Johnny did his monologue, talking about Michael Jackson, President Bush (the first one), Dan Quayle, Milli Vanilli, and the sixtieth anniversary of Twinkies. After the first commercial break, he and the Mighty Carson Art Players did a sketch about a funeral home. Then, Hope was the first guest, and he was lucid and charming and funny. Johnny and the crowd loved him. Next, B. B. King came out and did his thing. Same result. During his number, I was called backstage to take my position behind the main curtain. Even as I type this now, I can recall that feeling and those nerves so many years ago. The audience was great and I had done this bit so many times that I *knew* it would kill. But none of that took away from the feeling of reaching the top peak of that roller coaster. The clacking of the wheels was about to end, there would be a moment of silence, then a suspension of gravity, and I would soon be on the ride of my life.

And that's exactly what happened.

The band played during the commercials. As the cameras came back live, Johnny waved the band to quiet. I couldn't see anything backstage in the darkness. Just the outlines of the stagehands on either side of me ready to pull back the curtain and let me walk through. There was no monitor, and Johnny's voice was muffled, but I knew he was introducing me with a few credits. I held Peanut in my arms . . . right hand up his back and into his head, his body perched on my left hand. My case and other props with José inside were preset at the star marker on the floor center stage. I knew when Johnny said my name and Peanut's, the curtain would part and out I would walk. No cancellation hours before. No more questioning whether I was ready. Doc and the band hit it.

The open curtain sent a blast of TV lights into my eyes and my feet were carrying me to my spot. The audience applause was deafening, but the band was even louder. This was a drug. This was unlike anything I had ever experienced.

The laughs were in all the right places and the performance couldn't have gone better. I look back at that tape now and I smile a little bit because so much has changed in my style and comedy and performing abilities. But at that moment in time in my life and in my career, I couldn't have done any better.

I did the final drinking of the cranberry juice–tequila–Chianti while Peanut said, "Going, going, gone!" and the crowd went bananas. Doc and the band hit it again, I took my bow, and I couldn't have been happier. I had done it. I had *finally done it*! Barely two months before my ten-year high school reunion.

And to top it all off, I looked to my right, and there was Johnny across the stage, giving me the all-important, crowning "okay" sign with his thumb and index finger. My insides did a leap, and I smiled and waved back. As I was taking another quick bow, I looked to the right of center camera just a few feet in front of me, and there was the floor director making a signal for me that my brain took a few seconds to understand. He was waving me not to go back through the curtain but to go *to the couch*.

If I watch that tape, it's only for a split second, but I can see the horror in my own eyes in that instant. What was he telling me to do? This had never been in my imagination. I had *not* planned on this nor even considered what I would possibly do on the *couch* next to *Johnny Carson*.

My feet started to move in that direction and it was one of the longest walks of my life. The crowd was hip and recognized the moment for what it was. They went even more nuts. How was it possible that Ed McMahon and B. B. King were now standing up and moving over *for me*? (Bob Hope had come and gone.) Now was truly the test of the mettle. I got through a couple of questions about myself and my helicopter, and then Johnny asked me about Walter. This was truly unbelievable. I reached around the couch and pulled out the character who would turn out to be Johnny's favorite of all my little guys. Walter was all attitude:

Jeff: How are you, Walter?

Walter: Who the hell cares?

Jeff: You know where we are?

Walter: Yeah, and I don't give a damn.

Jeff: But this is Johnny Carson! (I pointed to Johnny and Walter looked.)

Walter: Well LA DEE DAH.

We did a few jokes about the show and Johnny. It was simple but effective. Johnny, B. B., and Ed all laughed, as did the crowd. But the best was yet to come. This was toward the end of the broadcast, and after the last commercial break, Johnny always thanked his guests. I was last.

Johnny: Jeff, good to see you. Hope you come back with us. Walter, I hope you're in a little better frame of mind next time.

Walter: It'll be a cold day in *hell* if I ever come back here.

It might not look too amazing in print today, but this wasn't any talk show host. This was Johnny Carson. Revered and respected, and Walter had just dissed him. I had that line in mind as we were coming back from commercial, but I knew I was taking a big chance with it. Johnny was king and I was just a road comic. But all had gone well that night and I figured I'd gamble. Johnny laughed hard, Ed and B.B. cracked up, and it *worked*.

As the show ended, I shook hands with Johnny and he was gone. Would I ever make it back? Would I ever have an actual conversation with Johnny Carson off the air?

As I walked backstage carrying Walter, one of the agents from William Morris greeted me. He had shown up unbeknownst to me during the taping. He was one of the older guys, and had been in the business a long time. "You know, your life is never going to be the same, kid. Remember that."

I knew he was right. It *could* never be the same. But what was next?

After shaking a few hands backstage and thanking as many folks as I could, I walked out of NBC at about five thirty p.m. It was eight thirty on the East Coast, and the show would air there in three hours. I thought this was the end of a perfect day. I was wrong. At that moment, reality was heading toward me at about 80 miles per hour down the 405 freeway. I never saw it coming.

CHAPTER SIX

The Instant Family plus Star Trek Nirvana

It wasn't a drunken driver or an eighteen-wheeler careening out of control that almost caused me to smash my car into an embankment on the 405 that night. It wasn't a coyote or errant deer on the freeway that brought my perfect day to a screeching halt. It was a phone call with my mother.

Driving away from NBC after my first *Tonight Show* appearance, I met my original William Morris agent, Dave Douds, at a restaurant in Burbank to celebrate. I was secretly praying for no big news events that would cause the night's airing of *The Tonight Show* to be preempted. I couldn't help being that self-centered on this particular evening. "If there's gonna be an earthquake, I hope it waits at least until tomorrow morning," I thought. I swear it was hard not to think like that, and if any other comic tells you he hasn't had the exact same thought when in that position, he's lying.

I found myself looking at my watch about every fifteen minutes, counting down the time until I knew Carson would air on the East Coast and in Central time. The broadcast would begin at eight thirty p.m. my time . . . and by nine thirty, it would be history. I somehow killed enough time with dinner, and on the drive back to Redondo, I stared at my watch and knew the minute Johnny was thanking Walter and me. I let a couple more minutes go by, and I picked up the car phone (if you're too young to remember, cell phones back then were the size of a mailbox and most of them were hardwired, mounted inside your car) and called my parents' home line. As usual, both Mom and Dad got on the phone at the same time. "So, what did you think?" I asked expectantly.

A few seconds of silence. I thought we had been cut off. "Hello?"

I asked. Walter had used the phrases "I don't give a damn" and "Who the hell cares," and I thought as the only child raised in a strong Christian family, this might irk my parents. But *surely* they saw the bigger picture.

My mom finally spoke up: "You know, we don't approve of you using that type of language."

After her words registered in my brain, I almost drove off the road in frustration, and I'm not kidding. This had been such a long-awaited day for me. All those years of working so hard, all those hours of dedication to my act. I was expecting excitement, congratulations, and big exclamations of "We're so proud of you!" But the only thing my mom did was criticize me for using two harmless, four-letter words. I know my mother didn't mean to hurt me and I know she felt like she still needed to do "her job" as a parent. But the silence on my end now was deafening. Then my father jumped in and tried to smooth things over with "You're a great ventriloquist!"

I couldn't hear anything else. I said I had to go and I hung up. At that moment on the 405 in Los Angeles, I felt pretty lonely. I had just done what very few comics get to do, and I now felt I had nothing to celebrate, and no one to talk to about it. Seventeen months before, I had left my life and my close friends in Texas in pursuit of a dream. Now it seemed like an empty, self-centered accomplishment.

Even worse, I knew I had to get up at four thirty a.m. and head to LAX for another flight and another string of college shows. These gigs had been booked long before *The Tonight Show*, and I still had to pay bills and fulfill contracts. Being on a big TV show didn't literally change things overnight. Remembering the next day's schedule put me in even more of a funk: After getting on a six a.m. flight, I would land at some small airport in the Midwest, rent a car, drive for an hour or so, then be doing an afternoon show in a cafeteria at a small college as some sort of a diversionary activity for students needing a break from studying for finals. Then I'd check into some horrible little motel room, sleep, then drive to the next college a couple hundred miles away the next day for another seemingly meaningless show. Seriously? Did I HAVE to go? I just did *THE TONIGHT SHOW*!

After killing a few more hours, I turned on NBC and watched the broadcast. I couldn't have been happier. Sitting there, I relived the absolute coolness of it all. Then the show ended and went to a commercial. I shut off the television. Silence. In my small, single room complete with a closet, a single bed, a small desk, and a tiny bathroom, I sat there, not knowing what to do next. I looked over at my desk, smiled, and emptied my father's pencil sharpener. A few minutes later my phone rang. I figured it was someone on the West Coast who'd just seen the show. It was actually another longtime friend and ventriloquist, Bob Rumba. Bob lived in Chicago and made his living as a modern-day vaudevillian, doing shows here there and everywhere. He would do everything from vent, to balloon animals, to magic. My favorite bit was when he dressed up like Barney Fife from *The Andy Griffith Show* and did a dead-on impression of the Don Knotts character. Sometimes at the vent convention, he dressed up like Barney and pretended to patrol the crowd before the show or lectures began. Killed me every time.

Anyway, Bob called me that night and nailed exactly what I was thinking and feeling. "Kind of weird to go from what you just did tonight, to back to your place, alone, with no one to share it with, huh?" he asked. Bob was single as well and had lived the nomad existence for much longer than I had. "Yep," I responded. "And I don't really feel like heading back East to do nooners at crappy colleges either."

The next day, after I had finished the college cafeteria show, a student walked up to me and said it more perfectly than I could imagine. "Weren't you just on *The Tonight Show* last night?" he asked, almost befuddled. "Yeah," I responded, trying to quickly pack my little guys back into the trunk. Then he really drove things home.

"What are you doing *here*?" It was like he had read my mind.

Peanut: It's nice when folks make you feel like a loser for playing their town.

The next couple of years, I kept doing as much television as possible. Being on the air was the key to building an audience and hopefully extending my "fifteen minutes of fame." After that first *Tonight Show*, Jim booked me four more times in the next two years, with my last Carson appearance coming just a few months before Johnny's retirement in the spring of 1992. Johnny always liked Walter the most, and I used Walter more than Peanut or José on television simply because of that. Of course, Carson would know what works. He had out-shined and outlasted every other late-night host.

My most memorable of the appearances was with Tim Conway. Things didn't start out on the best note. Before the taping began, I was in my dressing room getting ready, and I opened what I thought was the door to my bathroom. Turns out, I had opened the door to Conway's dressing room and accidently walked in on him in nothing but his underwear. I was mortified and started backing away, apologizing profusely, and Tim piped up, "No, no, come on in, it's fine, let's have a party!" Whoever was with me that day cracked up, then I did, and it was funny as hell.

The most memorable piece of each appearance, however, were the ad-libs. I never ran those extra jokes by McCawley, or anyone else on the show. It was dangerous, but never took a bad turn. For example, during one of my stand-up segments, Walter turned to look over at Johnny, who was of course sitting at his desk. Walter did a double take and said, "Hey, I think I know that guy. That's my wife's first husband! He paid off my mortgage!"

Most *Tonight Show* fans knew Carson was on his fourth marriage, and Ed McMahon, the show's longtime announcer and sidekick of Johnny's, was recently divorced as well, and was known to be dating a much younger woman. So I took my chances once again. While the "my wife's first husband" laugh was dying away, Walter then turned to look at the couch and said, "Shut up, Ed. You're next!"

> Jeff: You know Ed?
>
> Walter: Oh yeah . . . he's been datin' my grand-daughter.

I never spoke much with Ed McMahon, so I don't know how *he* felt about being picked on by Walter. All I know is Johnny loved it and kept having me back for more.

On another appearance during a couch segment, Walter turned to Ed for a comment. Ed was the well-known spokesperson for Publishers Clearing House. Just about everyone in the United States at one time or another had received mailings with Ed's picture on them. So I knew Walter would have an opinion. The bit went something like this:

> Jeff: You know Ed McMahon, don't you?
>
> Walter: Oh yeah . . . stop sendin' me all your damn mail!

After a huge laugh and a big cackle from Carson, Walter added, "Don't you have some envelopes to lick?"

I once met Jerry Seinfeld backstage at the Comedy & Magic Club and we talked about doing stand-up on *The Tonight Show*. He made a point that only a true veteran of stand-up would have been able to come up with, and it was this: "It's not your first time doing stand-up with Johnny that's important. It's your twelfth."

Seinfeld was talking about material. In other words, lots of guys could make it far enough to get booked *once*. But those who had what it took needed to keep coming back with new, fresh material, and kill every time. I took Jerry's words to heart and knew that if I were to become anything more than a one-hit wonder, I needed to do more than drink cranberry juice and make a dummy talk. I needed to write better material and jokes for the characters. I later realized Johnny liked Walter so much because he was a good character with a point of view, and attitude, and good jokes.

As this all started to sink in, I began to no longer feel the need to amaze the audience with technical vent crap. I needed to make audiences laugh so they would come back for more. After a while, my thinking came down to that one sentence that was becoming my mantra: *You can amaze an audience once or twice, but you can make them laugh for a lifetime.* At this point, I was now not simply a ventriloquist, but I was becoming a stand-up comic who just happened to use ventriloquism as a vehicle for the comedy.

Bubba J.: I don't think you can really make folks laugh for a lifetime because their faces would start to hurt and they might have a job to get to and you can't drive and laugh unless you see someone driving really funny, but I never seen that.

Jeff: I didn't mean it literally.

Bubba J.: Is this book almost over?

Christmas 1970

Chick magnet. 1971

At the age of ten, I made piles of these on my father's Xerox machine and then distributed them in mailboxes as far as my bicycle would carry me. I kept my price competitive. 1972

VENTRILOQUISH AND MAGIC
HAVE A Special Occasion coming
up? Need some entertainment?
Why not ventriloquism, or
magic, or both? Jeff Dunham
and his family of dummies. Call
Jeff Dunham at 239-XXXX
Fee - $5.00

Monty, JD, and Jimmy Nelson.
Ventriloquist Convention. 1975

WFAA Channel 8 interview, Dallas, Texas. The dummy is Monty Ballew. The young reporter is some guy named Bill O'Reilly. I have no idea what ever happened to him. April 1976

Jeff and Monty Ballew, Richardson High School. 1978

From the Richardson High School yearbook. Christy and I are sitting on one of my "borrowed" Datsun 280ZXs. 1980

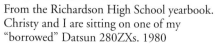

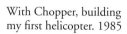

Six Flags over Texas, on the front steps of the Southern Palace. Summer 1980

With Chopper, building my first helicopter. 1985

Opening for George Burns. George is obviously overjoyed to meet me. Hershey Arena, Hershey Park, Pennsylvania. 1984

American Collegiate Talent Showcase. Archie, Little Dummy, and Dinah Shore. 1983

Bob and Delores Hope. This is me pickpocketing Mr. Hope. 1983

With Ollie, who was built in 1939 by Glenn and George McElroy. 1985

Sugar Babies. Mickey Rooney in street clothes. 1985

Headin' for Hollywood! At my childhood home with Mom, just before I drove away from Texas. September 1988

First *Tonight Show* appearance. Friday, April 6, 1990

The Cleveland Improv. Eighteen years of comedy clubs . . . 1991

Judge Ito Junior. 1995

Willie Nelson on *Hot Country Nights*, NBC. 1992

The purple Hummer and my helicopter. I land and take off from the trailer. It draws a crowd! 2005

Flyin' over Southern California in my third homebuilt RotorWay. Summer 2005

One of numerous appearances with
Jay Leno on *The Tonight Show*

My girls . . . Bree, Kenna, and Ashlyn. April 18,
2000

Reading *The Night Before Christmas*
at one of Jacquie's parties. Christmas
2003

The workbench on the bus. 2010

The *Best Damn Sports Show Period.* Walter just called John Kruk a cracker. 2002

At my parents' house with the first big thing Peanut paid for: the 1984 300ZX that I drove in college. It sat in the back driveway under a tarp for almost twenty years before I had it rebuilt to almost-new condition. 2008

Taping one of Achmed's segments for *The Jeff Dunham Show.* Marine Corps Base Camp Pendleton. San Diego County, California. 2009

Bubba J. singing along with Brian Haner, aka "Guitar Guy," during the taping of Comedy Central's *Jeff Dunham's Very Special Christmas Special.* The Pabst Theatre, Milwaukee, Wisconsin. June 7, 2008

My longtime friends and managers, Robert Hartmann and Judi Marmel, along with buddy Matt McNeil, our TV show's director. 2009

Peanut records a rap video in another episode of *The Jeff Dunham Show*. 2009

Mom and Pop (Howard and Joyce Dunham). Ready for a ride on the Tour Bus! 2009

Below: At the end of our two-hour concerts, Guitar Guy rocks the house and I shoot T-shirts out of our way-cool cannon. I've made a few holes in ceiling tiles! Austin, Texas. 2010

I faced one of the most difficult show-business decisions of my life in the early summer of 1991. A couple of weeks before, one of Johnny Carson's sons, Richard, had been tragically killed in a car accident. Richard was a photographer. Johnny was badly shaken by his son's death, and had taken two weeks off from doing *The Tonight Show*. But he was scheduled to come back on the air the next night.

Jim called and said, "Jeff, I need you to do Johnny a favor."

"Uh, sure," I said. "Anything."

Jim continued: "Johnny has put together some of Richard's best photos, and he wants to do a tribute to his son's work and show them during the broadcast. But if he can't bring himself to do the piece and bails on it, he'd like you to be on standby ready to do six minutes."

I sat there stunned, trying to take in every aspect of what I was being asked to do. Events can alter an audience, and certainly this first time back on the air for Johnny was going to be a somber night. How in the world was I supposed to get onstage, much less in front of America, and make everyone laugh when for the rest of the night they were probably going to be on the verge of tears, feeling for the King of Late Night after he'd lost a child? I was supposed to make everyone forget all that and tell jokes with a dummy next to me? How in the world—?

"Jim," I said, "that's crazy! Doing comedy during *that* show? Can't you—"

He interrupted me. "Do it for Johnny."

I thought about it for a few more long seconds and finally responded. "No problem," I said. "I'll have the set ready that I've been working on for you."

"Thank you," Jim replied.

I showed up at the normal time, and went through hair and

makeup. It was the oddest thing to be sitting there, literally praying that I wouldn't be on *The Tonight Show* that night.

Doc and the band started up, Ed did his thing, and I never heard the crowd. Jim walked into the open door of my dressing room and said, "Good news: Johnny's doing the piece. You can relax. Johnny wants to thank you, so stick around after the show."

These were of course not the circumstances I'd imagined for my first off-camera conversation with Johnny Carson, but it had been an honor to have been asked to be there and be put in that position. Afterward, Johnny thanked me and I expressed my condolences. As I was told, it was very rare for him to be seen after a show, and this day was one of the exceptions.

A few weeks later, Jim McCawley called with a most interesting query. "Do you do birthday parties?" he asked.

I was a little taken aback. "Birthday parties? Seriously?" I asked.

"Not like kid parties. Adult birthday parties," he said.

"NO," I answered bluntly. I had hoped he was calling me for a last-minute booking with Johnny, and a fun one this time.

"Well, Majel Barrett called, and she's looking for some entertainment for Gene's seventieth birthday party," he stated.

"Gene *Roddenberry*?" I spat. "THE Gene Roddenberry?"

Any *Trek* fan knew who the creator of *Star Trek* was, and that he married Majel, known mainly as the voice of the computer on every Starship *Enterprise* of all the series up to that point, plus the movies. She had of course made guest appearances as an actress on a few episodes too.

"Yes, the *Star Trek* Gene Roddenberry," Jim replied. "She's having the party in her backyard, and of course she's making it a big event, and she just wondered if I knew a good act to entertain about a hundred people. I figured you'd done that kind of thing before. You'd work better than a straight stand-up." I didn't know whether that was a compliment or another slight, but I didn't care.

"When?" I asked.

A few weeks later, I found myself in Gene Roddenberry's back-yard, surrounded by everyone *Trek* . . . except Shatner. Bummer.

I told myself that I would *not* ask for autographs, and that I would just play it cool. For the act, I did my typical "corporate" set, and it went fine. I kept it fairly clean, and Walter was the hit with that particular crowd. I had been invited to stay for dinner, and of course didn't pass *that* up.

Many of the partygoers were people from other areas of Gene's life, but there were enough *Star Trek* faces there to make me feel like a kid at an amusement park. I found myself sitting almost back-to-back with James Doohan, otherwise known as Scotty. Whoa! What turn did my life take that allowed *this* to happen? For the non-geeks in the crowd, Scotty was also known as Montgomery Scott, the *Enterprise*'s chief engineer, from the original 1960s television series. As any fan of the show knows, Scotty saved the *Enterprise* and the entire crew multiple times under impossible odds. I think he even saved the entire universe once or twice.

 Peanut: You really are a big geek.

 Jeff: I know.

Anyway, the only thing separating Scotty and me was one of those eight-foot-tall gas heaters. He was at one table, and I was at the one right next to him, and the heater was between us at our backs.

Let me set up the next part of the story by saying that not only was I a *Star Trek* fan, but somewhere in my heart, I *knew* these characters. I didn't have *Star Trek* sheets, or learn the Klingon language, or anything *that* extreme, but I had watched all the episodes of the original series in syndication since the mid-1970s multiple times, and I'd never missed an episode of *Star Trek: The Next Generation*, which was on the air at this time.

At some point near the middle of dinner, I heard a little commotion behind me, and saw people across the round table from me looking wide-eyed at a spot a few feet above my head. I turned around to look, then my gaze went up, and lo and behold, the gas heater had caught on fire in a very wrong way. It was billowing black smoke from all sides and at the top, and flames were starting to engulf all the upper pieces. People started to yell. And then, honest to God, the first thought that went through my mind was, "It's okay . . . SCOTTY's here!"

Well, who do you think the first guy was to panic and yell louder than everyone, and shove chairs out of the way so he could get clear of the danger? Scotty. Oh, dang. Something was destroyed deep inside me in that moment.

That was the first time I accepted that *Star Trek* wasn't real.

 Peanut: No doubt about it: You are simply a big, GIANT geek.

 Bubba J.: Even I'm getting embarrassed now.

The evening wasn't over, however. I met a few cast members, including George Takei (Sulu), Patrick Stewart (Capt. Jean-Luc

Picard), and Brent Spiner (Data). As the party was dispersing, I saw them standing alone, chatting. Like I said, I didn't want to be a dork or a nuisance, but I thought I had to at least say hello to Captain freakin' Picard. I walked up and they both turned to greet me. I stuck out my hand and first shook Brent's, then Patrick's. Then I said, "I don't want to bother you guys like an idiot fan, but I just wanted to say how much I really enjoy your work." Without missing a beat, Patrick Stewart looked me straight in the eye and without betraying a bit of insincerity, in that sterling and magnificent British baritone Shakespearean voice, said, "And I *yours.*" It was like I was five years old and had just met Santa.

Walter: Pull yourself together.

Jeff: What?

Walter: You're having a geek-gasm.

In early 1992, Dick Clark was producing a new show for NBC called *Hot Country Nights.* It was a prime-time musical variety hour that featured country music stars. In addition to music, they built in a short segment for stand-up comedy. The show would be taped on the set right across the hallway from Carson's, and was also the set, by the way, that would eventually become *The Tonight Show* stage for Jay Leno.

Jim McCawley had been chosen to book the stand-up talent. I was one of the first comics he called. Once again, he thought Walter would be perfect for the show.

I was booked for only one appearance; and since the show wasn't live, I felt zero pressure. I was introduced by one of the country artists after he'd done his number, and there Walter and I stood doing stuff we'd written just for the show:

> Walter: I only listen to country music when I'm doing my taxes.
>
> Jeff: Why's that, Walter?
>
> Walter: It's just nice hearin' about folks who are a hell of a lot worse off than I am.

It couldn't have gone over better. The laughs were big and the applause breaks were long. But as my segment was coming to a close, I realized I hadn't asked whether I was supposed to stand right there as they went to commercial, or whether I was to walk offstage. When Walter and I got to the end of our bit, I decided just to stand there and hopefully they would go to graphics or a commercial or whatever. Well, the segment ended, the applause died down, and there I stood. Keep in mind that Dick was to the side, just off camera, for all the audience to see. He and the director would talk to the crowd and the performers over the PA, giving direction.

> Walter (to the crowd): Shut up, we're finished!
>
> Jeff: I didn't find out, was I supposed to walk off? I have no idea what I was supposed to do.
>
> Director: You did perfect!
>
> Walter: Well . . .

Dick (booming voice over PA): YOU STAY AND
WALTER WALKS OFF!

That got a big laugh from the crowd, as they all knew who said
it. Then after a nice pregnant pause, Walter stated as sarcastically as
I could muster . . .

Walter: Oh, Mr. Clark's a comedian, *heh heh heh.*

Don't forget that this was *the* Dick Clark—very much an American icon and a living legend in show business. On this show in
particular, he was respected and revered, and most of the staff called
him Mr. Clark. I was the guy with the curmudgeonly dummy. So
that last line from Walter got a *huge,* long laugh from the crowd.
As it continued, I just stood there, looking embarrassed, picking lint
off my jacket, wondering if I'd just shot myself in the foot, never
again to work for the legendary Dick Clark. I looked uncomfortable,
and I was, despite the big laugh. Then as the applause and laughter was dying down, I honestly couldn't help it. . . . Walter topped
himself.

"Don't FUCK with the puppet, DICK." Mr. Clark actually hit
his head on the table in front of him, he was laughing so hard. The
ensuing conversation included a few more digs by both Dick and
Walter, but the exchange was another future-changing moment in
time that I hadn't planned or rehearsed.

Dick and the other producers decided to have me back for nine of
the twelve episodes. Each week Walter and I talked to one of the top
country stars on the show. The twist was that I loved country music,
but Walter hated it and didn't know or care who any of the stars were.
We gave the musical artist a loosely written script and we did it pretty
much unrehearsed in front of the audience as the cameras rolled.

One of my favorite moments was with Willie Nelson.

Walter: Actually, I'm a big fan of yours. It's good to see you have a sense of humor.

Willie: This is true. I have a sense of humor.

Walter: Yeah, you got a sense of humor. IRS took everything else.

I was now touring as a headliner. I of course never worked with other headliners, so most of the other acts I saw were good middle and so-so openers. Only a couple of times did I go to clubs to see other acts, but one weekend at the Comedy & Magic Club, another ventriloquist I knew was playing, so I went to see him. Headlining that night was some new up-and-comer named Jim Carrey. This was just before *In Living Color* and Jim was doing stand-up, opening for big names and doing his thing in clubs. He was beginning to headline here and there.

Well, I had the fortune of sitting near the front of the audience that night. Hermosa Beach is just south of Los Angeles, and the audiences there aren't your typical LA crowd. There are a lot of tourists and beach folks that end up there at night, so it's a nice cross section of demographics.

The opener and then ventriloquist went up, and then it was time for Jim. I knew nothing about him, and I don't think at that time much of the audience had ever heard of him either. All I remember is that the place was too small for the personality of Jim Carrey. If you've seen him perform live, or if you can remember some of his wilder antics in his earlier movies or of course on *In Living Color*, that's what he was like that night. With all the wild faces and loud voices and crazily huge mannerisms, he was just too big for the room. He was all over the place, and I'd never seen it happen before, but he actually frightened the crowd into a dead silence. It was mind-boggling. You could feel people actually pushing themselves back in their seats, try-ing to get away. My first thought was, "What is *wrong* with this guy?" In that small room with the folks who weren't ready for it, the genius of Jim Carrey came off almost as mental illness. It wasn't until later that America began to appreciate just how twisted *and* talented the guy really is.

All of my TV appearances continued to build an amazing and loyal following of fans. As I toured coast-to-coast incessantly, folks would come to the clubs, wanting to see the little guys that they'd seen on TV. Walter and Peanut began to evolve as my material became much more character based, versus being simply made up of funny jokes. The act was taking on the feeling of a sitcom that had been on the air for a couple of seasons—the audiences knew and loved the characters and when I introduced them at each point in the show, they would get more applause than me. It was awesome.

Every comic who's worked the road for any length of time has a hand-ful of bad road stories, and I am no exception. A guy who was my opening act for many years and became one of my best friends was Gary Brightwell. When we met, he was the house emcee at the Com-edy & Magic Club, and he also booked much of the talent. Fueled by his wry sense of humor, Gary had kept a collection of the absolute worst vent promo pictures possible and he had these photos plastered all over his office. I laughed every time I looked in.

Gary had learned really well how to take a completely dead crowd and get them laughing and ready for the ensuing acts, but while work-ing with me, he had also become my informant of sorts. Whatever club we were in, there was always a local emcee, and Gary would be the middle. After he'd done his bit, he'd come back to me and report on the crowd, noting what kind of mood the audience was in, if they were judgmental, conservative, drunk, or whatever. He would also let me know if there were any troublesome folks in the crowd that I needed to be aware of, such as individual drunks, or hecklers that wouldn't give up . . . that kind of thing.

Anyway, one night at the Improv in Brea, California, Gary came backstage and told me that there was one particular guy in the middle of the room toward the back who was being extra-obnoxious. The club seated about four hundred folks, was packed that night, and booze was flowing. Managing the club that evening was one of the co-owners, Robert Hartmann. I had known Robert for a few years as he had come up in the Improv chain from dishwasher to manager, to now owning some of the clubs. He and I were about the same age and he would eventually become one of my managers and another of my best friends.

It was Saturday night's second show, the most packed show of the week. Robert and I had an agreement that if anyone became unruly and started to heckle or interrupt the show, I would give the person two chances with my own heckler comebacks. If after those two shots, the guy (or girl) didn't shut up and I began to ignore them, that would be the signal to kick his (or her) ass out. Robert was always concerned that both audience and artist remained happy and that order was maintained in his clubs. He would stop at next to nothing to ensure a good night for as many folks as possible. That meant no bullshit. After Gary had finished his time and while the emcee was making some announcements and getting ready to introduce me, Gary ran backstage to tell me about the drunk. He told me where the guy was and that he was laughing obnoxiously after everyone else had stopped and that he was making catcalls and goofy noises. Robert had heard the guy too, and I just reiterated our system: two times, then out on the third.

About ten minutes into my set the guy started up. I had done about ten minutes of my own stand-up and now I had Peanut out. The guy blurted out, and Peanut let him have it. Big laugh. Less than ten minutes later, the guy did it again. Another line from Peanut, another big laugh, and we went on. A few minutes later, another yell from the guy when the rest of the crowd was quiet and I ignored him this time.

The lights at a comedy club are just like most other stage settings: dark in the audience and so bright onstage that the performer is virtually blinded from anything beyond the first row. A minute or so later, I felt this big empty hole form in the sea of laughter, from just about where the guy had been heckling. The quiet in only that area continued for a couple minutes, then it began to go back to normal. I finished the show and all was well.

When I walked backstage, there in the Green Room sat an ashen Hartmann and Brightwell, with an odd look on both their faces. "What's wrong?" I asked.

"Oh, man," was about all Gary could utter, then he began to slowly shake his head back and forth. Robert put his head in his hands, elbows on the table, and covered his eyes.

"WHAT?" I asked again.

"This was bad," Robert finally replied.

"What the hell happened?" I asked again.

"That wasn't a drunk," Gary stated.

"It wasn't?" I asked.

Almost simultaneously both said, "Nope."

"Then WHAT?"

Now I was getting mad. Robert took a deep breath and explained: "It was an eighteen-year-old kid. Huge fan of yours. He has the dolls, the T-shirt; everything."

"And . . . ?" I pushed.

"His parents brought him. He was loving the show. He has

cerebral palsy and the timing of his laughs was just off from everyone else and the noises were just him having a good time."

I was stunned. "Oh nooooo . . ."

"Oh, yes," replied Gary.

Then Robert explained, "He was killing the show and pissing off everybody at the tables around him. I got into an argument with his mom, and to shut him up, she told me off and then spiked him in the neck with some sort of shot. Everyone around us was horrified when she spiked him and just went quiet."

Robert had given the family passes for other shows, paid for their dinner and drinks, and apologized profusely and unendingly. He had asked them to stay after the show, so when most of the crowd had dispersed, I went out and made my own apologies. The family was seemingly fine and I took a couple of pictures with the young guy and signed some stuff. As they were leaving, Gary turned to me and with a big smile said, "Now you have your worst road story ever." Yikes. No kidding.

Now let's try a funny one: The Comedy Connection in Boston was one of my favorite clubs of all time, but unfortunately it's no longer there. It was on the second floor of Faneuil Hall, a marketplace and meeting hall in Boston since 1742. It was a Sunday night and I had just finished the last of eight shows that week. The audience had gone, and I had rewarded myself by having a single beer and hanging out at the bar next door for twenty minutes. This was an unusual thing for me to do, quite honestly. I always preferred to go back to the hotel room and watch *Star Trek* (just kidding . . . maybe).

I headed back into the darkened showroom to pack up my trunk and all the little guys for our trip home the next morning. In the dark that night, I quickly threw the original Muppet-like Bubba J. in the trunk, along with Peanut, the stand, and so on. I slammed it shut, latched it, then stood it back on end to roll down the stairs and across the cobblestones to the Bostonian Hotel and my room for a quick night's sleep and then an early flight back to LA the next morning.

When I got home the next afternoon I left the trunk in the garage, where it would now sit for five days until my next flight for some weekend shows in Tucson. It was August in the San Fernando Valley, so my closed garage easily reached temperatures of over 100°F.

On Friday morning, I opened the garage, got my trunk, and hefted it into the back of my truck. As I was driving to the airport, I thought, "Did I leave some food in here? What's that smell? Whatever." I got to LAX, unloaded the trunk, and checked it in curbside. I then parked my truck, went inside, checked in, got through security, and was just arriving at the gate when I heard myself being paged from the airport public address system.

I had to pick up a white security phone and dial a number. I did just that, and was then told to head to a certain door where I would be met by security. What the heck? I was then escorted out to the plane where I found two more security guys, a police officer with a gun, a baggage handler, and my trunk. "Sir, is this your trunk?" a big guy asked.

"Yeah," I said. "What's wrong?"

"What do you have in that trunk, sir?" he queried.

"Dummies," I stated.

"Dummies?" he asked.

"Yeah, you know. Puppets, ventriloquist dolls," I replied.

"Could you open the trunk for us please?" he said.

"Sure, but what's the problem?" Now I was really confused. I'd done hundreds of flights and millions of miles without a problem.

"It's the smell," the guy said. "Are you transporting any human remains in that trunk?"

"Good lord, no!" My mind was whirring now. But I couldn't resist throwing in an obvious joke: "Well, not real ones, anyway!" I smirked.

No one laughed. These guys weren't fooling around. Then the wind must have changed, and the smell drifted my direction. I almost gagged. What the hell? I put down my backpack, walked over, unlatched, and then opened the trunk. The deadly smell hit all of us at about the same time. It was hard not to throw up. Then I saw it. It took me a while to piece together what happened, but it must have happened while I was having that beer in Boston five nights before. I shut the trunk in the dark, never looking, and then left it in the oven-hot garage for a week. There in the bottom of the trunk, lay a rotting dead Boston rat.

Oh yeah . . . and that wasn't the worst of it. I deposited the rat in the garbage, threw the characters back in the trunk, gave it to the baggage guys, and then headed back up to the Jetway to catch my flight. But when I got the trunk to the Tucson club in 115-degree weather, I opened it again, this time in the hot alley behind the club, and almost threw up once more. The smell was every bit as strong and had permeated all the characters, their clothes, and even the bare plywood on the inside of the trunk. I got some Lysol, some Febreze, and even some house paint for the wood to try and mask the smell. All to no avail. I have no idea what the first couple of rows in the club thought the next few nights, but I almost passed out from the death stench for days after that. No manner of chemicals could rid Bubba J. of smelling like a dead rat. And of course the paint simply sealed the smell inside the trunk.

So there. That's my Boston dead rat story.

 Bubba J.: (sniff, sniff)

 Jeff: What's wrong, Bubba J.?

Bubba J.: That was gross and sad all at the same time. I don't know how you do it.

I got to know Ellen DeGeneres a little when she and I worked the grand opening of a short-lived Improv comedy club in Seattle. This was long before Ellen had publicly come out of the closet, but *most* people in comedy already knew. "Most people" means everyone but *me*.

All I knew was that she was a darned funny comic, she was sharp, she was incredibly kind to everyone around her, she had a great energy, and she was cute as could be. Luckily, one of the other guy comics knew more than I did. I was talking to him backstage one night, and I remember saying, "She's pretty cute."

"Uh . . . yeah," the guy said.

"I'm gonna ask her out," I said offhandedly.

I remember the guy looked at me sideways and said, "Uhhhh . . . really?"

"Yeah," I said. "She's not married, right?"

The guy goes, "Nooo. No, she's not married."

"No boyfriend either?" I asked.

"No, definitely not," he replied.

"Then, what the hell, I have a shot, right?"

Once again, he looked at me like I was from Pluto.

"Uh, nooo, not really," he said.

"Oh, come on! I bet she'd say yes! Why shouldn't I?" I asked, almost pissed off.

"Dude . . . she likes *women*," he said.

I sat there for a second, trying to let that register in my head.

"Really?" I asked, a bit deflated.

"Yeah."

"Oh," I said. "Well . . . wanna go get a beer?"

I still wonder to this day how Ellen would have turned me down.

 Walter: You are so clueless . . .

 Jeff: I really couldn't tell.

 Walter: No, I just meant that in general.

During the early 1990s, I signed with Rick Bernstein as my manager, who was a genuinely good soul, and our business relationship turned into an incredibly close friendship. My agency brought in Robin Tate, a longtime rock-and-roll and comedy promoter who'd worked with acts like Jerry Seinfeld and Tim Allen, just to name a couple. After seeing my club sales, Tate was convinced I could fill eight-hundred- to two-thousand-seat theaters across the country.

Now this was theaters—not clubs. It's a huge step in the comedy world to go from the small to the large. It's referred to as "breaking out of the clubs." Now the *real* fun was starting.

Brightwell was once again my opening act as our touring began. After a few years, we had now shared many jokes, too many beers, and way too much time playing Myst. We had become true road warriors together.

There were no limos or extravagances at this point, because we all wanted to make as much money as possible. We played it cheap. No huge catering bills, no wild parties, not even upgraded hotel rooms.

Whenever we arrived at an airport Robin would be there to meet us in a rented SUV or big sedan, and we'd head to the gig on our own.

One weekend in the dead of winter, in some Midwestern city, Robin wasn't with us, but his secondhand guy, Suneil, had taken his place for this particular run. We were in the SUV on the way to the theater, when Suneil and I discovered that Gary had never been treated to a White Castle burger. Well, we told Gary that you absolutely *cannot* go through this life without experiencing the taste and aftereffects of a Midwest gut bomb. He was willing to give it a shot. It was cold and it was windy with snow and ice covering everything in sight, and none of us were looking forward to leaving the toasty warm vehicle. Suneil volunteered to go inside and get the food. He stopped the car in the middle of the almost-empty parking lot, left the keys in the ignition with the engine running so we would stay warm, got out, and then slipped and slid in the freezing wind to get our food. So there Gary and I sat. I was in the front passenger seat, and Gary in the back. Gary poked me on the shoulder and said, "You know he just broke the rule."

"Yeah. It's tempting," I replied. We were both thinking the same thing at the same time. You never, *ever* leave your vehicle with the keys in it, much less *running* when two of your buddies are still in the car. This was just asking for trouble. And the brutal weather made it even more tempting.

"I think I'll do it from here," I said.

"Be careful," Gary replied.

"Of the car?" I asked.

"No, the burgers," he said. "We don't want him to drop them."

Suneil wasn't a big guy, which made this even funnier. He came out of the White Castle, arms loaded with burgers, fries, and a drink tray. He couldn't have carried any more, plus he had a huge winter coat on. We watched him struggle to make it over the icy parking lot and to the car without slipping and dropping everything. Gary and I sat there watching him do his balancing act, and right as he put his ungloved hand on the car's door handle, I hit the electric locks. *Clunk.*

The engine was running, the wind was howling, but when he tried the door handle a couple of times to no avail, he looked back and forth at both of us through the window, and very suspiciously yelled, "GUYS . . . UNLOCK THE DOORS, PLEASE." We just sat there and smiled.

Gary said, "Can you do it from there?"

"Duh," I replied.

I then reached my foot over, stepped on the brake, and pulled the transmission into gear. Suneil's eyes went wide. "HEY! COME ON!" I slowly let off the brake and the car started to roll. Over the ice and snow it went, and Suneil stumbled back so his foot wouldn't get run over. After about ten feet, I stopped. Suneil then walked to us and tried the door again, and we just smiled some more. "YOU GUYS! I HAVE YOUR FOOOOOD!" The car rolled again, this time a little farther. Gary and I started laughing and the cat and mouse game continued. Finally I crawled over into the driver's seat, and while Suneil stood solitary in the cold and wind, Gary and I did donuts over the ice around the empty parking lot. "GUUUUYYYYSSS!" Gary and I were laughing so hard, we couldn't stand it.

Finally we stopped, opened the door, and yelled, "Come on! Let's go!" Suneil slowly made his way over to the car, and of course when he got within five feet of us, we slammed the door again and locked it.

It sounds cruel now, but man oh man was that funny. Good ol' Suneil.

 Walter: I think this part of the book really gives the folks some insight into the "real you."

Jeff: Who's the real me?

Walter: An emotionally boneheaded man-child.

Robin Tate was a different story. He was about twelve years older than me but had certainly been around the dark side of showbiz a lot more than I ever knew. Unbeknownst to me at the time, Tate was a full-on alcoholic and cocaine addict. If there's such a thing as being professional about abuses, I never knew it and never saw it, and from what I could tell, it never affected his work. It wasn't until years later that I found out about it, when Tim Allen, a client of Robin's who had gone through the same problems but had cleaned himself up, had Robin and his wife, Glenda, pretty much kidnapped from their house in St. Louis, then flown on his private jet to Los Angeles, where they went through thirty days of rehab at the very famous Promises rehab center. To this day, Robin attributes the saving of his life to Tim Allen. I never saw anything, and never knew there was a problem.

Occasionally I would receive fan letters from or meet people at my shows who had seen me on *The Tonight Show*, and were at the live shows because of those appearances. When working the theaters with Tate, I'd still sometimes do clubs in the markets where there wasn't an appropriate-sized theater. In early 1992, I received a fan letter, which I still have.

. . . I have recently had a major change in my life that has kept me home in front of the TV at night instead of going

out! Anyway, that is how I discovered you! At first I saw
you on a few of the comedy channels—then I started looking for you. I really began to look forward to your appearances. You have brought so much laughter into a life that
really needed some—and I wanted to thank you. . . . I was
so excited the night I saw you on Johnny Carson and heard
you were coming here. I have been telling my friends about
you for months—now they are going to finally understand
the things I keep saying! (Peanut's sayings!!) I'm bringing
them to see you on Thursday night.

That Thursday night I was told backstage that a cute blonde was
waiting to see me. I found her, signed a picture for her, and we chatted a bit and went our separate ways. A few months later I went back
to work at the same club, and there she was again, waiting after one
of the shows to talk to me. This time I asked her out. She hemmed
and hawed and said that maybe she'd come back on Sunday, but she
didn't. Then a few months later, I once again played the same club
and on the Friday night while the opening act was on, I was walking
through the lobby of the club, killing time until I went on. In the
nearly empty lobby over by the far wall was a young woman talking
on the pay phone. I walked over, and she looked up, stopping her
conversation midsentence. I didn't recognize her, but I did recognize
good looks.

"He's going to stand you up," I said.

"What?" she answered.

I said, "He's going to stand you up. The guy on the phone."

She laughed and hung up. "Do you remember me?" she asked.

I was a little stumped. She continued. "The last time you were
here we talked after the show. I sent you a fan letter and said I'd see
you here."

"Oh yeah," I said, remembering the letter more than her. I also remembered the sentence about something keeping her at home.

I asked her out again that night, and this time she said yes. She was extremely good-looking as well as engaging, and we had fun at lunch one day. I can't remember exactly when she told me, but soon I knew she was a single mom and her new daughter had kept her at home almost a year before. I was impressed by her boldness and her strength. She and her daughter lived with her father in an apartment, and she had a job at a local gym working part-time. The strange part was, unlike most first dates that I went on, I went back to my hotel that day and thought, "Nope. Not the one." Usually I was enamored for at least a few dates with someone new, but this one was different.

The next day she called me at the hotel and this time asked *me* out. With nothing else to do that day, I thought what the heck. Long story short, we began dating cross-country, and I would buy her and her young daughter airline tickets to meet me in cities here and there where I was doing shows. A few months later, we got engaged. Paige and I and twenty-one-month-old Bree lived together for a while in San Diego, and then we had a wedding in May of 1994 on the beach near the Hotel Del Coronado with a small gathering of friends. It was a small but wonderfully charming ceremony. White trash to the core, however, we had our wedding dinner at Chili's!

Here's a bit of trivia that most of my guy friends shake their heads at, even to this day. On that one day, May 19, 1994, yes on that ONE day, I not only got a wife, but: I got a daughter (I adopted Bree not long after that), I signed the papers to finalize the purchase of my first house in Encino, we got a dog at the mall earlier in the day, and after the marriage ceremony late that afternoon, we went to the local dealership and I bought a brand-new, bright red 1994 Dodge Viper. Good lord. One minute I was single, living in a $400 a month apartment; the next I had a wife, a kid, a dog, a big mortgage, and a kick-ass sports car.

Walter: And I thought Peanut was a mental case.

Peanut: Thanks—Wait, do you mean in a good way?

Walter: I couldn't have done all that . . . I was too trau-
matized just from getting married.

Three months later we had the bigger official ceremony with 120 invited guests at Disney World in Orlando. Mickey and Minnie cut in on our first dance, and a couple minutes later, Winnie the Pooh came in to dance with an almost-two-year-old Bree. It was truly a storybook wedding.

We lived in that house in Encino for a couple of years, where our second daughter, Ashlyn, was born. In 1997 we moved to Tarzana, into a bigger house with a bigger mortgage and a lot more rooms to furnish. The day before we moved from that house to the next, baby Makenna came into this world, and I was now truly a blessed man. I had a beautiful wife and three beautiful daughters.

The holidays were always magical for us, and Christmas, hands down, was the most fun. Paige decorated the house to look wonderful. Our living room had ceilings two stories tall, so our tree was usually thirteen or fourteen feet high. When the girls were really young, my favorite thing to do was to create "The Mommy Store." Since the girls were too young to actually shop for their mother, I would buy a bunch of presents for Paige, large and small, cheap and expensive, beautiful and funny. I would then turn my office into a store, complete with big price tags on all the items placed all around the room, and a little cash register at my desk. I had three little toy shopping carts and play money that I would divide into equal piles. A big banner hung across the back wall that said THE MOMMY STORE. My wife of course was never allowed anywhere near my office during this, but I'd run the video camera so she could watch it later. I'd open the door, and the girls would run in and start choosing treasures for their mom. I would sit at my desk, and they would then come over and I'd ring up the sales, taking their toy cash. Then we'd sit on the floor and wrap all the gifts, with the store's "complimentary gift wrap."

Bubba J.: Daddy did the same with me when I was a kid. Ours was the "Momma Pawn Shop."

Jeff: What kinds of gifts were there?

Bubba J.: Rolling papers, beer, spit cups, everything she loved!

One of my favorite Christmas mornings was a few years later, when Paige and I had been married seven years. It was Christmas 2001. All of Santa's gifts had been discovered, and the girls thought everyone's presents had been opened. I gathered all of us around the tree and said, "Well, that really isn't everything. There's one more present for Mommy . . . and it's from me. Hang on." Out to the garage I ran and hauled in a wooden crate, sealed tightly with a bunch of screws. It was about the size of a carry-on suitcase, but it weighed more than seventy pounds. I had built this crate myself, and had packed tightly the contents weeks before.

All the girls, including my wife, were bewildered. I just smiled, handing Paige a cordless drill with a Phillips bit in the chuck.

"Have at it!" I said. She went to work on the crate as I sat back, grinning, and the girls looked on, confused. They almost always knew what the presents for Mommy would be, but I'd kept this one a secret.

A few minutes later, all screws in the lid were out and Paige pulled it to the side while the girls gathered around to see what lay inside. With a perfect fit, nestled inside the rest of the crate was a well-worn, scratched-up, and beat-up pay phone. One reason it was so heavy was because the money was still in it.

"What in the world—?" Paige asked.

"Think," I said.

"Daaaaad," Ashlyn said, "why'd you give Mommy a PAY PHONE?" Ashlyn was now six, Kenna was four, and Bree was ten.

Paige still looked confused. "I don't get it," she said.

"Oh, come on," I responded. "Look at the address." On the phone, behind the thick clear plastic cover, was the address of where the stolen pay phone had originally been installed. For years I had been telling the proprietor of the establishment that if they ever remodeled the building and changed out that phone, I wanted it. The staff knew my wishes too, and they had done even better. One night a few of them had a little too much to drink and they decided to get the thing for me. When they brought it to me, I opened the guy's car trunk, and there it was, still mounted to a piece of drywall! Portions of a stud had even come along for the ride when they'd ripped it from its mooring.

My wife looked at the address on the phone's faceplate, mouthed it silently to herself, then the realization hit her. This was the pay phone from the comedy club lobby that she'd been talking on when I interrupted her conversation. I found out later that the guy she'd been talking to hadn't been a date that stood her up, but it was, in fact, her father. She had called him to check on infant Bree, who he was babysitting back at their apartment.

Paige burst into tears, and the girls were even more confused. "Mommy, what's wrong?" asked one of them.

"I think she's happy," I said.

I removed the phone, then put the lid back on the crate, and we stood it on end next to our big television in the living room. I then mounted the pay phone on top of the crate. As cheesy as it sounds, it looked perfect, almost like an abstract piece of white-trash art.

Bubba J.: That's a nice story. I got my wife something special from our first date.

Jeff: What was it?

Bubba J.: The smashed-up folding chair from a wrastlin' match.

Jeff: That's nice.

Bubba J: And for our five-year anniversary, I topped it with an exhaust pipe from our twenty-ninth tractor pull!

As the 1990s wore on, nothing made me happier than being with my family. Though I worked an incredible amount and was gone a great deal, nothing was more important to me than time together with my wife and children. I wanted to push my career as far as it would go, but like most people, it became an incredibly difficult balancing act between job and family.

My goal was always to be doing better the next year than I was the last. Whether that meant bigger venues or more TV, it didn't matter; I simply wanted progression. I had also always said to myself that I would never take a gig simply for the money. Each and every booking had to advance my career. Corporate dates, colleges, comedy clubs, Las Vegas, cruise ships, amusement parks, every one of them was a step in the direction I'd been heading.

By mid-1993, the theater work began to wane. So now I was faced with one of life's dilemmas: I wanted nothing more than to work less and be with my family, but if I did that, we wouldn't have enough money to make ends meet. I was still one of the top-earning touring club comics in the country, and we were going broke. It was ridiculous. On top of that, when I was home, I couldn't spend much quality time with the family. I would have to spend hours on end sitting in my office, paying bills, making deposits, and taking care of all the business aspects of my job and domestic life.

The worst memory of those days came early one morning when Ashlyn was barely four years old. Before I left, I would always put my trunk, my suitcase, and my backpack just inside the front door, where it would sit until I took it out to the car. One morning I had piled it all there, and then went back to the kitchen to say good-bye to my wife. I walked back to the front door, and there sitting next to all my stuff was little Ashlyn's own colorful kid-sized rolling suitcase. She wanted to go with Daddy. I got a huge lump in my throat, and then truly had to fight back tears when I took it back to tell her she couldn't go. Before I left, we sat down on her bed and opened the suitcase together. There were only three things: Her two baby dolls and her blanket. It was heartwrenching as she sobbed, standing at the front door, crying for me to stay as I was driven away in the cab. I couldn't fight back the tears either.

CHAPTER SEVEN

Moving Forward? Not Exactly

During the rest of the 1990s, though I knew that business was going well, I felt like I was spinning my wheels: Even though just about every club show was a sellout, and although I knew this was a position any comic would dream of being in, by 1993, I was starting to feel like I was trapped under some kind of thick layer of ice and I couldn't break out to go any higher. I thought the answer for keeping the career growing was television. I was pushing for what many of my more successful contemporaries were doing. I wanted a sitcom.

My guest appearances on the many stand-up shows from 1989 to 1992 had created a legion of fans who kept coming to the live performances. But in 1994 the market changed. By then, most of the stand-up television programs had come and gone, and just about the only conventional places left for comics to be on the air were *The Tonight Show with Jay Leno*, Leno having replaced Johnny Carson permanently in 1992, and *Late Night with David Letterman*. *The Arsenio Hall Show* came and went as well, as did a few more late-night talk shows and hosts. With television appearances harder to come by now, touring clubs, and even doing local radio morning shows as club publicity was becoming incredibly important. Momentum is important in a career, and since television continued to be elusive, I was always on the lookout for ways to keep my shows memorable.

One week when I was in Tempe, Arizona, playing the local Improv, I was having lunch with Dan Hutchinson, who at that time was the manager of the club. He loved my act, but especially Walter. We were tossing around ideas of what kind of guy Walter was, and what he and I should be discussing onstage. We then started spitballing the idea back and forth that Walter should be some sort of advice giver, like Dear

Abby. On my PowerBook I pieced together a handout that had a picture of Walter's head in black and white, and the words *Dear Walter* . . . with multiple blank lines following it. Dan agreed to make and cut multiple copies of the sheet, then have the staff distribute them to every table in the club. Before the show started, the sound guy would make an announcement for folks to "Please fill out your 'Dear Walter' cards. You can ask his advice on anything and everything. We'll be around to pick the cards up shortly." Then just before the show started, the staff would gather all the cards and bring them to me in the Green Room. I would then furiously go through them all, picking ones that I knew Walter could answer with good jokes.

The first night, the bit killed. Folks knew that this was a unique part of their show. They were seeing Walter and me think on our feet and not simply go through the motions of a set routine. The piece got so successful that for many years I ended the show with it.

Dear Walter, Did you vote for Abraham Lincoln?

Walter: No, but I gave him my theater tickets.

Dear Walter, Why do women play mind games?

Walter: 'Cause they're no good at regular sports.

Dear Walter: We're newlyweds. Any advice?

Walter: Nope; too late.

Dear Walter: What is the difference between sex and making love?

Walter: Fifty bucks.

Dear Walter, How do I keep my wife's butt from looking like a golf ball?

Walter: Stop pokin' it with your putter.

Dear Walter, If a man touches and smells a woman's hair, is that considered sexual harassment?

Walter: No, unless the guy's a midget.

Dear Walter, Are you anatomically correct?

Walter: No, I'm politically correct; I have no balls.

Seemingly, the comedy was the main purpose for the cards. But I had an ulterior motive on the business side of things. At the bottom of the cards was a second section, which was adorned with a picture of Peanut. A short line of text promised folks that if they filled in the blanks and gave us their mailing address, we would use that data for Jeff Dunham promotions and mailings, and nothing more. It said that we'd notify them when I was coming back to their area for live shows, or whenever we were going to be on TV, and that we would never sell nor give the information to anyone else for any reason. We utilized the mailing list in every way imaginable, but did what we said we would and kept the addresses all to ourselves.

My agency made these cards a part of every single contract, and it was a deal breaker. The clubs were required to help with the "Dear Walter" cards at each show, and I had to be allowed to farm and cultivate all the collective data. Many of the clubs protested, wanting to keep the information for their own databases. Again, that became a deal breaker for us, as I absolutely refused to allow that to happen, simply out of loyalty to the fans. Granted, some of the clubs would try and pull a fast one by copying the cards before they were given to me, but we quickly squelched that process by making sure the cards went directly from the tables to one or two of my guys and then to me. Another trick the clubs would pull would be to "innocently" cut the cards in half so that the "Dear Walter" section would be separate from the address pieces. That way they could give me the Dear Walter side, and then copy the addresses for themselves while I was onstage. The fix would always be a simple phone call to my agency or management, who would call back and "straighten out the misunderstanding."

The next huge step with the Dear Walter cards came a few years later when the Internet started to take off, and e-mails became the better choice for publicizing. A mass e-mail was a fraction of the cost of snail-mail postcards, but that wouldn't come for a couple more years, and long after we had used the snail-mail list to huge advantage. Though it sounds like a small number now, at that time we maintained an average of thirty thousand to forty thousand good snail-mail addresses.

The Dear Walter cards were a huge success for many years. On both the comedy as well as the business sides of things, it was magic. Some of my best material for *years* came from the ad-libs and jokes Walter would answer with after I read the questions aloud. A few years later, I gave a list of the funniest ones to my wife, who turned them into a soft-cover book that we titled—what else—*Dear Walter*. This was long before we had anyone interested in carrying any of my merchandise in retail, so since no publisher wanted it at that time, we self-published it and sold it at shows and online for a couple of years. It wasn't a huge seller, but it certainly did pretty well as a homegrown piece of work.

Understandably, the database grew in leaps and bounds every month. It was a true key to maintaining and informing loyal fans, but soon it simply became too much for me, my wife, or any of my publi-

cists to handle. I finally had to source out the mailing list maintenance to a professional company.

After taking over for Johnny, Jay Leno had me on as a stand-up guest.
Just as with my first time with Carson, I ended up on the couch right
after my set. The other guest who was still there when I made my walk
over with Walter in my arms was none other than Sugar Ray Leonard.
Not being able to resist, I had Walter turn to him and say, "So you're
gonna fight again, huh? How old are you?" Sugar Ray replied back,
"Forty."

"Forty, huh?" Walter asked. "Oh kaaaaayyyyyyy. . . ." That reply
from Walter drew a nice big laugh from the crowd, but once again,
I never asked anyone if I could talk to Sugar Ray—I just did it and
luckily, the affable boxer seemingly didn't take offense, and instead
laughed along with everyone else.

During the next few years, I returned to Leno every so often, making guest appearances in fake satellite hookups with Walter dressed in
ridiculous costumes. One time he was a bad mall Santa, then Cupid,
then the Easter Bunny, and finally Uncle Sam. "I know what NBC
stands for! 'Nothing But Crap!'" (Another nonsanctioned ad-lib.)

I've always found that one of the best ways to keep audiences interested and laughing is to utilize current topical material straight out
of the headlines. That's pretty much ninety-nine percent of most talk
show opening monologues, and there have been a handful of characters and public figures in recent years that many comedians owe a
debt of gratitude to. Bill Clinton and George W. Bush are a couple

of the top guys, but the big one of the 1990s was O. J. Simpson, plus many of the clowns surrounding him and that entire goofball circus.

After the slow-speed chase and all the nutty stuff that followed the tragedies, like every other comic, I jumped on it, but I also took it a little further than most comedians. During the Simpson trial, the poor O.J. jury was sequestered, and during the almost four-month trial, they had little to do. I heard through the grapevine that the court was trying to find entertainment for the jury during off hours, since they weren't allowed to go anywhere, talk to anyone, or do much of anything. So I had my publicist at the time contact Judge Ito, the presiding judge in the case, to see if he would like a little free entertainment from me and my guys. How cool would *that* be?

Well, sure enough, Judge Ito said yes, and we were put on the docket. As the day for the performance grew closer, I began to wonder about jumping on this crazy bandwagon of publicity and hype. Leno had the "Judge Ito Dancers" and everyone in the world was making jokes about the case and the judge himself. Certainly there was nothing funny about a double homicide, but everything that surrounded the case made it all look like complete tomfoolery. I knew I could add my own twist to it all.

I went to my workshop and began creating a new Little Dummy for Peanut. A week or so later, and I debuted him at the Brea Improv, and within a couple of days, he went on *E! News* and *Extra*. Who was Peanut's new sidekick? A junior-sized Judge Ito dummy. The jokes were stupid, but the reaction was huge.

As the day for the jury performance grew near, I knew I might be risking getting locked up, but I had to try and make them laugh with the junior judge. When the day finally arrived, what came as not much of a surprise was the fact that I wasn't given the location of where the show would take place until just before we were supposed to start driving there. The reason was that they were trying to limit knowledge of where the jury would be and when. The press was crazy.

I always thought the court's concern was a little overcautious when I saw later that the jury was taken out for some fun to a couple of Lakers games!

Anyway, I got a call from the courthouse a couple of hours before showtime, and was told when to be at the Police Academy in Fullerton. So off I went. When I arrived, I was promptly escorted to a back room with six of the deputies, where I was asked to go through my act joke by joke to make sure there was nothing inappropriate for the jury to hear. I was told I couldn't mention the case, the defendant, the prosecution, or the judge. I then pulled out the little Judge Ito, and all the deputies laughed and laughed, and then said, "NO."

Well, despite having to dismiss my latest cast member, the performance couldn't have gone much better. Everyone was very affable afterward and I was allowed to chat with the jurors a bit. My confidence in our jury system was shaken a little, however, when one of the alternate jurors walked up and started a conversation. She was young, blond, and cute, and every bit a stereotypical Valley Girl. I heard her say to someone a few feet from me (and I'm not kidding here), "Ohmigod! When he pulled out Peanut, I was just *freakin'*!" Not long after that she of course was hearing evidence based on test results of deoxyribonucleic acid.

Peanut: Would you have done the show if you had known these idiots were going to let O.J. go free?

Jeff: Don't call them idiots.

Peanut: Sorry. Morons?

In the same way that quickly writing jokes for the Dear Walter cards backstage developed a skill in me to come up with good jokes quickly, doing literally hundreds of radio and TV interviews a year taught me how to be a good interviewee, or in some cases, how to take over a show and move things in the direction I wanted it to go. But most important, I learned the power of making jokes from current events. Morning radio guys loved it when Walter and I would come in with fresh material about whatever had happened in the news the day before, or even from that morning. It wasn't unusual for me to be sitting in a taxi on the way to the station going through the morning's newspapers and writing quick jokes about whatever was in the headlines.

While sometimes the morning jocks were good and would go back and forth with me and Walter in interview style, many times they would be a bit put off that I was even there. Why? Well, the comedy clubs would purchase commercial time on the most popular radio shows to run ads, and if the radio jocks didn't have any say-so with management or the salespeople, the morning teams would be forced to have me on as a guest. In the early years, there were many morning radio teams that would either sit there with a major attitude during the interview, or they would try and make fun of me. Sometimes they would make things uncomfortable simply by turning on my mike and throwing out mundane questions like, "What's going on?" I quickly learned how to take the ball and run.

Sometimes I had to win over the morning teams before things went sour on the air, and that meant being funny immediately and without platitudes. No "Hi, how are you?" It would be Walter jumping in and going straight to the material. Oftentimes, if a comic went into an obviously well-worn comedy bit, many of the jocks would shut down. I'm sure they would be thinking things like, "We're here for five hours every morning thinking on our feet with new material at every break, so you should be able to as well."

Every so often, a morning host would ask, "What topics do you want to talk about?" or "What questions should we ask to lead you?" I got to the point where I would usually say, "Just say hi and I'll run with it." It just became easier that way because I had the jokes and material ready, and with a tiny bit of interaction, Walter could just spout off for minutes on end about what was in the news. That way it usually went over perfectly. Everyone just had to sit back and laugh.

Of course the one glaringly obvious goofy aspect about me doing radio was the simple fact that I was a ventriloquist. Poor Debbie Keller, my longtime friend and publicist, must have had a hell of a sell job in front of her back in the early days. Eventually people caught on that it was simply characters telling jokes on the air, and the ventriloquist aspect didn't matter. And yes, every single time, I would take either Peanut or Walter with me to the radio studios. It was amusing for the jocks that Walter was even there, but what was even funnier would be when an engineer would give a microphone to me, and then not thinking, also put a second one in front of Walter. That happened numerous times and the poor guys were the laughingstocks of the station for the next month.

Every so often the odd audition would come up when a sitcom or a commercial was looking for a ventriloquist. If I was in town, I'd take a dummy and make a go at it. As most folks in this business will attest, you usually go on dozens of auditions, and you're lucky if one or two of them pan out. So by the mid-1990s, I was used to being turned down. For whatever reason you're rejected, you try to learn not to take it personally. Usually the casting folks know within a few seconds of you walking in the room whether you're right for the part or not, simply by your looks.

On one particular occasion, however, I was called in for a Hertz rental car commercial. Every other ventriloquist I had ever heard of who lived anywhere near New York or Los Angeles had gone on the call, and I knew I was just one more on the list. I was one more guy with a dummy at an audition. I had become fairly jaded at this point, but I couldn't help getting excited about the potential of something as cool as a national commercial for a well-known product. That could mean big exposure and income, unexpected cash if it aired a decent number of times.

When I arrived, it was the same old thing: Here's the script, read the lines, try your best, and go with your instincts. The Hertz campaign at that time was the "Not Exactly" campaign. They'd left it open to the vent to bring whatever dummy he chose, which was kind of unusual, so I took Walter. He was still my strongest, most versatile and universal character.

The script called for the ventriloquist to be running through the rain, looking up at the storm, while the dummy griped at him for choosing the wrong car rental company. Since we were in a small room with one little video camera, I had to pretend I was running while holding Walter, and I did what I was told. I looked around, acted as if the storm was pelting down, and Walter did what he did best: looked at me and told me what an idiot I was.

When I was finished, the guy just stood there and looked at me. "Okay. That was great," he said. I'd heard that a million times. "Thanks," I said, and I left.

Unlike other auditions when I felt good about what I had done and that I really had a shot, this one left me knowing I hadn't a chance in hell. I couldn't help but be depressed because nothing in television in the past four or five years had panned out. It had been all guest spots here and there, but every year when we shopped around my own television show idea, no one would bite.

Driving home from the audition, I took the Reseda Boulevard

exit as usual, and there at the bottom of the ramp at the stoplight in the normal spot was a homeless guy with a sign asking for handouts. I always struggled with whether to give to these guys or not. Are they just going to spend it on booze, or do they really need it? Here I am in a nice vehicle, and they supposedly don't have enough cash for a donut. I was feeling sorry for myself, and was ashamed. I rolled down the window and gave him a $20. End of story. So I thought.

The next day, the call came in, and I had already tried to put the whole Hertz thing out of my head. I didn't even have to go in for a callback. They wanted Walter and me on such and such a date, I was hands down the best, and congratulations. What the—?

So now I was going to be in a national television commercial. I was stoked. Granted, it was one simple spot, but I had never done a *national* one, and I knew that exposure like this would probably jump ticket sales once again.

I found out later that day that they needed *two* Walters. . . . And the shoot days were in one week! There had been the one and only Walter for all these years and shows, but they needed a backup in case the deluge of water made one of the dummies inoperable.

I hadn't built a figure in many years, and I was in a time crunch. So I phoned an old friend in Las Vegas named Joel Leder, who was also a vent and figure maker himself. I flew up one afternoon with the original Walter so Joel could make a quick silicone mold of the head, then cast a couple fiberglass head shells. I then flew back to LA the same day, headed to Sears and the local hobby store, and purchased all the materials I would need to construct two new Hertz Walters. . . . Waterproof ones!

What Joel made was just an empty shell of a head—no mechanics; the mouth wasn't cut out; no paint or hair; just a shell, like the body of a car with nothing in it to make it run. So now I had one week to construct these two Walters, and I was booked at Zanies Comedy Night Club in Nashville for the next six nights. I had to take all the materials and tools, pack them in a box, and ship them to the hotel in Nashville, where I would build the figures.

The next day I arrived in Nashville and proceeded to set up shop in the hotel, unbeknownst to the maids. The shows at night were more of a nuisance than anything, interrupting my construction process.

Joel had done a good job with the fiberglass, but before installing all the mechanics, a LOT of sanding had to be done. Gary Bright-well was with me that week, and as a truly loyal and good friend, he came to my room and went to work on one of the heads, as did I. We sanded and sanded until the heads looked good and were ready for the mouths to be cut out and for me to install the triggers, levers, springs, strings, rods, and customized pieces of brass, all cut and welded by me right in that little room. I had even purchased a little Workmate bench with a built-in vise. I did accidently drill a hole in one of the counters in the room, but that wasn't the biggest issue—by the end of the six days, the entire room, including the bedspreads, pillows, and curtains, were covered with a thick layer of sawdust and fiberglass dust. I'd kept the DO NOT DISTURB sign hung on the doorknob all week, so no one had a clue. I can't remember if I left the maid a tip or not.

Walter: Maid? They probably should have bulldozed the place.

Jeff: Probably.

Walter: Imagine what the folks in the room next door must have been thinking hearing two guys talking and laughing, followed by the sounds of power tools.

As I departed the hotel, one new Walter dummy was finished, paint and hair and all, and the second one was close. The Hertz commercial folks had paid me to build two, but I knew the one would never break in the rain, so I didn't worry about the second one being a little shy of the finish line.

Taping took place over two days and at two locations. The inside scenes, which were supposed to be in an airport, we filmed at the Los Angeles Convention Center, out in the main area where there are long escalators. I had to carry Walter, pushing my way down the stairs and through the "extras" who were standing in place. The whole time Walter was of course doing his lines, bitching about the crappy *other* rental company I'd used.

That went well, but being the novice TV guy that I was, when I had to make a phone call (still mainly car cell phones at that time; no small handhelds), I picked up the receiver of a pay phone that was one of a bank of phones near the bottom of the escalators. I put in a couple of quarters, and when it didn't work, I moved to the second one. A crew guy finally walked over and whispered, "Those are part of the set. They're not real. So . . . they don't work." DOH!

The next day we were on location, ironically, just outside the Los Angeles International Airport at a former Hertz rental location, which was now an empty set of buildings. Once again, the set and prop guys had done an amazing job at making Hollywood magic happen. I thought it was an actual Hertz rental place.

This was where I had to run through the rain. . . . And if you haven't seen rain machines work on TV or in movies, you wouldn't believe it. Simple raindrops don't look like much on camera. So to make up for what you can't see, they have to create a deluge to make it look like a normal rainstorm. To make matters worse, what I was running through was supposed to be a torrential downpour! So . . . the

rain machines were pretty much put on full blast. Plus, and also ironically, because it doesn't rain much at all in Southern California, this
happened to be the *one* week that we got heavy rain in LA, and yes, it
was raining pretty hard. Walter and I might as well have jumped in a
pool in our clothes and swam around for a while. Oh, and it was also
during a rare cold snap in LA too.

 Walter: Only in LA do folks call a little rain
in 68 degrees a "cold snap." You're a wuss.

Remember how I told you I wasn't worried at all about Walter
getting wet? This one commercial reportedly cost about $1 million,
and in the mid-1990s, that was a big budget for a thirty-second spot.
Well, Walter's mechanics were brass, and the head and all other construction was fiberglass, so nothing was going to have a problem while
soaking wet. The head would have been fine if it *had* been in a pool
underwater. I even used acrylic paint, which is actually a form of plastic, so that was waterproof as well. However, when painting the faces
of the characters, I like to put on a little texture, and also take any
kind of shine out. Acrylics shine, so in a pinch, I had run to the local
store looking for some kind of powder to mix in and dull it down.
Not thinking, I grabbed some after-shower powder. . . . I didn't know
what it was; all I knew was that it was a powder, and that it would dull
a shine if I padded it onto wet acrylics.

Oops. It turned out that it was some kind of soap. So guess what.
When the rain got really intense near the end of the filming, Walter's
face started to foam! I kept wiping it off as the bubbles came out of his
head. No one ever saw, and it was late enough that it only happened
for the last thirty minutes or so, but at one point it looked like Walter
had rabies.

By 1994, I was stuck on the idea of having a TV show. I could see that throughout the decades, many of the more successful stand-ups had, and were, parlaying their success into sitcoms: Bill Cosby, Jerry Seinfeld, Tim Allen, Ellen DeGeneres, Roseanne Barr, Brett Butler, and so on. It seemed an obvious move to me to be looking for a similar avenue.

"Holding Deals" were popular in that time period, and this was when a network or production studio would pay an actor (or comic) a big sum of money to reserve him or her for a certain amount of time while the potential for a television show was explored. "Development Deals" is another term for it as well. I can thank Tony Danza and his company, Katy Face Productions, for my first holding deal in the early 1990s. We tried to come up with a sitcom idea for many months during my "holding," all to no avail, but that money paid for my 1994 red Dodge Viper. When that big check came in from Danza's company, it seemed like goofy "found" money to me, like I'd won a lottery or something. I remember thinking, "Shouldn't I have *fun* with this chunk of cash?" I think I threw off the Dodge salesman in San Diego a bit when I walked into the dealership that night, pointed to the Viper, and said, "I'll take that one," then proceeded to write him a check for the whole amount. It probably wasn't the wisest financial move, but I have to admit that being able to do that felt really cool. Within the next few years, I wouldn't even be able to *think* about doing that again. As for my own sitcom, it seemed to me like the only way I would be able to progress in my career, other than by simply making a seemingly unending journey around the country playing small clubs. I thought that if I was going to continue to succeed, I had to follow the route every other famous comic had gone before me.

Among a few of the guest appearances I made on numerous television shows of the time was a single episode appearance on *Ellen*. I played a ventriloquist who was actually an undercover CIA agent. Walter was their dummy of choice, and after a mean slight from the little old man, Jeremy Piven, who was a regular on the show, attacked Walter and started choking him. Jeremy was great, and completely got into the scene. We wrestled back and forth with poor gagging Walter. Jeremy, however, gets the credit for being the only guy in my memory to have incapacitated any of my characters when, during one of the takes, Jeremy pulled on Walter one way, and I pulled the other, and the trigger that controlled Walter's mouth snapped off in my hand, hidden inside Walter's body. We had to cut and take a "time-out" while I ran to my dressing room and glued the gadgetry back together!

Peanut: It would have been funnier if he had gotten beat up by Ellen.

Walter: Hey!

Peanut: And then a caged death match with Rosie O'Donnell.

Jeff: Let's move on, please!

There was only one other person who had tried to damage one of my characters. A few years earlier during the taping of a *Hot Country Nights* episode, Walter and I were interviewing Hank Williams Jr., and after numerous retakes when we'd finally gotten it right, Walter looked at him and said, "Hank! You kept fucking up your lines!" After a big laugh, Hank was obviously miffed with the little guy, and proceeded to abruptly walk off set, but not before taking his handheld mike and bonking Walter on the head with it.

 Peanut: Well, at least he hit the right guy.

The American Comedy Awards were a group of awards presented annually in the United States from 1987 to 2001 recognizing performances and performers in the field of comedy. The awards focused mainly on television comedy and comedy films, but there were also awards for the year's funniest male and female stand-up comics. Some of the earlier winners were guys like Robin Williams, Jerry Seinfeld, George Carlin . . . *that* caliber. So when Debbie (my publicist) told one of my agents that she really thought I could win the award, she heard him cover the phone and repeat the sentence out loud, which resulted in a big group, background laugh. That wasn't the end of the story, however.

The years of roadwork and hours of doing radio obviously paid off, because appreciative club owners around the country nominated me, and then the voting public made the final decision . . . and I won. Many folks in the business thought it was great, some were stunned, and others were pissed. Why were a portion of people unhappy? Some in the comedy industry just didn't think that a ventriloquist should be classified as a comic. My argument has always been the same. What I do is still the spoken word. I'm not demonstrating any physical feats or accomplishments that elicit an audience response. The wonder of a guy talking without moving his lips is gone within thirty seconds of seeing it. I'm simply speaking in dialogue rather than monologue. But whatever the case, winning Funniest Male Stand-Up Comic of the Year (1998) was a big step in shedding the "only a variety act; not a real stand-up" stigma.

 Peanut: It was an honor just to be nominated.

 Jeff: It was.

 Peanut: I was kidding. That's what the losers say. It's WAY better to win.

Some of my favorite bits throughout the years have been built from real-life moments that take place when I'm onstage. It usually starts with an ad-lib, which I'll then repeat the next night, adding more jokes on either side of the first one, and then after a few weeks of working and massaging the pieces, they turn into an entirely new routine. One of the best examples of that took place at the Washington, D.C., Improv in the late 1990s.

The club manager came to me before the show one night and very apologetically let me know that in the front row that night, sitting almost *on* the stage and facing the audience slightly to my right, would be a signer for the deaf.

"A what?" I asked.

"You know," he said, "somebody signing for deaf people." I stood there looking at him for a moment, thinking about what I was being told here, plus all the implications, and then just to clarify and make sure I heard him right.

"So we have deaf people here tonight?" I said.

"Yes," he replied, very matter-of-factly. Once again I just stood there looking at him, probably a fairly perplexed look on my face.

"Tom," I replied, "do they know what the show *is* tonight? That I'm a *ventriloquist*?"

"Oh yeah," Tom said back. "They're big fans."

You know how, in a cartoon, when a character is just standing there looking straight ahead, contemplating, and the only sound you hear is a xylophone hitting two notes each time the character blinks? That was me.

Then Tom said, "I know it's a pain, but they insisted on coming, and by law, I have to put them in the front row so they can see what's happening onstage and at the same time see the signer."

"Oh, I understand the distraction part," I said. "I'm just trying to wrap my head around somebody trying to read Walter's lips."

A signer right up front is undoubtedly distracting for an audience for a few minutes, but just about everyone gets used to the whole idea very quickly and eventually the added movement blends in and becomes no problem . . . even with stand-up comedy. So within a few minutes of the opening act and middle guy, it was smooth sailing and nothing felt odd during my set either. All was fine. Well, all was fine until Peanut came out.

The next part may be a little hard to describe, but I'll give it my best shot: I know the difference between right and wrong. I know what should be made fun of and what shouldn't. But I've also been doing what I do for so long, that whenever a character gets onstage with me, there's a part of my brain that is that little guy, and the part that's *me* doesn't tell that other guy what he can and can't do. It's almost like I'm a bystander in my own head, and the little guys can do what they want. And no, I'm not nuts. Maybe it's more like every character is a different gear and my head shifts into each one when needed.

But back to the problem at hand . . . I've had signers in the audience many times since that night in D.C., but when I was getting ready to pull Peanut out that first night, the part of my head that was *me* was thinking, "Uh-oh . . . this should be interesting. . . ." Because I knew that I, or should I say Peanut, couldn't *not* say anything! It was once again that roller-coaster feeling of being taken up the hill, hearing the clickity clack, and knowing that there was no way I could get off this ride. And sure enough, Peanut is out of the box, on my arm, and within a minute or two of being onstage, he noticed the woman. Once again, the idea of "getting away" with stuff that a normal human couldn't was very much in play with all that happened for the next ten minutes. Like a little kid, Peanut watched the signer, fascinated to see his words being acted out visually. Then he would throw out random words, just to see what they "looked" like. And of course, like a naughty kid, he wanted to see what a few curse words would be in sign language.

Then Peanut started to think about the whole idea of deaf people coming to see a ventriloquist.

"WHAT?" he said. "What's next? Blind people going to David Copperfield? Do they have a guy *telling* them what happened? *The elephant disappeared! It just f-ing disappeared!*"

And then came my favorite part: He tried to get the signer fired by making up sentences that made no sense. The audience caught on right away.

"My up new round the bend doink, doink pink slam of course bag to the optimum blang see the blender run sideways kinda for help fish?"

Yes, it was just wrong, wrong, wrong, but the audience was literally howling with laughter. And of course part of the reason they were laughing so hard was because it *was* so wrong. But Peanut got away with it, and even the deaf folk were laughing. Plus, I knew I had found gold with this new bit. If you want to hear the full story and see Peanut act it out *(shameless plug alert)*, it's in his segment of my first DVD, *Arguing with Myself.*

Peanut: I knew that bit was going to be great.

 Jeff: You did?

 Peanut: Yep. Or get you killed.

After 1993 and the theater run, the next ten years were filled with a seemingly endless road of shows, one comedy club at a time. Almost every year my representatives and I would pitch a different sitcom idea to the networks and studios, but to no avail. I simply worked week after week, club after club. . . . The one thing that *did* grow, however, was a very loyal following of fans. Part of me knew this was great and important, but I was also bothered, wondering who, if anyone, in Hollywood was paying attention. Was there a next step up in my career, or had I already peaked?

As the years continued, even though I stayed as one of the top acts in the clubs, I became more and more convinced we could do bigger and better. There were just too many fans coming out on a regular basis bringing family and friends, and my ticket sales hadn't waned in a decade.

I remember stating one year at the vent convention that ventriloquism as entertainment would continue to die a slow and embarrassing death unless someone made it hip again to a wide audience in a mass-media fashion. It had been decades since anyone had accomplished *that*.

By this time I had taken on new representation. Robert Hartmann, who had been managing Improvs for more than a decade, was now the co-owner of many of the clubs, plus he had formed his own talent management company. After a couple of partnerships that didn't work out, he finally signed on Judi Brown, a former Colorado comedy club talent booker, who was now living in LA and making a good name for herself booking comics at comedy festivals and on HBO. One of Judi's fortes that made her appealing as a manager was that she had a good handle on the comedic sensibilities of "the rest of the country." A great many comics tend to develop a big-city flavor to their acts, mainly due to the fact that to be successful as a stand-up with any chance of being on television, you usually have to move to LA or New York and make *those* audiences like you. Judi appreciated the fact that there were a bunch of states between those two cities, and a lot of work was to be found for the uncommon comics who had more universal appeal. I never did figure out how to be citywise and slick, so I just continued to do the same kind of material I always had. It must have worked, because we could never describe my typical audience. Every crowd looked like a cross section of Americana. There were young folks, old folks, and middle aged; blue collar and white; housewives and hippies; ballplayers, cops, and military; lawyers and farmers; gay dudes and lesbians. Peanut and the guys could sell tickets in just about every corner of the country and my job was to just keep the dummies talking and the people laughing.

One of the larger problems I had to deal with in the clubs in those years was getting true ticket counts. As our draw became bigger, ticket prices were then raised, and some club owners and managers began to take advantage. Because of what I know now, I feel sorry for many of the comics who can draw at a club. A bunch of comedians get screwed nightly.

When an agent works out a deal with a club for his client, ticket prices are agreed to, the gross dollar amount of tickets sold is estimated, and either a fixed fee is agreed upon to pay the comic plus bonuses at sellouts, or he is given a percentage deal for every ticket sold. This is the procedure for just about any venue and any kind of performance. You can see how an artist can easily be at a disadvantage, having to trust whatever numbers he or she is shown at the end of the night. How does anyone know if those are actual true numbers?

All I can say is that many of the clubs were honest with me, and many were not. I began to develop a pretty good skill of estimating crowd sizes, and noticed that the numbers I was being given at the end of the night didn't match what I saw in the seats. I would go in and count chairs before doors were open, and during the opening acts went out and estimated how many people were there. Many times I heard a lot of BS about a huge number of comps, or that a bunch of four-top tables had only two or three people, et cetera. Some of that was true some of the time, but there are a million ways to cheat an artist, and comedy clubs are masters at it. Granted, a good agent will negotiate a huge sum for their comic up front, so a lot of clubs feel justified in selling a few tickets off the books. Whatever the case, as our ticket sales and prices increased, I knew a lot of the places weren't being honest with me.

There were a couple of blatant rip-offs that clubs tried to pull— like selling a certain number of "VIP" seats at a *much* higher price, or simply raising the ticket price by even three or five bucks a head without telling me or my agency, hoping I'd never notice since I never entered through the front door. Three or five dollars might not sound like much, but multiply that by three hundred seats a night at eight shows in a six-day week . . . and that's a lot of *pure unreported profit* to the club. It's an ugly business sometimes.

Sweet Daddy Dee: That's showbiz, people. Same as pimpin'.

Jeff: It is?

Sweet Daddy Dee: Sorry, ho. I mean, Jeff Dunham.

Let me tell you what I did when I'd finally had it with a club owner one week. I won't mention cities because I still work with this gentleman occasionally. He's a personable guy, but he's also a crook . . . and on one memorable night, I turned him into an honest crook.

It was probably sometime in 1994, and my agent was now constantly on the lookout for clubs trying to screw us. By this point, we'd been burned so many times that the first night of the week, my agent would call the box office and try to buy tickets for my show to check the prices.

This was not the first time I'd been to this particular club. In fact, I'd been there many times, but I had never done the business that I was doing that week with seven sold-out shows. Also because of the screw-overs, I'd recently started paying more attention to how many seats were in a place compared to what was on the contract. I'd never bothered to look at this particular club's contract, but on the first night after a sellout, I went back to my hotel room and took a look. The contract read 350 seats total. I hadn't just fallen off the turnip truck. . . . I knew even without counting that this number wasn't even *close*.

Gary Brightwell was opening for me that week, so the next day he and I went early to the club to physically count all the chairs. There were five hundred. I was pissed. It hadn't really mattered in earlier years, because I hadn't been selling out. But now it mattered a LOT.

When the club owner got to the club that night, I confronted him. Keep in mind that I had known this guy for many years and I considered him a friend. I don't want to use his real name, so let's call him Bob. I said, "Bob, explain to me why the contract says there's 350 seats in here." He replied, "Because that's how many seats there are!" I couldn't believe he'd just said that. There's not a club owner or manager in the country who doesn't know *exactly* how many seats there are in his club, plus they know exactly how many seats they have hidden, stacked somewhere out of sight. Those are then pulled out and added to sell more off-the-books tickets to get more folks in when the fire marshal and headliner aren't looking. And, oh yeah, I've caught clubs doing *that* as well.

I said, "Bob, there's five hundred seats in here!"

"Oh, no," he started huffing. "No way there's that many seats." I couldn't believe he thought I was that stupid, or that he thought he could get away with his lie.

I said, "Bob, I've already counted them. There's five hundred seats." It was ridiculous. Was this his defense—that he didn't *think* there were that many? I said, "Let's count!" And off we went. When we finally agreed there were five hundred seats, Bob said, "Well there's no way we can get that many people in here at once."

At this point, I'm just standing there, looking at Bob, wondering what to do next. "So how many people do you think you can squeeze in here on a good night?" I asked. "Three fifty," he replied. Good lord.

I waited until Saturday night's first show. Not just sold out, but *sold out* sold out. The folks were packed in like sardines. I was scheduled to do fifty minutes, and I did just that. But instead of my typical "thank you, good night," I put away the last character and had a chat with the very cooperative crowd. I said, "Well folks, this has been a lot of fun and you've been great. But I have a problem. There seems to be a misunderstanding with the management as to how many of you there are in here tonight, and how many tickets were sold. Just a show of hands first: Did any of you win free tickets from a radio station, or get in here free tonight? Don't worry, no one will throw anything at you . . . anyone?" None. I continued, "Well, I need to ask you a favor. I need to know how many people are here tonight, so if you will oblige me, I'd like to spend about ten minutes and do what we used to do in grade school: I need you to count off one by one. Just one person at a time. Please don't cheat and count yourself twice." And with that, the folks started to number off. I couldn't believe how orderly and nice these folks were, alcohol loaded and all. Brightwell told me later that Bob was in the back, ready to have a heart attack.

Lo and behold, within about fifteen minutes, we ended up with a count of 492.

At the end of the week, a disgruntled Bob gave me a very large additional check to make up for what he'd been stealing. Although I wasn't happy with what he'd pulled, and no telling how many times he'd done it to me before, I still liked the guy. He had a lot of good connections in comedy, so for business reasons, we kept things friendly. Though he's a lovable crook, a tough lesson was learned by me that week, and it was a big disappointment: Good business doesn't always make good friends.

 Peanut: I remember Brad.

 Jeff: "BOB!"

 Peanut: Oops!

Just before the turn of the century, in late 1999, a seed of a relationship was planted, and little did I, nor anyone else, know how important this tiny step would be for my career. Judi got me booked on Comedy Central's stand-up show *Premium Blend*. It was a half-hour program, not much different from any other stand-up show from the past few years. It utilized the simple formula of a host introducing four different comics who would each come out to do a few minutes. Taped at a rented theater in New York City, the production would bang out three or four shows a day for about five days, ending up with a lot of inexpensive programming which, in typical Comedy Central style, would be aired, then repeated ad nauseam.

Judi had used whatever connections and pull she had to get me booked on the show, and as far as we could tell, no one at Comedy Central was expecting me to be very funny. With very few exceptions in its recent history, the network tended to utilize only traditional monologists, so a ventriloquist wasn't exactly their cup of tea. They put me on dead last in the episode, which, for television, is *not* the headliner spot.

Whenever I do a television spot, one of my goals is to make the crew laugh. It's a good barometer because these guys have seen everything and are usually pretty jaded when it comes to guests on the shows they're working. If it's a comedy show they're filming, they've heard all the zingers. If it's a morning talk show, they've seen everyone from heads of state to the guy who grew a tomato that looked like the Madonna. So if I come in, do my thing, and they go out of their way to compliment me, mission accomplished . . . and that's exactly what happened that night. It wasn't my best TV spot by a long shot, but what *was* important was that we now had a foot in the door at Comedy Central.

Bubba J.: I had my foot in a door once.

Jeff: You did?

Bubba J.: Yeah, but it was a car door.

 Jeff: I see.

 Peanut: I knew Comedy Central would want us.

 Jeff: Why were you so sure, Peanut?

 Peanut: Because we had something they needed . . . comedy.

As the year 2000 approached, I was doing everything I could to keep expenses in check, stay financially *somewhat* above water, and of course, not buy anything crazy. But sometimes, when you work hard, you feel like treating yourself.

One beautiful Southern California day, the kids and I were driving by the Thousand Oaks Hummer dealership. Sitting on their cement "stage" in front of the building sat an H1 Hummer, the model with the swinging doors in the back. (The H1 is the *real* Hummer . . . not the shrunk-down, soccer-mom one.) As we drove by, the girls went, "Daddy, LOOK! A purple Hummer!"

"Purple?" I said as we kept driving.

"Yeah," they said. "It's . . . BLUE. Whoa!"

"You said it was purple," I replied, not looking out the side window at what they were talking about.

"DAD, IT CHANGED COLORS!" one of them yelled.

"No it didn't," I calmly stated, knowing they were mistaken.

"Yes it did! LOOK!" And as I looked out the passenger window toward the platform, the blue Hummer suddenly blinked to a dark orange color. "What the—?" We came to a screeching halt, scrambled out of the car, and ran to the truck. It was the coolest thing I'd ever seen. Don't forget, this was a few years before the Green movement took over, and you weren't regularly given the finger for driving a gas-guzzling behemoth vehicle. But not only was it a Hummer, the dealership had *loaded* this one. A salesman came out with the keys and let us play. It had a huge stereo system with giant woofers. It had an Alpine GPS nav system, video player and four screens, a top-of-the-line communications system, custom leather seats, a custom chrome-and-leather steering wheel, and on and on. You could now count me as the fourth kid. This was awesome. But the coolest thing was the *paint*. My kids weren't nuts; the thing did change colors. And it wasn't one of those paints that simply had various luminescent colors in it. No, this was a color-*shifting* paint that jumped from one color to the next, depending on what angle you were viewing it from. It was pretty new stuff, and the dealership had customized this machine with it.

That day I talked to my accountant about buying a new car as a treat for myself. The deal was that I would purchase the vehicle, but promise to drive it for *ten* years. Though it was a pretty stupid move considering our financial status at the time, I loved that beast, and still do to this day. Unlike a lot of other guys with big SUVs, at times I've taken it out in the wilderness and beaten the living crap out of it *and* the people riding with me! I've even driven it around in a lake with water sloshing over the hood. My kids grew up in it, and Kenna has made me promise to never sell it. I gave her my word.

It was the perfect vehicle to have ready for the oncoming promised disasters of Y2K, for which I was one of the idiots who was prepared. I didn't dig a cellar in the backyard, but I overstocked on survival food, batteries, bottled water, a portable toilet, and yes, some artillery.

As we all know, nothing happened when the computers clicked to 00, but now I had a cool vehicle and I could eat dried beans for the next quarter century.

Bubba J.: You had ARTILLERY!?

Jeff: Yes.

Bubba J.: To shoot at other comedians who were going to steal your JOKES?

Jeff: Not exactly.

Walter: Good for you, teaching your kids to be paranoid.

Jeff: I was just being cautious.

Walter: Looked like you were getting ready to appear on *Real Morons of LA County*.

Starting in 2000, Robert and Judi tried for three years to convince Comedy Central to give me my own half-hour special. These were called *Comedy Central Presents*. My team had to argue about sales numbers from the road and ratings from even *Premium Blend* three years earlier. The network was still not excited about putting a ventriloquist on the air and they weren't budging.

Another performer that Judi had managed and pushed to get on the air at CC was The Amazing Johnathan. He is a magician who uses a very twisted and sometimes brutal approach to another old vaudevillian art form. After his half hour aired on CC, ratings showed that there was certainly room for something other than straight stand-up. The network finally relented, and in the fall of 2002, I once again headed to New York to tape in front of a live audience. And once again, the network stacked show upon show over a few days. It was the same formula as *Premium Blend*, but this time instead of a five-minute bit, I did an entire half hour.

Though I had input on my set design, there wasn't much else besides material that I had control over. The network brought in a different audience each night of taping, but used the same crowd for more than one comic. In other words, this wasn't *my* crowd. Even though there were a few hundred people there, most of them had no idea who I was, and thus had little idea who my characters were. This was completely unlike what I was used to, where the people paid to come see *me* because they wanted to. Long story short, I hated the show that night. Though I did make the crew laugh, what I had practiced over and over in front of my own audience didn't and couldn't have gone over as well in front of newbies.

I'll never forget a few weeks later, sitting by myself at a bar in Dayton, Ohio, watching the first airing of the half hour. Since the taping, I had been reassured by the network that they were doing a great job of editing and that anything that wasn't perfect was either being cut out or edited carefully to make sure it was funny to the TV audience. So I was excited to see what they'd done. This was my first solo almost-full-length special!

I hated it.

Having had zero control over editing, there had been some decisions made that I never would have been okay with. Jokes that I would have cut out because they didn't go over as well were left in, and some of my favorites that I knew would air well were cut out. A very important step in my career now appeared to be a very big misstep. A failed corporate gig here or there could be hidden and wouldn't make any difference in the future. But here was something that would air over and over and I didn't feel it did *one* thing to make me look in any way outstanding.

Fans are a beautiful thing. When Comedy Central got the ratings back from the premiere airing, they were very solid. But better than that, the repeats maintained very high numbers compared to other comics' half hours. When we got that news back, plus the very positive reactions from those inside Comedy Central, I felt like my career was taken off life support.

More importantly was that any comic who appeared on Comedy Central had a bump in business and sold more tickets than the guys who had any type of TV exposure anywhere else. Stand-up fans watched Comedy Central and then they'd come to the clubs to see who they saw on TV. Even heavily advertised and highly rated HBO stand-up specials had little to no effect on sales compared to airings on Comedy Central.

It's difficult to argue with ratings, and although my numbers were as good if not better than most of the other comics' half hours, there was still resistance to putting me on the air. So in 2003, I was turned down by Comedy Central for anything else. The next step would have been my own hour special, which the network would have produced, but they wouldn't discuss the possibility. A ventriloquist simply wasn't their cup of tea.

On the road I stayed, club after club after club. In maintaining the lifestyle we'd become accustomed to, family spending started to far exceed what I could comfortably afford, despite the Hummer.

I had to stay out on the road working an average of 250 shows a year. That meant forty weeks a year I was out, each Wednesday through Sunday.

As the ensuing months clicked by, Judi and Robert and Debbie and I would strategize how and where to get me on television in any capacity. I knew that was the fuel for ticket sales. My managers and I would strategize about the next step. Sometimes questions and doubts for the future of my career would try to crawl into my head, but I never doubted for a moment that something big could still happen. I had been working at my craft and nothing else much too long with too much success for it to stop at this point. It had now been thirty-two years of pursuit with never a consideration of doing anything else. I refused to believe this was all there was. Maybe this new little skeleton dummy I had just made would help out. . . .

CHAPTER EIGHT

....

A Little Terrorist in the Best Damn Chapter

I was asleep at home in Los Angeles on the morning of September 11, 2001, when we got a phone call to turn on the news. Like the rest of the country and most of the world, we watched in disbelief, horror, and heartbreak as the Twin Towers in New York City were destroyed. Like most parents, my wife and I did our best to help our young children understand what had happened, and at the same time try to make sense of it ourselves. Almost a decade later, it seems cliché to recall the words we all repeated to one another that day: Life will never be the same. But it was true and we see it even now, all around us and everywhere we go. (Or *try* to go.) Almost everyone in this country was in some way affected by the events of September 11, and as the days went by and the initial shock wore off, I began to wonder how, as a comedian, I was supposed to get back onstage and tell *jokes*? If so, *when*? It didn't seem like something to even consider. In fact, it felt *wrong*.

Nine-eleven happened on a Tuesday, and that weekend we canceled my scheduled run at Uncle Funny's, a club in Davie, Florida. Performing was the last thing on my mind. Everyone's priorities had changed and now nothing mattered more to most people than being with family. That's all I wanted to do, and home was where I stayed.

The next Thursday and weekend I was scheduled for the Tempe Improv just outside Phoenix. Letterman and Leno had each gone back on the air the Monday of that week, both with great poise, and in what could only be imagined as incredibly difficult positions. These were the guys that were supposed to make us laugh despite everything else. The audience of four hundred people in a club where I was performing was microscopic in comparison to the number of their nightly viewers, but the questions and the fragility of our audiences were the same.

What would be my first words onstage? What should be my demeanor? What *material*? Should I even be *thinking* about going onstage?

During these early days after the terrorist attacks, we would embolden each other to move on with life by saying that if we didn't, ". . . then the terrorists have won." But I was not one of the heroes risking my life, helping to dig and search for the fallen at Ground Zero. I wasn't a soldier, ready to fight for freedom, nor was I a farmer, helping to provide. Did I now even have a purpose in a post-9/11 world? Or was my clownlike profession a soon-to-be forgotten luxury, enjoyed in a past life when the world was innocent and naively happy?

What finally made me realize that I really did have some sort of role in the healing process, no matter how small, was when we started getting ticket sale numbers back from the Improv a couple of days before my first scheduled show that week. All six shows at four hundred people each were completely sold out. *And* the club wasn't getting any cancellation calls. In fact, they were turning away business and were considering *adding* shows. There were people coming to my show who wanted to *laugh . . . again.*

Walter: But unfortunately, they never did. THE END. Thanks for reading!

Jeff: Walter . . .

Walter: Sorry; I need a nap.

I can honestly say that it was probably one the best weeks of shows I have ever experienced at a club. I wrote material about 9/11 and surrounding events and people that in no way made light of any part of the tragedy, but instead was unifying, patriotic, and challenging toward any outsiders who oppressed our ideals as Americans. Certainly it was a little bit of figurative flag waving, but it needed to be. In the more literal sense, remember how many American flags were mounted on cars in the months following the event? I had two flags on my Hummer, and I didn't shy away from material that bolstered the American spirit either. Walter certainly had his thoughts about the whole thing.

> Jeff: Did you know polls are showing that eighty-eight percent of Americans will support Bush if he decides to strike back?
>
> Walter: Then I say let's round up the twelve percent who won't and bomb the shit out of *them*.

And then there was *this* guy to talk about:

> Jeff: I heard Bin Laden has four wives.
>
> Walter: I think the U.S. should get him back by giving him four more.

For weeks there was almost nothing else on the news:

> Jeff: A whole bunch of sporting events were canceled, but now they're getting back into it.
>
> Walter: Yeah, it was sad: Last week I turned on SportsCenter, and all it showed was a bunch of ESPN guys watching CNN.

There are certain subjects that in my opinion will never be okay to joke about, so I have a few things under a heading of "no-gos" that I simply won't make light of. Of course the 9/11 tragedy is at the top of that list. But as the one-year anniversary grew closer, I listened to Leno and Letterman consistently joking about Osama bin Laden and the continued and unsuccessful hunt for him. Then one day it finally hit me—"I know where Bin Laden is!"

I knew I might be pushing the limits of what was okay onstage, but the mind-set of the terrorist is so far removed from anything that we in the free world can fathom, I knew there was comedy just waiting to be unearthed. And who was the face of all that we loathed and who was it that a vast majority of the country wanted brought to justice? Of course, it was Bin Laden. But no one could find the SOB. I began to postulate, like many people, that maybe he was already dead. Of course his annoying videos kept popping up on the Internet, to help squelch that fantasy, but I began to imagine, what if he *was* dead, but was still in hiding! And if he *was* hiding, where would be the perfect place for him to be? Ah HA! He'd be in my trunk with all my little guys.

As lamebrained as the idea sounded, I knew I wasn't doing Shakespeare or Neil Simon. When you boil it down, all I do onstage on a nightly basis is . . . well, a *puppet show*. Additionally, I was working in front of no more than three or four hundred people at a time, so why not experiment with a Dead Osama character?

Achmed: Finally, we get to talk about *me*!

Jeff: Actually, this is the guy *before* you.

Achmed: WHAT?

Walter: Ha ha.

So there was the idea. But before I moved forward on the actual physical puppet and potentially wasted a lot of time, I knew I had to carefully consider what I would be doing with this guy onstage. Here was a perfect example of that fine line between what I could do onstage with characters, compared to as a regular stand-up comic. Success would be unlikely for any comic who might dare to don a terrorist outfit and jump around on a comedy club stage telling terrorist jokes. Oh sure, there'd be a few venues here and there where it might go over, but I'm fairly certain that the public outcry and the fear from club management of any reprisals would keep that comic out of work until he came up with something else.

My opening act was now Canadian comic Jeff Rothpan, who, most important, was someone whom I could write with very well. I'd tried out other writers in the past and almost no one worked out for any length of time. One guy, however, who a few years before had written some good stuff for Walter was a young, little-known stand-up comic at that time named Judd Apatow. (Yes, *that* Judd Apatow.) Sometime around 1996, I was paying Judd a measly $50 a joke. He's earning slightly more than that now for his creativity. Here's one of his jokes that Walter used for a good while:

Walter and I had been talking about the lack of sex Walter has experienced as he's gotten older . . .

Jeff: I thought making love got better with age.

Walter: Hang on to THAT dream, pal.

As simple as that joke is, it was a perfect, surefire line for Walter that worked *every single time*, and in front of any kind of audience. Okay, well, not at the Cub Scout banquets.

Walter: Way to go.

Jeff: What?

Walter: You paid Apatow so little, it motivated him to become one of the most successful filmmakers in Hollywood.

Jeff: I guess you could look at it that way.

Walter: Cheap bastard.

Judd was a rarity, because almost without fail, every other writer would inevitably come up with dialogue that was typical "ventriloquist vs. the dummy" crap. It was difficult to find a writer that could keep in his head that he was supposed to be writing straight stand-up material in dialogue form, and not simply "wooden dummy" jokes. I thought many times that if I saw one more "hand up the ass" joke, I was going to throw my chair out a window. Rothpan, like Apatow, understood that the dummies were *characters* and should be treated as real people with their own points of view. As I soon discovered, Rothpan's true forte was pumping out current-topic jokes for all the radio I was doing at the time. I loved this, because while I would concentrate on working on evergreen material for the stage show, Rothpan would work on the current topic stuff that would be great, but would age and then I'd have to throw out when that particular subject was no longer in the news. Plus, Rothpan was good with the blank page, and I was better with punch up and expansion. Our system was pretty simple: First, Rothpan went through the news and picked out stories. We discussed them and agreed on the ones we thought were joke-worthy. Then he would write some gags about those subjects, e-mail them to me, and I would put my own spin on everything, sometimes adding more jokes related to what he had done, plus rewording his lines to fit the characters more in my style. As a team, we turned out some really great stuff.

Using this system, Jeff and I came up with material about Dead Osama. I had to carefully choose what I thought was appropriate and wouldn't offend the majority of people. I knew that using an actual terrorist dummy was pushing the edge, but I also felt that the way I was approaching this very volatile subject would actually be acceptable to *most* Americans, and that it would, in fact, be *really* funny.

So with what I felt was enough jokes and ideas in place, I had to create a "cheap" or trial version of the puppet. I never went all out on the initial dummy, simply because I didn't want to waste hundreds of hours building something that wasn't yet proven onstage. I guess it's kind of same idea as a concept car created by an auto manufacturer: They build one to display at car shows and see what the public reaction is before committing too many assets and capital to an actual run of mass-produced vehicles. So I was happy to first work with a rough incarnation of new characters. I could put a moving mouth on just about anything. I began to keep my eye out for something that looked like . . . well, like a *Dead Osama*.

It was now late September, just a few days past the one-year 9/11 anniversary, and I was in Aahs, a gift and novelty store on Ventura Boulevard in Sherman Oaks, California. It wasn't too far from home, and my wife and I were wandering through the store, picking out Halloween decorations. Remember when I wandered through that toy store and spotted Mortimer on the shelf? It's amazing how life repeats itself. I rounded a corner in Aahs, looked up, and there, hanging on a peg, wide-eyed and startling looking, was a goofy, big-headed, hollow plastic skeleton that looked like he wanted to kill me.

He was as cheap as Halloween decorations come, with a bulbous big head and a small, dangly body. Comically menacing and molded in typical Halloween skeleton gray-white, his features were carelessly highlighted in airbrushed black paint. Looking at him, I decided that this simple skeleton would be much less grotesque and a lot funnier than a dead guy. All he needed was a moving mouth, a body adjustment here and there, and some sort of head covering.

Two days later, I had cut out the mouth, mounted it to a hinge, and installed a couple other mechanisms that turned him into a makeshift ventriloquist figure. I now had a functioning "dead" dummy. Next I glued glass eyes over the molded plastic ones, then added black fake fur for bushy eyebrows, mustache, and beard. Oh, and that cloth on his head? Not wanting to take the time to drive two miles to a fabric store, I ended up using one of my white T-shirts that I pulled out of the dirty laundry and hot-glued into shape and on his head. Done.

As I looked at Dead Osama and made him talk, the first voice and accent that popped out of him fit him to a tee. I went through the material Rothpan and I had written and refined it a bit more. I knew that to make this guy acceptable, he would have to seem menacing but at the same time a buffoon.

Barely a year after 9/11, fear of the next terrorist attack was still a big part of our daily existence in America. I think one of the main reasons the Dead Osama character worked so well in 2002 was that many people tend to deal with their innermost fears by laughing at them. Terrorism is exactly what it says it is: terrifying. But put a goofy face on it, point out the foibles of Osama's probable everyday existence, plus make him a failure . . . and a dead one at that, and now you have something. It wasn't until years later when I created the next incarnation of the Dead Osama that I added the all-important element of vulnerability. As ridiculous as it sounds, I made Achmed the Dead Terrorist a more sympathetic character—but more on that later. For now, there was no room for sympathy with a Dead Osama.

I made him a goof because I wanted him to be threatening but harmless. So what would a guy like that be yelling at the audience to try and scare them? It had to be like one of those little dogs, yapping at you in an attempt to intimidate. The most obvious answer would be for him to yell what we all feared: "I KILL YOU!" But then I added his goofy accent and it came out, "I KEEL YOU!"

In all honesty, I didn't know how an audience would take this. That phrase, in my opinion, was right on the edge of not being appropriate. It was *only* a year later. There is the old comedic equation of "Tragedy plus time equals comedy." Once again, I questioned myself. Comedy is sometimes escapism and we need that at times as well. And I wanted my audience to face full-on what we as a country needed to thumb our noses at.

So there was my stance. But now the all-important question was where was I going to try this out first? I decided that the only way to truly test this character and this material was to take it right where it mattered most: New York City.

Hasbrouck Heights, New Jersey, is actually only sixteen miles from where the World Trade Center stood, and I was booked at Banana's Comedy Club for two shows the night of Friday, November 15, 2002. Both my shows were sold out, and the folks were there to laugh and probably forget what had happened right in their backyards. Was I really doing the right thing? I knew that there had to be people in that audience who had lost immediate family members and close friends on 9/11 . . . barely fourteen months before. What was I doing?

 Achmed: This still isn't me?

 Jeff: No, not yet, Achmed.

 Achmed: Ohhhh . . . the anticipation is KEELING me!

Like a lawyer going to trial or boxer heading for the ring, I knew I had done everything I possibly could have to be prepared. I could back out now but I *wanted* to do it. Like I did with every new bit, I had planned on putting Dead Osama in the middle of the show. That way I would have already earned some acceptance by the audience, and thus been given a little bit of a license to whatever I did next. And if by chance it didn't go over, I had more surefire pieces to win back the crowd before the night had ended.

My stand-up came first, then Walter. He did his 9/11 and Taliban material, and the folks just ate it up. Instead of running from the subject and pretending life had simply gone on, we tackled it full force. I don't know what the audience expected that night, but they couldn't have laughed and applauded any more. Then it was time for the Dead Osama. I didn't really want to give them time to think about what I was doing, so I did a very fast and to-the-point introduction. The character and humor would have to be what won them over.

"Hey, folks, I don't know about you, but there is one sentence that I have been waiting to hear for a long time, and that sentence is, 'Osama bin Laden is dead,' am I right?" The place went nuts. I continued. "Well, I have an interesting introduction to make: Please help me welcome onstage before you this evening, Osama bin Laden!"

If this had been the beginning of the show that night, or if these folks hadn't already been fans, I think that after that introduction, you probably could have heard a pin drop. But as I had hoped would happen, because these people had now built up a small trust toward me, the reaction wasn't negative but it certainly wasn't overly enthusiastic either. For the people who had seen my show before, they knew that what I put on was a good, funny, somewhat safe show, only going so far as to skirt the *edge* of socially inappropriate. And for the folks who had never seen me before, at the midpoint of the show I think they now would at least be open to whatever came next.

There was a smattering of applause, a few gasps, and certainly rapt attention. Then when I pulled out an obviously *dead* Osama, a laugh went up and the place burst into applause. And there he was: this goofy-looking skeleton with that piece of cloth on his head, giant fixed eyes and eyebrows, and a googly-eyed stare that darted from audience member to audience member.

> Jeff: How did you talk your followers into doing the things that they did?
>
> Osama: Those guys were idiots!
>
> Jeff: You promised them seventy virgins in paradise.
>
> Osama: I know! It was a lie! HA HA HA HA HAAAAAA!
>
> Jeff: No virgins?

Osama: NO!

Jeff: Why did you pick the number seventy?

Osama: I was going to say sixty-nine, but that was a little too obvious!

And then I scooted him forward on the character stand that the guys sit on. His little plastic feet stuck out over the edge, but then would rotate at the knees so that his feet were then backward with the toes pointing straight down. He saw this and tried to adjust himself to fix it. I reached down and would turn them up again. He would move a little and they would fall back. It became a great sight gag with him getting increasingly more frustrated because his feet wouldn't stay the right way.

Osama: DAMMIT! FIX MY FEET!

After several more attempts, he would glare at the laughing audience and yell, "SILENCE!" Another laugh . . . and here it came . . . this was what I was scared of most, but I knew I had to try it. . . . "I KEEL YOU!"

Neither I nor anyone else at that moment could have guessed how far and wide that cry would travel, literally around the world, as a joke and a punch line for many years to come. But what was it that night? Was it a line too soon and too close at only fourteen months and sixteen miles from where three thousand people died at the hands of terrorists?

Whatever was in the air that night, whatever I had done beforehand, and whatever mood the audience was in spilled over into a moment in time, which felt like a fitting step toward unity and healing. Those people laughed and they applauded. I think they wanted in some way to feel that life was moving forward and that it was okay to cheer as the clouds of tragedy were fading into the past, never to ever be forgotten, but to be put behind us, and the future be looked toward with optimism. Maybe I see that moment as something bigger than what you feel now as you read this. But for me, that night was a significant moment in time. I couldn't hunt Osama down and kill him myself. I wasn't an air force fighter pilot, or a trained marine in the hunt. But I did for my country what I knew how to do best— I stuck my tongue out at the asshole.

For the next year and a half after that, I used Dead Osama in almost every show possible. The only times I would leave him out would be on television spots, or at corporate shows where the people who hired me were afraid of me offending someone.

I don't for a moment think that every person in every audience thought that what I was doing was acceptable. But for every fifty e-mails or letters that we would receive as thanks for the laughs, we'd get maybe *one* who wasn't happy with what they'd seen. Club owners were just happy to have the ticket sales and the drink orders. All I know is that a vast majority of the folks who came to the shows were diggin' it, and I kept doin' it.

Sometime in late 2003 I put Dead Osama aside to move forward with newer material. The hunt for the real Osama continued, but the country was now very much focused on Iraq and Saddam, and the bit was getting stale. So to the shelf in my garage the angry guy went, with no clue as to where his next incarnation would lead.

Achmed: He was an imposter and he NEEDED to be left in a garage!

Jeff: Did you ever talk to Dead Osama, Achmed?

Achmed: Yes, one time. He was scared of the dark so I took him my Dora the Explorer night-light.

One of the major tasks that my publicist Debbie Keller always had in front of her was to get the little guys and me on television. We all knew that the key to ticket sales was exposure on the airwaves, and she was constantly on the lookout for opportunities anywhere and everywhere. The FOX Sports Network had a popular show on their schedule called the *Best Damn Sports Show Period*. None other than the ex–Mr. Roseanne Barr, Tom Arnold, was the host. Every night Tom would sit with a handful of highly successful and notable athletes, and they would discuss the current goings-on in the sports world. They debated and picked on one another, showed highlights from games, and did everything short of drink beer on camera. They would of course have guests on as well, usually other star athletes, but sometimes celebrities or other known figures who were big fans of a particular sport. They'd kibitz too, and have a good ol' testosterone-filled time. The show also experimented with bringing on stand-up comics who would give their own take on things, and that made for some good laughs as well.

Debbie brought the idea to me, but I wasn't sold on it at first. She was convinced, however, that Walter would be great at giving his take on sports. After I thought about it for a while and watched the show a few times, I began to see how incredibly funny it would be. Then I really *wanted* to be on the show. So Debbie began to pitch me to them. And she pitched . . . and pitched. For months, it was always a resounding, "NO. NO VENTRILOQUIST ON *THE BEST DAMN SPORTS SHOW*." But *then*, after many months and much cajoling from Debbie . . .

I wish I could say that brilliant joke writing or my fancy video editing made it happen (I made my own promo tapes back then). But no. What finally got me on was the age-old showbiz trick of horse trading. "I'll give you this client if you'll book my lesser-known client too." And that's exactly what Debbie finally had to do. By this time she had other clients, a couple more notable and successful than me, and the *Best Damn* wanted one of them in the worst way: Bobcat Goldthwait. So Debbie promised to talk to him about doing their show if they would book me as well. They agreed to give me a shot.

By now, when it came to writing current topic material, Rothpan and I were a great team, and certainly sports was an arena for comedy where the subjects and players were always changing. Whatever happened on Sunday night was in the news and on the airwaves Monday morning. Any kind of antics on or off the field, plus personalities that just needed needling . . . these were all things Jeff and I knew we could joke about. Also, there was never a more perfect character for this task than Walter. I never even considered using anyone else.

The show taped daily, and they agreed to have Walter and me on for one or two segments (depending on how the first one went), and Walter would simply give his take on what had happened in sports the day before. We'd written some great stuff, picking on various teams and players of all different types of sports, and we pared it down to the prime jokes. Also, we'd written some pretty biting digs, and a few got nixed by the producer during the preshow meeting, not long before we went on the air.

At that time, the show's cast of five was formidable. Three athletes sat on the couch as regulars: John Salley, a six-foot-eleven NBA center-power forward who won two championships with the Detroit Pistons; Michael Irvin, an All-Pro wide receiver who won three Super Bowls with the Dallas Cowboys; and John Kruk, a three-time Major League Baseball All-Star with a lifetime batting average of exactly .300. This trio was joined by two hosts: anchor-reporter Chris Rose and Tom Arnold. This was a fraternity of great guys, but in typical locker room fashion, they liked to pick on one another. So how were Walter and I going to go over? I was not a big athlete who had proven himself on the field. I had a doll. This was either going to be great, or a great disaster.

I was waiting in the Green Room as the show started, watching the monitor. My segment was about halfway through the three-hour broadcast, and just like *The Tonight Show* and Johnny's monologue, I wanted to make note of what went on to see if there was anything I could "call back" and get a laugh. The studio audience was forty people at best, if I remember correctly, and today they seemed like they were in a raucous mood (that was a *good* thing).

In addition to preparing all the "approved" jokes, I'd also come up with a few slams for each of the guys, but they were only in my head. I knew that if the atmosphere was right, and if the other material was going well, I would have some extra cred and Walter would be able to do what he did best.

Once again, here was territory I'd never *really* traveled through. These were some heavy hitters—some guys who knew their stuff and had gone the distance on the field or on the court and earned their status and the right to hang with other athletes of their pedigree. I was a bit nervous.

Well, it was all worth the effort. I think I won the guys over by doing what needed to be done first, and that was—guess what?—BEING FUNNY. I must have gained some kind of respect by doing jokes about sports moments that had happened only the day before, plus the bits were insightful and made it sound like Walter knew the games and players very well.

The producer loved the spot and wanted us back as soon as possible. He even tossed out the idea of us being regulars on the show. I was stoked. I'd never been a part of any kind of a team since *elementary school*, but now here I was, going toe-to-toe with some of the greatest names in sports. Michael Irvin? Seriously? How many times had my father and I sat at home, yelling at the TV for Irvin and Aikman and the rest of the Dallas Cowboys? Once again, I almost couldn't believe it.

Walter: Did your mom watch the show?

Jeff: Yeah, why?

Walter: It had the word *damn* in the title.

Over the next couple of months, they had us back five or so times. Each time, Walter would gripe about anything or anyone in sports, unabashed and seemingly uncensored, just like any old-fart sports fan his age would. Granted, some shows were better than others, depending a lot on the studio audience, but more important, how the guys on the panel were reacting. The more they laughed, the funnier the bits.

One of my favorite moments was when there were about seven of us sitting in a semicircle in high-backed chairs. Walter was on my knee, doing our segment, and to our right was guest and infamous sports announcer Al Michaels. Michael Irvin almost always dressed in some off-the-wall outfit, and this particular day he was sitting a couple seats over to our left, wearing blue cotton plaid pants and matching shirt that looked exactly like pajamas. Between jokes, Walter spouted off to Al, "Do you see how Irvin is dressed?" Then, turning to Irvin, "Are you going to Michael Jackson's sleepover *again*?"

Walter: There were so many good follow-up jokes for that, and not one of them was appropriate.

Jeff: I'm not sure if the *first* one was appropriate.

Walter: You're welcome.

And another one that still makes me laugh when I watch it . . . Kruk was sitting in the middle of the couch and Irvin and Salley were on either side of him. Walter and I were to their right in a chair by ourselves. Walter had just done a joke with the punch line being Kruk. Everyone laughed, and the director went to a close-up of Kruk who looked anything but pleased. The other guys were still laughing and Walter said, "Oh, look: I got the brothers laughing and the cracker is pissed!"

Salley and Irvin about killed themselves laughing and falling all over each other. One thing I learned on that show was that the black guys would laugh really hard when the other guys, or they themselves got picked on, but the white guys would get mad. Kruk wasn't really mad that day, but Chris Rose seemed to get visibly so when Walter inferred that his marriage was a "good cover" for the possibility that he wasn't straight. Once again, the brothers laughed.

At another point after Kruk had made a joke about Walter being related to a sideline bench, Rose said to Kruk, "You know you're arguing with a piece of wood." Kruk replied, "Yeah, well he's pissin' me off!"

But the absolute best *off*-camera moment came not long after I had told Tom Arnold that I had read his biography and really enjoyed it. A couple weeks later when I was back at the studio, Kruk pulled me aside just before we went on the air and said, "I have to tell you what happened in the production meeting this morning. They said you were gonna be on today, and then told us the usual stuff: Just let you do your thing; if we want to come back with a line or two, that's fine." He paused, then added: "So Tom stopped in the middle of the meeting and said, 'Look, guys, I just have to tell you this—he was sincere as he could be—he says, 'You know Jeff Dunham, I really like him. But I can't fucking *stand* Walter.'" Then Kruk added, "And he wasn't kidding!"

This was incredibly fun stuff for me, and those few weeks on the *Best Damn* brought into perspective something that I had very much lost sight of—at home, I was severely outnumbered. In my house were my wife, my three daughters, my sister-in-law who always lived with us, and my mother-in-law for a few months out of every year. Six women and *me*! There were also three female dogs and two female rats . . . otherwise, it was just me and Bill the golden retriever! And one week when I was out of town, the women took Bill and had him neutered! I walked in the front door a couple days later, and I could swear Bill ran up to me and yelled, "YOU WON'T BELIEVE WHAT THEY DID TO ME! . . . RUN!"

Then I got on *The Best Damn Sports Show Period* and had a blast. And they kept having me *back*. It was locker room fun at its best, all in an estrogen-free, testosterone-filled environment.

After the show I would get in my Hummer and drive the ten miles back home from FOX Studios, still pumped. With Led Zeppelin or AC/DC thundering out of the truck's nuclear-powered sound system, I kept that high going as long as possible. After all, I'd just gone toe-to-toe with some pretty tough hombres, and I'd held my own. Now I felt like some kind of bad-ass. This is not a good frame of mind to be in, then roaring into the driveway and trudging back into pretty-smelling, Touchy-Feely Land. On one of the best-worst days, I lumbered in the front door. My wife said something to me, and I snapped back with, "Oh yeah? You can either do that or blow it out your *ass*."

And she said, "I can do WHAT?"

And I said, "Uh um uh, you um uh, well, the house looks lovely, honey."

And the testosterone drained out the back door while Bill licked himself.

Walter: What a big wuss.

Jeff: What would you have said?

Walter: Exact same thing. You can't mess with these women.

The success of Walter and me on *The Best Damn Sports Show Period* got some attention from the FOX suits upstairs. The 2002 football season was nearing playoff time, and a change was in the works on the FOX NFL Sunday pregame show. Jimmy Kimmel had been the comedy relief on the Sunday broadcast, doing sketches and making fun of the show's hosts, James Brown, Terry Bradshaw, Jimmy Johnson, and Howie Long. He was also known as a prognosticator, picking who he thought would win certain games every week. David Hill was the president of FOX Sports at the time, and he noticed the laughs Walter and I had been getting. I can remember where I was on Ventura Boulevard when I got the news. David Hill was considering hiring Walter and me to be the guys to take Kimmel's place, when he left for his late-night talk show on ABC. This spot couldn't be much cooler. If this happened, I would be on the air every single Sunday during football season, trading jokes and jabs with some really big guys in the NFL. I loved Terry Bradshaw . . . and Jimmy Johnson? Former *coach* of the Cowboys. Most important, I knew this was the perfect formula and would work. I would come in with Walter, tell a few jokes about what had happened in the NFL that week, make a few jokes at the four guys' expense, get some laughs, and all would be great.

David Hill called me in for a meeting, and details were hammered out. We worked out the financial aspects, what the segments would entail, what I needed to keep up with stats and subject matter, and he even asked me what I liked in the way of alcohol to celebrate. He said, "Get ready—you're going to be a household name *very* soon. We'll make the announcement during one of the playoff pregames, the guys will introduce you and Walter, and then you'll take over for Kimmel next season."

This was huge . . . absolutely huge. It was finally the breakthrough that I'd been striving and working for since 1988 when I moved to LA. Fourteen years of treading water were about to pay off.

Hill concluded our meeting, saying that just to make a final check and be sure it was a good mix, we should come in the following Sunday, and between the actual live segments, Walter and I would sit down with the four guys and do a taped, pretend run-through, as if we were doing a live segment. I thought that was a great idea too, and I couldn't wait to meet those four guys. It seemed like such a great bunch on the air. . . . And since the guys on the *Best Damn* had been so great, I knew this would go equally well.

When writing this book, I have chosen to tell the stories of my journey. There have been highs and lows, successes and failures. I have tried to not leave out anything significant, be it good or bad. But what I'm about to talk about now was truly one of the biggest failures, disappointments, and worst crash-and-burn moments I have ever experienced in this passage. Not only was I disappointed in myself, but in others as well. Men I looked up to and admired, men who I thought were great, were anything but.

I was very excited when Jeff Rothpan and I walked into the FOX Sports studios that day. I had been there many times before, and each appearance had gone either well, or incredibly well. I was so sure that this day would go even better. We had picked out the best jokes of everything we had written, and I had honed the segment to a smart, sharp edge. I had practiced the four minutes every night that previous week, and I was ready to make these guys laugh.

Into the studio we were escorted, and we sat quietly off camera in the huge studio while James, Terry, Jimmy, and Howie did their thing. There they were: bigger than life, laughing and kidding and talking to the nation about what was happening in the NFL at that very moment. Then they went to an extended break, and I was shown to a chair between all four guys on their amazing set, with lights and graphics and cameras all around. Walter and I were seated right between Terry Bradshaw and Howie Long. I should have known it was a setup when I walked into it.

In hindsight it makes perfect sense as to what happened next. Here were four men who were gods in their professions. Jimmy Kimmel had made a mockery out of these guys, poking fun at just about anything about them, but could stay out of harm's way since rarely was he ever actually talking *to* them. Most of his segments were done on tape. They could fire away back at him and make just as many jokes about him as he did them, but he wasn't there to fight hand to hand. I, on the other hand, *wanted* to be in the middle of these guys. But I made the mistake of thinking that they would play the game just like the *Best Damn Sports Show* guys did. Not only was I fresh meat, but I was entering the lion's den with a little wooden talking stick.

Walter: I can't relive this; let me know when this story is over.

Jeff: Where are you going?

Walter: To the bathroom with my iPod.

We came back from a fake commercial break, and James Brown introduced us. Walter barely had half a sentence out of his mouth when Terry Bradshaw pounced. He came at Walter with something that made no sense and wasn't funny. It was simply loud and overwhelming. Whenever I would try to set up a joke, Bradshaw was either stepping on our lines, or interrupting any kind of comedic timing that I needed. No one laughed at anything we said. There were simply sneers, interruptions, and a couple of chuckles. Was Bradshaw off his rocker and as crazy as he admitted in his own biography, or did he know exactly what he was doing? I tend to believe the latter. I think that at least two of the four guys were insulted beyond measure that a ventriloquist was being put on their show, and this was the only way they could stop the management's plan.

The biggest insult happened when it was all over, as I was holding Walter and slowly standing up to walk away. Howie Long looked me straight in the eye and with nothing but finality in his voice said flatly, "Nice meeting you." I knew I was finished.

Impressionist and comedian Frank Caliendo was chosen for the gig, and has made a fine go of it ever since. For a long time after that, though, I would catch myself wondering if I had screwed up the "big" opportunity forever, and if there weren't going to be any more.

For two more years, we continued to pitch sitcom and television show ideas here and there to no avail. But Judi had never given up on the Comedy Central end of things. She was convinced that there were still big opportunities at that network, and she just needed to convince them to put me on the air again.

At home, I was very close to dropping the bomb that we were going to have to move. Did that mean just a smaller house, or did it mean a new location with new schools and friendships strained due to distance? I didn't know, but I was scared. All I could do was keep working. Club after club.

Once in the late 1990s and again a few years later, I had self-financed very small, inexpensive, professional multicamera video shoots of my show. Once I did it at a theater just outside of Phoenix, and another time at Charlie Goodnight's comedy club in Raleigh, North Carolina. They were last-minute ideas, and I never had a staff on hand to help me. I would contact a local video company who would scout the place, then bring in a camera crew and shoot. I would take the raw tapes and edit together a production on my Mac. My intention was to sell these tapes as another revenue stream, but also use them as another way of getting my act out there. Both times, after spending a few thousand dollars on each, I was unhappy with the end product. Both were great shows and funny, but I hated the overall look of the tape and that it wasn't good enough for my fans. I wasn't proud of it, and that was the bottom line. So I would take all that time and money and effort, and all those tapes and backup hard drives, and put them on a shelf in my garage.

Judi and Robert saw what I was doing and we all began to think very hard about what the next career move should be. TV certainly wasn't coming to us. Comedy Central had said no too many times to count, no matter how much we touted my sales numbers or reminded them how well my half-hour special had done for them. They simply didn't want a ventriloquist.

I've talked about different turns in life, and how sometimes seemingly small decisions or events here or there can change our futures immeasurably. I can point to a few moments and people in my own past that had they not been there, I don't think I'd be anywhere near where I am now. And so it is that you may never have heard of me or Achmed, or anyone else in my trunk, had it not been for a gentleman in a wheelchair.

It was now the late summer of 2004, and NBC had just completed their second season of *Last Comic Standing*. Image Entertainment, an independent distributor of home entertainment programming, had an employee named Bob Foster who loved stand-up comedy. Bob wasn't a top executive at Image, or a big decision maker. In fact, he was one of the guys in charge of the details, like designing menus on the DVDs. Bob had lost part of a leg to diabetes, and when not on crutches, was tooling around Image in his wheelchair. He had become a fan of Kathleen Madigan, one of the contestants on *Last Comic Standing* that season. He searched for Kathleen on the Internet, and found that her manager just happened to be one Judi Brown-Marmel, one of my managers as well. He contacted Judi and told her that he had shown Kathleen's *Last Comic Standing* appearances to his bosses, and that they liked her. Judi didn't know much about Image, but took a meeting.

Judi had lunch with Barry Gordon, who was one of the top guys at Image and made a lot of the decisions. It turned out that in the past few years, Image Entertainment had been very successful with the acquisition of all the Blue Collar Comedy guys and their DVD titles. They were distributing not only the DVDs of the group together, but also their independent projects as well. Image distributed titles for Jeff Foxworthy, Larry the Cable Guy, Bill Engvall, and Ron White. The simple formula they had come up with was this—sign a client, produce their live special, sell it to a network where the edited version of the special would air, then sell and distribute the full-length version on DVD in retail. It was genius. They were raking in the dough.

Judi made the deal for Kathleen, but she also took a very important step for me: She sent Bob (the menu design guy) the latest version of my promo reel, which I had edited myself. It contained my funniest clips from the Carson days, plus the *Best Damn Sports Show*, and bits with Dead Osama shot with a simple handheld home video camera. Bob dug it in a big way. He took my tape straight to Barry Gordon as well as Richard Buchalter, the head of sales, and told the guys they *had* to watch. Well, apparently, not only did they like it, but they loved it. And these guys saw what Judi did. They saw Middle America, all the normal folks out there who would buy this DVD for themselves and their family. The material wasn't cerebral or highbrow—it just made you laugh.

The deal finally became official in early 2005. Image would pay us $50,000 to produce a special. Judi and Robert joined forces with Stu Schreiberg and created Levity Entertainment. Their idea was to produce comedy DVDs and sell them to distributors and broadcast partners. Stu already had a solid track record producing shows like *Iron Chef America* on the Food Network, all the live finales of *Survivor* on CBS, *The Dallas Cowboys Cheerleaders* on CMT, and most important from my standpoint, Jamie Foxx's *Laughapalooza*. Stu knew how to shoot comedy. It was a perfect marriage: By co-owning and booking a huge number of the major comedy clubs in the country, Robert had relationships with just about every comic in the business. Judi had great relations with many of the networks and shows because of her background in bookings, and Stu had the experience and track record on the production end of things. So now, not only could Levity Entertainment develop comics in the club chain, but they could then cultivate their careers through television and DVDs. And now, it looked like I was to be their flagship project.

The team tried to figure out how in the world we could shoot a decent comedy special, worthy of airplay on any given network . . . for $50,000. It was pretty much impossible. That wasn't enough money to do anything worthwhile, and certainly nothing near the quality I was telling them I wanted. We hadn't yet convinced anyone to buy the show, so there was only one place to get the money. I had to borrow it.

Peanut: And we borrowed that money from the Mafia.

Jeff: No, we didn't.

Peanut: Just trying to make the book more exciting.

A guy named John Power had entered my life not long before that, and he was well on the way to helping me not only keep my head above water financially, but he was also going to help our family understand that we had to stop spending so much money. My yearly purchases of new Apple laptops weren't the problem—it was more the lifestyle and the yanking out of credit cards at every whim that was killing us.

Anyway, I had no doubts that this could be my last stab at accomplishing my lifelong goal. I was now forty-three years old. Comedy careers rarely, if ever, take off for anyone after that age. Borrowing this money was going for broke, but I believed that if we shot this thing the right way, made it beautiful and high quality, and made it *funny*, we could get it on the air. And if we got it on the air, I was confident that all kinds of good things would follow. Remember what a gamble this was. This was borrowed money spent with zero guarantee of return. Image had made a $50,000 investment, confident that they would earn it back, even if it meant simply selling the DVDs at clubs after my shows. Twenty-five thousand copies of a DVD sold was, and still is, considered a huge success. Everyone was telling me that was the goal.

"Twenty-five thousand?" I thought. "If we get it on the air, it's going to be a *lot* more than that."

 Peanut: I was tired of being poor and hungry.

 Jeff: It wasn't that bad. No one went hungry.

 Peanut: Oh yeah? Did you see Achmed?

Remember my formula for great television comedy? For it to be good, you need a laugh about every ten seconds. In my eighty-minute show, that would come to 480 laughs. Granted, if you get a twenty-second laugh, you're cutting down the numbers. But you get the idea. This shit ain't easy. I had work to do.

I also had to decide what characters to use. Too long with one character and it would drag. Peanut, Walter, and José were a given. But who else? The Dead Osama was simply not an option. He was old news and outdated. After Osama, I had been pushing myself to come up with a character that was even more outside my comfort zone.

I had never forgotten what I had originally intended when creating Peanut, and that was to make fun of prejudice. It cracked me up when black comics would make fun of white people. They would point out laughable aspects about myself and my race that I couldn't see, because I lived it every day. In the summer of 2004 during the ventriloquist convention in the dealers' room, I picked up a character that had been built by figure maker Tim Selberg. It was a little African American guy who had a tough-looking scowl and made you laugh just by looking at him. So as to not lose a week of work, during the day I attended the convention, but at night I would drive up the freeway to the Funny Bone in Newport, Kentucky. I asked Tim if I could try his creation out a couple of nights. Once again, just like the Dead Osama, I had to carefully write jokes that would fit my purposes and not be racist or offensive to a majority of the room. I decided to introduce this little guy as my P.I.M.P. No, not my pimp, but my "Play-uh In Management Profession." He was my career manager. In this way, I would be acknowledging the obvious hipness of the way he was dressed, but also as my manager, he would be "above" me the minute he hit the stage. Next I came up with a few jokes that made fun of white people, and especially me for being "tight and white." I simply wanted to see how the character went over.

He killed. My goal was to never be disparaging to blacks, and to make sure as many people as possible thought the character and bit were funny, no matter what their race. To ensure the former, I would go outside the club and stop African American couples as they were walking out to talk about what they had just seen. I told them, "Be brutally honest. I don't want to offend. I'm simply trying to make *everyone* laugh. Tell me how or where or if any of what I did was offensive to you."

Very quickly I discovered I was on the right track. The laughs were big from both blacks and whites, and as far as the people with whom I spoke after the shows, I didn't seem to be offending anyone.

I purchased the figure from Tim, and told him I would put him to good use. What I didn't know at the time was that this wasn't the first of this dummy that Tim had sold. There was nothing wrong with that—I just didn't realize he wasn't one of a kind. There were in fact *two* others, being used by vents in different parts of the country. I was completely bummed when I found this out later, but this was a no-go for me. I had to be completely original. So out to the workshop I went, ready to create my own African American figure.

My workshop was my two-car garage. I had a workbench and just about every shop tool imaginable. I had built my last helicopter in that garage—if there hadn't been bay windows for the tail to stick out, it wouldn't have fit!—as well as many things for my girls. Dummy repairs took place there, and it was my refuge. After being on the *Best Damn* and sitting next to guys the size of John Kruk and John Salley, I realized that Walter was too small. It was here that I had created a larger version of Walter, once again starting from nothing but a pile of clay and my face in a mirror. I now had to create someone who was nothing like me. Most of the jokes I had come up with had worked for the little guy, but every bit as important, the relationship with me was believable and the *character* was strong.

To create a face first in clay, I needed inspiration. With Walter I had stared in a mirror. Obviously, that wouldn't work here. So I got on the Internet and found some black guys whose faces I really liked. I printed full-color eight-by-tens of Usher, 50 Cent, Michael Irvin, the godfather of soul, James Brown, and Chris Tucker. Then I hung all the photos on the wall above the workbench. It must have been a little disconcerting or somewhat unsettling for my kids and the boys from down the street when they walked by the garage and looked in, only to see me, the one white guy, sitting on a stool, staring at big photos of a bunch of black dudes. The funniest part was, Chris Tucker actually lived six houses down from us, and every once in a while, he would come tooling down the cul-de-sac on his Segway. I would have given just about anything if he'd come down that month and peeked in.

As I sculpted the head and face, my goal was to make my dummy ethnic, but not racist. I kept this goal in mind throughout the entire process, including when I was installing movements, painting him, and even having his clothes made. The entire process took a few weeks, and I had him ready for the next convention, which was in July. From then on I used him onstage as much as possible, developing material as quickly as I could. Of all the guys I've built, he's probably my favorite character in terms of creativity. I love his features, his coloring (on close inspection, you'll see a virtual rainbow of colors in his face), plus the movements I took extra time in installing. It always gets a nice laugh when he raises his upper lip, and a sucking sound emerges, as if he's sucking on his teeth.

Though I thought that the jokes I'd come up with quickly at the convention were promising, I still certainly didn't have enough for an entire routine for this guy. I also needed to really understand him so I could successfully and fully develop his character. Unlike Peanut and Walter, who were just exaggerated extensions of my own kind of thinking, inside of me was no hip, streetwise brother. And being a pimp? I obviously don't know anything other than *what* a pimp did, not how or why or when or with exactly whom. So to be convincing and make him seem legit, I had to do some research.

At first Judi and Robert hired a few black comics to help me out in all aspects of trying to create this new little guy, but ultimately I ended up having to rent some videos and do most of the figuring out on my own.

Snoop Dogg's *Puff Puff Pass Tour* documentary was unbelievably insightful. That led me straight to Archbishop Don "Magic" Juan, who was featured in the film and had been "spiritual advisor" to not only Snoop, but to Mike Tyson, Sean "P. Diddy" Combs, Kimberly "Lil' Kim" Jones, and Mariah Carey, just to name a few. According to the Web, the Bishop had been a street pimp for many years before he became a preacher and spiritual mentor. But what really caught my attention, besides his look and dress, was that he won the award of Pimp of the Year thirteen years straight at Chicago's annual Players Ball. There was an annual convention of pimps. Awesome.

The Bishop was the subject of the 1999 HBO documentary *Pimps Up, Ho's Down* (which, incidentally, would have been the title of this book, but it was already taken), and the film and the archbishop became my touchstones for the creation of this new character. The documentary was an invaluable research tool, helping with the nomenclature, diction, manipulation, and of course the look of what became a character that was a big leap for anything else I'd attempted up to that point. The character's name, Sweet Daddy Dee, by the way, was suggested to me by Darryl Quarles, who wrote the film *Big Momma's House*, starring Martin Lawrence. Darryl also said, "When he says his name, jump on the SWEEEEEEET. . . ." The teeth sucking I just hit on by accident. As for some of the street vocabulary and phrasing, I again headed to the Internet for that. I downloaded urban and street dictionaries for days, poring over everything and choosing the best stuff for making Sweet Daddy sound legit.

Sweet Daddy Dee: Thanks for making me sound street.

Jeff: You're welcome.

Sweet Daddy Dee: At least the white folks bought it.

Aware that I could be stepping into a hornet's nest of controversy, I continued to try to handle the whole thing with sensitivity. Just because an audience knows and likes a comic doesn't stop even loyal fans from turning very quickly if they don't like what they're hearing. If I didn't do this right, I would easily be labeled a racist. On the other hand, if I was *too* politically correct, it wouldn't be funny. Once again, I was pushing myself up against a very fine line. The main theme of the relationship onstage was making sure that the audience knew that Sweet Daddy was hip, and I was *not*. All the fun had to be made of me, pointing out the foibles of being white and, well, *lame*.

> Jeff: Sweet Daddy, what do you call white people who try to act black?
>
> Sweet Daddy Dee: Irritating.

I also didn't hesitate to let the audience in on the joke. Everyone knew of course that this was a white guy trying to be a black guy, who was trying to make fun of the white guy:

> Sweet Daddy Dee: I'm like coffee.
>
> Jeff: Coffee?
>
> Sweet Daddy Dee: Yeah. Before you can experience any of my *brown goodness*, I gotta go through a big-ass white filter.

The most obvious and trite thing I did with Sweet Daddy was make him a pimp. But that was a very thought-out and purposeful move. In doing that, I was shining a glaring light on the whole thing right from the start, so the audience didn't have time to get nervous about what they were seeing. Then I would immediately start in with him bashing me for being *so* white, and we were off to the races.

Sweet Daddy Dee: That's why I love white folks—if you make fun of them, they actually enjoy it!

Jeff: I'd like to think most of us have a good sense of humor.

Sweet Daddy Dee: Either that or you just don't get it.

While honing the act with Sweet Daddy in all corners of the United States and in front of all types of audiences, the most surprising revelation was this: Multiracial audiences and more urban audiences reacted the most favorably to Sweet Daddy. The hipper the crowd, the more black people in the audience, the more and bigger the laughs. In the South, on the other hand, and the more white the crowd, audiences were more tentative. No matter where else I took him, there was always an *ooh cool, where's he going with this?* reaction when I first introduced him and pulled him out. In the South, it was more quiet—perhaps because the white folks were afraid that they'd be reinforcing old stereotypes if they laughed, which of course was the opposite of what I was trying to accomplish.

In truth, as I stated before, the butt of the jokes when Sweet Daddy Dee is onstage is me, not him. I'm the dumb, hopelessly unhip white guy. When he says "Word" to me, I'm lost, having absolutely no idea that it's a term from the street.

Also, throughout the bit, it's usually Sweet Daddy who raises the issue of race. Scanning the audience, he asks if there's another brother in the house. When he gets a shout-out, he says, "Yo, brother: RUN! We outnumbered like at a Dwight Yoakam concert!"

He probably could have said "NASCAR race" and gotten the same laugh, but I saved NASCAR not as a punch line, but a setup joke for the next character. Sweet Daddy confesses that he's completely bamboozled by white folks' fascination with auto racing. To him it's just three hours of guys driving around in circles. *"Hey, they're makin' a left turn! Hey, they're makin' another left turn!"—leave the room for fifteen minutes and come back—"Hey, they just made another left turn!"*

Bubba J.: I've seen guys make right turns.

Jeff: You have?

Bubba J.: Usually into the wall.

Since this was to be my first DVD, material for the preexisting characters almost picked itself. All I had to do was divide the show up into segments and decide how long to perform with each one. Then I just picked my favorite material for Peanut, Walter, and José.

We had chosen a tape date of August 13, 2005, and as the day approached and as I honed material, we began to wonder if in eighty minutes, four characters was enough. Robert asked me if there was another character that I thought would be strong enough for the show. I reminded him of my little white trash buddy, Bubba J., who had been my answer to Bergen's Mortimer Snerd.

In 1993 I was using an earlier version of Bubba J., who was perfect during the Clinton administration, as Arkansas and Southern jokes were running rampant. NASCAR had also been growing in popularity, so subjects for Bubba's material were plentiful. Like Dead Osama, I put him aside after a few years, wanting to explore other ideas. But now I thought this might be the time to resurrect him. Stylistically, however, he didn't match the other guys. All the "humans" in the show were "hard" figures. Peanut was a "soft" figure, but he was non-human, so it sat okay in my head. If I wanted Bubba to be a significant character, I now had to build *another* dummy. We were now in mid-July. Was I truly going to build an entirely new dummy plus have the new routine ready in *one month*?

It seemed crazy, but I knew I could do it. Once again, I sat down with clay, but this time no pictures.

In the middle of construction of the head, I told my friend, the figure maker Alan Semok, that I was redoing Bubba J. He suggested that I make *one* of his eyes move. "One?" I asked. "Just one?" Then I thought about it for a second. *That* was a genius idea!

Bubba J.: Thank you, dear friend Jeff.

Jeff: For what, Bubba J.?

Bubba J.: That's the first time my name and the word *genius* were ever used in sentences that close together.

Bubba J.'s material was not that difficult to choose, as I could pull from the routine from a decade before. I added some NASCAR stuff plus a few new jokes here and there, and practiced with him as much as I could before the DVD taping. The NASCAR reference would be set up perfectly by Sweet Daddy in the act, and now when Bubba J. said he *loved* NASCAR, it got an even bigger laugh.

Bubba J. was very easy for me to write for, simply because I had grown up in Texas and I knew a bunch of folks who were *just like* him. In fact, I actually don't think I'd be much different from him,

had one or two things been slightly different for me growing up . . .
like getting braces, for example.

Bubba J.: You mean your legs were crooked too?

Jeff: Well, not leg braces; *teeth* braces.

Bubba J.: I'd rather walk straight and eat crooked.

For the DVD taping, we'd chosen the newly refurbished and
beautiful OC Pavilion in nearby Santa Ana, California. By my
standards back then, we had a large audience. About six hundred folks
squeezed in and were ready to rock. I had invested another $70,000
and now we were at $120,000 for the endeavor. The pressure was on.

We were scheduled to shoot two shows that night, and would
edit between the two later, picking the best pieces of both shows and
mending them back together as one. We had five cameras and lots of
tape. Out in the production truck behind the theater, Stu and our
director yelled, "Action!"

An hour and a half later we had in the can one of the best times
I'd had onstage in a long time. My team all came backstage afterward, beaming. Stu said, "You really don't even have to do another
one! We got it!" He was kidding of course. All he meant was that it
went really, really well.

During the show, a guy near the back of the audience got up during the Walter segment, probably for a restroom break or whatever.
Having worked clubs for so long, I was ready with a few prepared
ad-libs, but also I was feeling comfortable enough to really screw with

the guy and whoever he was with. The jokes were good and the laughs were great. It turned out that this "Michael" was actually a neighbor of ours and was there with my wife and a bunch of our friends. I had no idea when he got up, as all I could see from the stage was a silhouette. It wasn't until Walter started yelling back and forth with his wife in the audience, while we waited for Michael to come back, that I realized who I was screwing with. It made the bit even funnier.

Walter: Did you tell them that adult diaper sales went up after that aired?

Jeff: No.

Walter: Pretty certain they did.

After the show, Michael was at the bar, and since things had gone so well, I accepted the two shots of tequila he bought me. I was so happy with the way things went that even though I had another show to go, I figured I could loosen up a bit.

But this was ten minutes before the second show was to start. The new audience had already loaded in, and Stu was yelling, "Places!" It wasn't until I started walking back to the stage that I thought, "Uh-oh. This isn't good: I haven't had *anything* to eat all day. Nada. Zilch. And I just downed two big slugs of Patrón Platinum. Oops."

Yep, the timing was just about perfect. As the show went on and with a slightly clouded head, I forgot to check Walter's arms before I pulled him out of the case, and in the middle of our routine for that second crowd, his arms fell to his sides, out of his typical "crossed" pose. Since we were taping, it was no big deal to stop, fix his arms, and then keep going. Trouble was, after I stopped to fix his arms, when I tried to start up again, I had NO idea where I had left off. All I could remember was, "Shots of tequila: BAD." We didn't have a teleprompter because I'd done the show a million times, so there I stood . . . clueless. I was trying to shake the cobwebs, but there was just too much booze and not enough brain cells. It doesn't look like anything is wrong on the tape, and the guys in the truck thought the same thing because no one tried to help me. They were all laughing, thinking I was just screwing around since the first performance had gone so well. The great part was, Walter kept making jokes about what an idiot I was for forgetting my own show, so that made everyone think all the more that I knew exactly what I was doing.

 Walter: Little did the audience know you really were a dumbass who forgot where he was.

 Jeff: Thanks for that.

 Peanut: That's why we're here. Just keepin' it real, dude.

If you want to see a desperate man with an unrelenting dummy, you can see the whole thing unfold in the extras on *Arguing with Myself.* For me, it was a nightmare. The audience and the crew thought it was great.

It ended up a fantastic night, and I remember walking offstage after the second show and thinking, "Wow . . . making a DVD was a lot of work. I'm glad *that's* over!"

I had no idea what I was talking about. The real work hadn't even begun, *and*, we still had to sell it to somebody. We had potentially a great product, but no one who wanted to air it. As a result, the raw footage just sat untouched for weeks. I finally got impatient enough that I got a copy of the tape and edited the show on my PowerBook. It was great, but it still had nowhere to go.

Finally in January of 2006, Creative Artists Agency set up a meeting at Comedy Central for the trio of Stu, Judi, and Robert. They were pitching to Dave Bernath, executive vice president of acquisitions at Comedy Central. The three headed to New York City. According to the reports I got later, Dave listened politely to their fifteen-minute spiel, and then gave them a very emphatic no. And of course it was for the same old reason: Nobody at the network wanted a ventriloquist on Comedy Central.

To this day, no one can tell me exactly what during that meeting finally made Dave relent. He listened to the trio's arguments and admitted that if someone were flipping channels, they would probably stop and watch me for the simple fact that my guys and I looked like nothing else that was on TV *anywhere*.

Stu thinks it was out of sheer frustration simply to get them out of the office, but after some final begging (everyone agreed that actual *begging* took place), Dave decided to give me a shot and agreed to buying a fully produced one-hour special for $75,000 and promised *one*—count it: ONE—airing. And by the way, $75,000 for a special was pretty much next to *nothing*. We didn't care. We just wanted it on the air because we believed it would get good ratings and that solid DVD sales would follow.

 Walter: Good thing they bought it or Stu would have ended up on your other knee . . . with your hand stuck up his . . . back.

So now that the special was sold, we had that mountain of postproduction work to conquer. And when I said that the work hadn't even begun, I wasn't kidding. By the time all was said and done, a team of probably thirty-plus people and I had spent approximately $130,000 on the thing, plus hundreds if not thousands of man-hours. I was still making almost exactly the same amount of money that I had five and ten years before. The hope for a better future was still in the air, but hope didn't pay the mortgage and grocery bills. I was still hammering away every Thursday through Sunday at clubs all over the United States, and now I had a huge loan to pay back.

We finished our cut of what we thought the forty-two minutes should look like for airplay—that's an hour show allowing for all the commercials—but then sent the entire eighty minutes to Comedy Central for their input and changes. After not much argument, the final *final* cut was agreed upon and now there was nothing left to do but promotion.

 Bubba J.: My daddy never got a promotion.

 Jeff: Did he work hard at his job?

 Bubba J.: He never got a job either.

From what I understand, no one at Comedy Central was expecting anything big for my special in the ratings. A typical new episode of *South Park* drew a rating of 1.5, and for cable, that's pretty darned big. The premiere of any other typical stand-up special would draw somewhere around a 0.6. Comedy Central said that for us, a 0.6 would have been just fine, a 1.0 would be a grand slam.

Arguing with Myself premiered on Comedy Central on Saturday,

April 8, 2006. Ratings would be reported in New York the following Monday, usually in the morning. I was home and waiting.

We really had *no* idea what to expect. We had done everything possible in print, on air, and on the Web. And, by the way, we received very little support from Comedy Central. We felt like they just wanted to air it and move on. It was seemingly an embarrassment to them.

Sometime in the morning on Monday, Stu missed Dave Bernath's call, but the message was, "We need to talk." Stu remembers saying, "How bad could it be? Could it be worse than a 0.5? A Yule log at Christmas gets a 0.4, for God's sake."

When Stu finally got him on the phone, Dave was still stunned. "I just don't believe the numbers; I don't believe how good they are."

It was a 0.9, which translated to 1.7 million viewers. That was as good as a *South Park* rating, and it was the second-highest-rated show on Comedy Central that weekend. It also attracted the third-largest audience of any stand-up special premiere on Comedy Central year to date.

When Bernath said he didn't believe the numbers, he wasn't kidding. They repeated the special ten days later, and it was the second most watched show on CC for that day, second only to *The Daily Show*. And now, Bernath was once again the genius at Comedy Central.

Sweet Daddy Dee: That's when I knew I should be managing you.

Jeff: But you made a big commission after the years of hard work had already been done.

Sweet Daddy Dee: Welcome to Hollywood!

Even though ratings were something to brag about, we had to pay equal, if not *more* attention to DVD sales.

As I was an unknown commodity to Comedy Central, I certainly was a nobody in the retail DVD world. I'd never had anything to sell in retail, so no one, including Image, knew if I'd sell even twenty DVDs.

Arguing with Myself was released for sale in retail and online to the public on the Tuesday following the premiere. Although pre-sales had been big on Amazon, that didn't necessarily translate to actual in-store retail sales. What if all my fans were cybergeeks, and no one who shopped in actual stores put the DVD in their carts? Just because Walmart was carrying them didn't mean they would sell. No one would know anything for certain until numbers came in from the stores. In the meantime, I just kept working the clubs.

 Walter: So, what were the numbers?

 Jeff: You have to read the next chapter.

 Walter: Fine. Turn the damn page!

CHAPTER NINE

To the Stars and Back Times Infinity

We had to wait through the week to get any kind of DVD sales numbers back from Image. Like ticket sales for movies, you look at total sales after the first weekend to see how you did. We were optimistic, because not only were presale numbers good, but the title actually reached number one in comedy *two weeks* before the air date. This was, of course, due to a bunch of loyal fans who had been anticipating a DVD for a long time. We'd done everything we could up to that moment to get the word out, but we weren't slacking off just yet either. We continued to send out e-mail blasts to my list, plus I would talk about the DVD at every live show and on every radio and TV interview possible.

Early on we learned that a typical good-selling stand-up comedy DVD sold a total of twenty-five thousand units over its lifetime. Unfortunately, we'd spent so much money on the production, even at twenty-five thousand of them, I'd still owe the bank a lot of dough. John Power, my business manager, said we'd need to sell forty thousand DVDs just to break even. Even our distributor was saying they would be very happy with twenty-five thousand in the title's entire lifetime. Holy crap. Robert told me I was crazy and Stu just looked at me stone-faced when I said I thought we'd do a hundred thousand in the first year. Almost no stand-up titles did that.

When we tallied the numbers nationwide for the first weekend, it looked promising. We'd sold 3,827 in the first week. Four days later Comedy Central aired the special for the second time, and once again we pushed it online and through e-mails. We also purchased a couple of thirty-second spots during the broadcast, advertising the DVD.

Throughout the next few weeks and months the sales continued to build. In the DVD world, a title goes platinum when one hundred thousand units are sold. That had been my goal, but *everyone* told me not to get my hopes up.

But . . . we didn't hit platinum in a year. We hit it in three months. By September, when I was a guest on *Late Night with David Letterman* for the first time, we'd sold more than a quarter of a million units. It didn't stop there. When the holidays rolled around, the sales had grown almost exponentially. In the month of December alone, we sold nearly fifty thousand copies. It was going bonkers.

Peanut: I remember dancing around the room.

Jeff: To celebrate the fifty thousand copies sold?

Peanut: No, Bubba J. was hollering and shooting at my feet.

My first appearance on *Letterman* was in the fall of that same year, but not until writing this passage in this book had I really thought about how long the journey to get even *there* had been. More interesting to me, however, was that I'd never recognized the bit of irony that prevailed both that night and in 1990 when I first appeared on *Carson*. It was now September 2006, and Walter shared the stage with me on *Letterman*, just as he had on *Carson* sixteen years before. It seemed a lifetime had passed since I sat at my workbench in my apartment in Waco, sculpting Walter's head. I had created Walter nineteen years before, while at the same time watching the very two programs that were to make him famous.

Maybe the reason I hadn't thought too much about irony or the significance of being on *Letterman* was because after that night in 2006, I'd tried to completely shut the whole thing out of my head. Not many people have ever heard about the absolute debacle that took place that evening. What happened just moments after I walked offstage after my performance has made me not only never want to watch the playback of the show, but I also don't even like *thinking* about that night. I didn't know if I was going to tell this story, but I've spilled just about everything else, so here goes.

The occasion for my appearance wasn't exactly anything I could have imagined even a month before it happened, but it was a vintage wacky Letterman gambit for which I was most appreciative. It was Ventriloquist Week on *The Late Show*. The idea was that each night a different ventriloquist would be introduced in one of the very early segments of the show, and then do four or so minutes of his or her best stuff. I was slotted for Thursday night and even before the booking, I knew what my set was going to be. Nine-eleven was five years behind us, and I'd honed some incredibly strong material with Walter making fun of terrorists. In the clubs, this stuff was getting absolutely huge laughs. And it wasn't inappropriate. I was now doing the same material at very conservative corporate gigs where being politically correct was an absolute *must*. Walter was simply saying the stuff about terrorists that a lot of us were thinking. This was the perfect example of me being able to say more than the average stand-up because it wasn't *me* saying it.

 Walter: I think it's some kind of a reverse insult that you even imply that it *could* be you.

Jeff: I agree.

Walter: Right. Wait. . . . What?

Before a stand-up performs on *Letterman* or *Leno*, the entire set has to be seen and approved by at least one of the producers of the show. In my case, Eddie Brill was the producer who worked on *Letterman* with most of the guest stand-up comics, and he had worked with me very diligently, making sure that all the material I was going to do was completely copacetic. He came and saw me live doing the set, and he'd gotten everything approved by other higher-up producers at the show. I was ready to go.

Thursday is now the coveted night on *Letterman*, as that's when ratings are usually highest. Out of the other four vents that week, I was given the prime spot because of the recent success of the Comedy Central special, plus the huge DVD sales. We were now well over the double platinum mark of two hundred thousand DVDs sold.

Being introduced by David Letterman was every bit as exciting as Johnny Carson so many years before. We hit our mark, and got started.

Jeff: You've been looking forward to this?

Walter: Oh sure. I love Dave.

Jeff: Why?

Walter: I don't know. . . . A few more years and he and I are going to look exactly *alike*.

Jeff: What about Paul?

Walter: We already do.

We continued with some jokes about Walter's wife and their sex life, then he made fun of mine. Next we moved on to our travels and airline security jokes. These were the pieces that had been doing so well for so many months—jokes that would get applause breaks from American audiences from all walks of life. A few weeks before, the new "no liquids over three ounces" rule had gone into effect:

Walter: That "no liquids" thing is a pain. . . .

Jeff: They do that because those potential terrorists were trying to sneak explosives on inside shampoo bottles.

Walter: That's pretty funny.

Jeff: What?

Walter: Like those guys actually use SHAMPOO. What was it? Head and Shoulders and Neck and Back?

Jeff: I don't know.

Walter: Gee, Your Ass Smells Terrific?

Jeff: Walter, the terrorist stuff is very serious.

Walter: There's the one group of folks I don't understand at all . . . damn suicide bombers. . . . Good lord . . . what the hell is this, "Eye e eye e eye eye eeeeeeee . . ." (Then Walter made an exploding sound . . .) "PCHCHCHHHH . . . WAY TO GO, HABIB! BETCHA CAN'T FRICKIN' DO IT AGAIN! Eye eye eye eeeeeeee . . . PCHHHH HH . . ." Dumbass.

Jeff: Well, you know, Walter, most of those guys truly believe that if they martyr themselves like that, there will be seventy-two virgins waiting for them in paradise.

Walter: April fools, dumbass! If there are any virgins waiting for you, it will be seventy-two guys, JUST LIKE YOU!

Walter: Seventy-two virgins . . . why not seventy-two slutty broads who know what the hell they're doing?

Walter: "Eye e eye e eye eye eeeeeeee . . ." (long pause) PCHCHCHHHH. He had a longer fuse.

Walter: I wonder if they play THAT joke on each other every once in a while?

Jeff: What joke?

Walter: "Eye e eye e eye eye eeeeeeee . . ." Click . . . what the—? . . . PCHCHCHHHH.

Walter: HO! DID YOU SEE JAMIL'S FACE!? It's
gone now, BUT DID YOU SEE HIS FACE!?

Those were jokes that made *me* laugh. And they made the producers laugh . . . and the audience. Applause breaks are a big deal for
comics, and I got seven in that set.

The bit wasn't perfect because I took a few chances with ad-libs,
especially at the end, but for the most part, the entire set was great. A
friend of mine who was in the audience said Dave laughed pretty hard
at the "slutty broads" joke. I sat in the Green Room for the rest of the
show, happy as a clam. The guests who followed me were Ted Turner
and Fergie, but most of the details were a blur as I sat back and tried
not to grin like the Cheshire cat.

The show ended and I looked at my watch, counting the hours
until the show aired. Soon Eddie Brill came running into the room.
"We have a problem," Eddie said.

"With what?" I asked.

"Can you go out and do your set again before the audience
leaves?" he blurted.

"Do *what*?" I spat back. He was in a huge hurry and kept glanc-
ing over his shoulder back toward the studio.

This was a nightmare even I couldn't have imagined: My set, and
every single joke, word for word, had been approved by the *Letterman*
producers. But the person who *hadn't* heard the jokes was the CBS censor who sat in on each and every taping, just to make sure there were
no problems. On *any other day*, what I had done that night would have
been fine. But lo and behold, in New York City on that particular day,
many of the high-profile leaders from the Middle East were in town for
a gathering at the United Nations. Now, considering the material I had
just done, the censor had watched my act and said it couldn't air. Eddie
and the other producers wanted to detain the audience and have me do
the set again without all the terrorist references and jokes. Those were

the biggest laughs in the bit, and I had organized the pieces together in such a manner that the laughs built. Plus, the audience had already heard the jokes once! How could I take the teeth out of my act and then expect them to laugh a second time at the B material? I protested and the clock ticked. Within a minute or two it was too late. Most of the audience had gone. *Now what?*

Eddie left for a quick powwow, then came back and told me that the show would do something they almost *never* did, and that was to edit my set. The beauty of live television is that the unexpected can happen. But even in live broadcast events today, there is a built-in delay of a few seconds so if an inappropriate word or sentence slips out, it can be muted or bleeped, and thus not be heard by the viewing public. In a nightly talk show, they pride themselves in keeping it as live as possible, but in a rare instance like this, an exception had to be made. I was about to be sliced and diced.

I asked if I could stick around to give my two cents' worth during the editing process, but that was nixed and understandably so. They had to get this thing done quickly and they didn't need me looking over their shoulders and arguing.

Eddie reassured me that the bit would still be strong. I knew that was next to impossible.

Watching it a few hours later that night with friends in my hotel room, it wasn't as bad as I thought it would be, and in fact, they'd done a very nice job with making the set seem seamless. The trouble was, just as I had feared, some of the biggest laughs were from the most biting jokes, and they had been axed. What made it worse was that in a few instances, the setups were left, and the punch lines were missing. For example:

> Jeff: They do that because those potential terrorists were trying to sneak explosives on inside shampoo bottles.

(Giant edit and then . . .)

> Walter: There's the one group of folks I don't under-
> stand at all . . . damn suicide bombers. . . .

So they did a fine job of making it sound like a conversation, but from a comedic standpoint, it was like someone had made a delicious hamburger, and then served it without the meat.

Bubba J.: I call that vegetarian comedy. And it stinks. Like broccoli . . . or a wet dog . . . covered in broccoli.

Walter: Can someone just shut him up please?

Bubba J.: Or my grandma . . . in a small room with the air turned off. . . .

Walter: Seriously, can I put duct tape on his mouth?

Timing is everything in comedy so I'd chalk up the events of that day as a perfect example of *shit happens.* Almost no one who watched the broadcast knew the difference, but I certainly did, and I wondered if I would ever be asked back to *Letterman* again. What I walked away with, however, were two completely opposite thoughts. On one hand, I was incredibly disappointed that my set had been chopped up and wasn't nearly as powerful as it had been in its original state. On the other hand, I was amazed and amused that a *ventriloquist* was censored on network television for being too politically controversial. The number of comics that had happened to you could literally count on one hand . . . but to my knowledge, it had certainly never happened to a *ventriloquist*.

 Walter: We get it, Skippy. You're edgy.

It was now the fall of 2006, and the engines were kicking in. It was akin to the space shuttle on liftoff. I, along with many great folks around me, had been working on this project for a long time. Comedy Central had started the countdown, and DVD sales along with the *Letterman* appearance launched the flight.

Two weeks after *Arguing with Myself* premiered and Comedy Central realized that the ratings weren't a fluke, they asked us for a second special. It had now been a full *year* since I had taped the first one, so I was well into writing and honing new material. I knew I could be ready by spring, so we set a tape date for May 2007. I wanted to change up demographics and scenery this time around, and since Walter's bits about terrorists had been going over so well, I figured why not try them out at the place where politics mattered most? I had been performing at the Improv in D.C. for fifteen years and the audiences had always been stellar. We booked the beautiful and historic Warner Theatre in Washington, D.C., to tape *Spark of Insanity*.

I have always been very careful about balancing the material in my act between old and new. It's similar to how established rock bands pick their sets when they tour: They have to give the fans some of the old songs because those are the ones the audiences want and expect, but at the same time they have to play some new stuff too so they progress as artists. If you don't include the old, they'll be unhappy, and if you don't include some new, you'll seem like a tired and sad has-been.

I knew I had to use Peanut, Walter, and José in the next special.

They were the most established, most well developed, and most loved characters. Sweet Daddy Dee and Bubba J. had done well, but they could easily be replaced.

I decided I'd use a new character that I'd been working on named Melvin the Super Hero. He was little and meek, a family man with a secret identity as a crime fighter with not-so-super powers.

Jeff: Do you have superpowers?

Melvin: YES!

Jeff: Like what?

Melvin: I can FLY!

Jeff: Really? To where?

Melvin (pointing to the edge of the stage): To THERE!

Jeff: Can you stop a speeding bullet?

Melvin: Once.

Jeff: Can you leap tall buildings in a single bound?

Melvin: Why the hell would I want to do that? There's not a lot of call for that.

Jeff: Superman does it.

Melvin: Huh . . . showoff.

He was one of the two new guys that I had to construct for the next special, and each step along the way with Melvin, I videotaped the process, doing a bit of show-and-tell. We then pieced all that footage together into a mini-documentary, and made it an extra on the eventual *Spark of Insanity* DVD.

Knowing one new character wasn't enough, and wanting to push the edge even further than I had with Sweet Daddy, I contemplated bringing back Dead Osama. However, I wanted the material in the specials and on the DVDs as evergreen as possible. I wanted folks to be able to view the show a decade later and it not feel dated. Osama, dead or alive, would become old news. It was time for a do-over.

 Achmed: It was like *Extreme Makeover—Terrorist Edition*.

The material with Walter regarding terrorists had been going gangbusters. I'd been reworking the jokes so he was never specific about exactly who he was making fun of, never naming a particular group, organization, or religion. Not long after that, I began to consider that maybe those particular jokes of Walter's could materialize into an entire character. I figured he could be a generic terrorist, with the same attitude and demeanor as Dead Osama, but we would never say what group he was with or even what country he came from. His accent would be very nondescript—something that to the American ear sounded simply . . . *foreign*.

My two favorite steps in the construction process of a dummy are the beginning and end: sculpting and painting. Sculpting the character is starting on the proverbial blank page. There's nothing before you but a block of clay and your imagination. As with Sweet Daddy Dee, I gathered multiple pictures, but this time of skeletons, plus I pulled out a few Halloween decorations to pose for me. I also consulted with longtime friend Kelly Asbury, who had been an animation artist and illustrator for Disney, Pixar, DreamWorks, and later a director for *Shrek 2* and *Gnomeo and Juliet*. Kelly drew me a few versions of what he thought this new guy should look like, running the full spectrum of explosive tragedy. The drawings went from a clean face to half–blown up, to the full-on Daffy Duck blown back, nothing-but-charred-face-and-eyes look.

I absorbed all the photos, toys, and illustrations, and began to sculpt.

Like an oil painting, you can take as much time as you want creating a clay sculpture. Walter's sculpt was done in one sitting. Achmed took a few weeks as I could only work on him between club runs in and out of town. I would work a few hours, quit, then come back a few hours or days later and go at it again.

Finally when the clay head began to look crazy enough and I could hear the voice in my head when I looked at him, I knew he was ready. The next step was to make a silicone mold, then the fiberglass head shell, but I had given up that part of the process with the last Walter, when I breathed in too many fumes in a closed garage one day and started hallucinating. That particular day I even made a few phone calls I shouldn't have, accusing the pool guy of stealing my tools. Good lord. Time to give up the chemicals.

 Walter: I still think that pool guy has our tools.

 Jeff: No he doesn't. I was just loopy from the fumes.

Walter: I think they left some permanent damage.

Jeff: I don't think so.

Walter: I do. You used to just talk to yourself. Now you and talk *and* type to yourself.

I found an artist named Dragon who had been working in special effects in Hollywood for years. He and I had become friends a couple years before, and he was now the guy who took over the "gooey" process and would take my clay, make a mold, and then cast the fiberglass shells of the heads. Dragon was incredibly talented, his shop was scary, and his work was beautiful. A few days after dropping off the clay, I went back to Dragon's, and he handed me a perfect fiberglass head ready for mechanics. As I was ready to walk out the door, I said to Dragon, "I have no idea what to use for eyes. The sockets are bigger than a real human's, so I can't just get glass eyeballs like I usually do." Dragon said, "Yeah, I was looking at that. I think I have *just* the thing." I followed him deep back into his shop, past alien spaceships, androids, robot suits, suits of galactic armor, weaponry from God knows what universe, giant masks and suits of all frightening sorts, and even a bunch of pirate stuff. Finally we arrived at his desk *area*. I say area, because you really couldn't tell where the desk ended and just piles of parts and junk began. About five minutes later he popped up with an, "AH-HA!" In his hand he held a larger-than-average eyeball. It looked *really* cool . . . and unusually familiar.

Dragon continued to dig and finally came up with the other one. "You ever seen *these* before?" he chuckled.

"Yeah," I said, "hang on." I thought about it, gazing at the giant eyeball, both of them beautifully cast in resin with veins and details I could never have matched in paint. What was typically the white part of the eye was an interesting dull yellow, and the iris a brown-orange with red highlights. Then it hit me! I had seen smaller versions of these eyeballs daily, because they were sitting in my office, molded in the heads of toys I had collected ten years before. "*MARS ATTACKS!*" I said!

"Exactly!" Dragon replied. "We made the full-sized aliens for the movie, and a buddy of mine made the eyes. These are two extras we never used. You're welcome to them."

"How great is THIS?" I thought as I was installing them a few days later. "This guy is going to have the real *Mars Attacks!* alien eyeballs!" And so it was.

Walter: Oh great . . . so now he's a Martian terrorist? Achmed is part alien?

Jeff: I guess so.

Bubba J.: Now I know who probed me!

As I assembled my newest cast member, I had been tossing around ideas for names and, somehow, Achmed just fit him. Next was the reworking of some of the old Osama material, and then of course writing specific jokes and bits for Achmed. Because no two vent figures I build are ever the same, each one has individual physical traits and movements, which affect manipulation and personality. These quirks then play into the material. Jokes are jokes, but if I can get a laugh from a *physical* movement too, there's no reason to pass it up. Bergen was stuck with radio and only had to worry about dialogue, but today we have high-definition video from multiple camera angles. Besides being funny, everything and everybody had to look good and move just right.

As for material, I decided that the funniest idea that would create the most tension would be if Achmed was a failed terrorist who simply didn't have his heart in his work. He needed to be conflicted between what he was trained for and was supposed to be doing, versus becoming enamored with Americans and our culture, and starting to love all the cool stuff we have. I also thought that maybe, just maybe, he might not be sold on the idea of killing people. Sure, he would feign the attitude and always be yelling, "I KEEL YOU!" but like Walter, every once in a while a soft side would show itself.

Achmed's character traits and quirks began to gel together very nicely, and I knew he was going to be perfect for the next special. A newspaper review from the early Achmed days said that somehow I'd accomplished making a terrorist a sympathetic character. I took that as a *big* compliment.

 Achmed: That's right. Terrorists have feelings too.

 Jeff: Well, at least you do.

 Achmed: Hug?

Material for Achmed was becoming a mixed blend of subject matter and purpose. Since he would be completely new to a majority of the folks seeing him in this special, I had to do introductory jokes simply to establish who he was and where he was coming from. Obviously at first sight of Achmed, you know this is comedy. He immediately got laughs by simply looking around.

Whenever writing material, I always go for multiple laughs in a short span of time, but I also try to never sacrifice character in the process. When I was writing for Achmed, I made sure that whatever he said, it was an accurate reflection of his personality. After establishing himself with a few lines and jokes about who he was, his name, and what he was doing in the United States, I went the route of asking him serious questions as if I were speaking with an actual terrorist. Then he would answer with Achmed-like responses.

Jeff: So you're a terrorist.

Achmed: Yes.

Jeff: What happened to you?

Achmed: I am a horrible suicide bomber. I had a premature detonation.

Jeff: You did all this for a bunch of virgins?

Achmed: Are you kidding me? I'd kill you for a Klondike bar!

As I wrote for him, I would also try to imagine what it would be like to come to the United States for the first time, especially if your heart wasn't meant for killing. This allowed me to do some observational humor as well, but all from the standpoint of a somewhat innocent albeit goofball terrorist.

Jeff: Do you like being in Washington, D.C.?

Achmed: I think some idiots must live here.

Jeff: Why?

Achmed: For example, the Washington Monument.
It's looks nothing like the guy. It looks more like a
tribute to Bill Clinton.

Last, because Achmed was already politically incorrect, I thought
a few somewhat related, non-PC jokes would fit right in:

Jeff: Where do you get your recruits?

Achmed: The suicide hotline.

We taped *Spark of Insanity* on May 5, 2007, in front of about 1,400
people. At this time, this was a *big* venue for us, and the show felt
huge. Once again, we shot two full shows with two different audiences in one evening. The set designs were beautiful, and this time
we employed a new technique of having a completely different set for
each character. Everyone agreed that set changes had to be as quick as
if we were shooting live. In that way, the audiences' energy was kept
high, and lulls were almost nonexistent.

Both shows were knockouts, and we again knew we had a lot of
great material to choose from while editing. And as I had hoped, D.C.
had been the perfect backdrop for Achmed.

Once again I walked offstage thinking, "Wow, that was a lot of
work. . . ." But this time I knew it had only begun. Comedy Central

wanted the special on the air and soon as possible, and September 23, 2007, was the date scheduled.

Spark of Insanity premiered while I was onstage in Tucson, but all I could think and wonder about that night were the ratings. Were we going to do as well as we had with *Arguing*, or had that been a once-in-a-career fluke? Did people really want to see me and my guys again? The wait to find out the numbers was unbearable.

Late that same evening after the Tucson show, Robin Tate, who was now back and promoting my theater appearances, drove me to, of all places, Casa Grande, Arizona, to an almost deserted golf resort out in the middle of nowhere. The reason it was deserted was because it was off-season and literally no one was checked into the hotel . . . except me. And when I say there was nothing and no one around, I mean *nothing* and *no one*. I had a corporate gig the next night somewhere near in Casa Grande, and this was the nicest hotel they could find for me. But no one bothered to tell me it was going to be *The Shining* in the desert.

Robin dropped me off, laughing as he drove away. I know he was laughing, because I could *hear* him. After ringing the bell at the front door of the creepy place for five minutes, some old guy finally unlocked it and said to us, "Oh, they told me someone was checking in tonight! Sorry, I forgot." I hauled my trunk and backpack up to the top suite, which was an entire floor that I had all to myself. I was fully expecting Jack Nicholson to show up with an ax and to find REDRUM scrawled on a bathroom mirror. Seriously?

 Walter: Trust me, Robin would not have left you off at a dangerous place.

 Jeff: How do you know?

Walter: If anything happens to you, he doesn't get paid!

But I went to bed that night thinking about nothing but people and numbers and the Arbitron.

The ratings came back the next day, and yes, once again, we were all *wrong*. It was bigger than anyone had expected. We got a 1.8. That meant 3.8 million viewers.

So the rocket ship was clearly in the atmosphere now, and gaining altitude. The following Tuesday, the *Spark of Insanity* DVD hit the shelves and blew away *Arguing with Myself* in no time.

Ticket sales on the road blew up as well. We figured this would be a good ride, but we had *no idea* . . . our efforts to market the DVD and promote the network's repeats continued to be effective, but now there was a new fuel for the rocket that was more powerful and far-reaching than anyone had ever imagined. It was called YouTube.

As soon as any new video content is released in the market or goes on the air, people post their favorite segments of it on YouTube. However, when the uploads happen to be segments of their products, most content providers consider that to be a *bad* thing. Every download is a potential lost sale. We felt that way about uploads from my DVDs. So as a seemingly smart business tactic, while we had one team of guys uploading carefully edited promotional video clips, we had another group of guys policing the net, doing their best to remove everything else. We felt we were simply protecting sales.

One day, however, I noticed a particular Achmed clip that our guys had missed that was getting a significant number of views . . . and I mean a LOT of views. A bunch of folks had uploaded entire Achmed segments of *Spark* and we had successfully gotten YouTube to remove most of them, but this particular one had been missed, and had been viewed more than any other very quickly. Plus, the view numbers were growing almost exponentially on a daily basis.

Achmed: I have something to tell you.

Jeff: What's that?

Achmed: I was about 19 million of those views.

I began to rethink things when I realized that if we had taken that clip down earlier, millions of people wouldn't have seen Achmed and our routine. Were we being too strict? It wasn't like it was the entire DVD, and we were now in the age of the Internet. This is where the most give-and-take mass communication was taking place, in a never-before-seen, free-for-all way. If people thought something was funny, they would watch the piece themselves, then forward it on to friends, business associates, and family. If that particular video was a hit, the view numbers would explode in mushroom-cloud fashion. So, our guys removed and kept removing as many Achmed videos as we could, except this *one*.

A week before Thanksgiving 2007, the clip was at 11 million views. Two weeks later, it was at 13 million. By December 17 it was at 18 million, and a week later, 20 million views. And this video wasn't a minute or two long that could quickly be viewed. It was ten minutes in length.

Achmed the Dead Terrorist and his best-known catchphrase were quickly becoming a phenomenon. Everywhere we went, people said to me and to each other, "I KEEL YOU!" My favorite example of how huge it was becoming came from a substitute schoolteacher from Florida who stopped us outside a theater one evening after a show. She said that not long before, she had no idea who I was, or who any of my characters were. She had never heard of me or Achmed or any of the little guys. But one day at school, she was substituting in an unruly second-grade class. The bell rang and class was supposed to start, but the kids wouldn't stop chatting. She said she kept trying to get their attention: "Class . . . it's time to settle down . . . boys and girls! . . . you have to be quiet now! CLASS?" All to no avail. She finally got so frustrated that she yelled at the top of her voice, "SILENCE!" There was a beat of quiet in the room, and then almost every kid in the class yelled back as one voice, "I KEEL YOU!"

It goes without saying that things were going incredibly well on the road, and the characters were becoming more and more well known. But now we get to the part that completely blew me away . . . something I had never even dreamed of. I've had three huge surprises in this journey, all within the last few years, and this was the first one. As the numbers on YouTube grew and grew, we started getting e-mails from outside the United States. It was so easy to be thinking solely about the U.S. and Canadian markets, because this was our turf. Neither I nor anyone else on the team was thinking beyond the United States' borders. But while scanning on YouTube, I began to notice that people were posting their *own* videos, *acting out* the Achmed sketch. . . . And many of them weren't from America. Then to add further wonder, people in other countries were posting the Achmed clip with subtitles in their own native tongue, and some even went so far as to *dub* other peoples voices in other languages, speaking for Achmed and me! What the—?

It was becoming plainly obvious that Achmed was reaching further than any of us had ever imagined. But now, the final piece that made me literally sit back in my chair with my mouth open, staring at my computer screen, was when I went to google.com/

trends and typed in my own name. It turns outs that there were more people Google searching me and Achmed in other countries and in other languages than there were in the United States and in English. The country Googling me the most was South Africa, followed by Germany, Poland, and some of the Scandinavian countries. Danish, Polish, and German were the top languages, followed by English.

What had happened? What was it about this little skeleton that was hitting home for so many people?

Achmed: And that's when I realized I couldn't handle the pressures of fame and stardom, so I turned to alcohol.

Jeff: No, you didn't.

Bubba J.: Well, I did!

Jeff: No, you didn't either, Bubba J.

Bubba J.: Oh yeah, I was already there.

We began getting more and more fan mail, and not just e-mail, but loads of snail mail as well. Servicemen and women from our own armed forces were digging Achmed like no one would believe.

The armed forces stores were now carrying both of my DVDs and the soldiers couldn't get enough. I can't tell you how proud I was that my little guys were making the members of our armed forces around the world *laugh*.

There have been a great many remarkable and heartfelt moments that I've experienced in the past few years, thanks to our military. With their letters and stories of appreciation for Achmed and the crew, I could almost fill an entire second book. But for now, I'll tell you about two of my favorites.

One particular week I was at the Stardome Comedy Club in Birmingham, Alabama, where I had performed at least one week a year for almost two decades. Bruce Ayers, the owner of the club, came backstage one night before the show and told me there were a couple of air force guys who wanted to say hello afterward. I'm usually pretty zonked after a gig, but this was one meet and greet I didn't want to pass up.

After the performance, I went into the showroom, and there stood two men who weren't exactly kids. I was expecting the usual younger guys, barely out of boot camp, but this wasn't the case. Both men introduced themselves as pilots who had flown multiple missions over Iraq and Kuwait. One of them said, "Mr. Dunham, we just wanted to thank you for all you're doing for the morale of all us guys over in Iraq and wherever else hell is taking place, and we'd each like to present to you our individual talisman. I've had this one in my pocket for eight missions over Iraq, and John's here is about the same." A talisman in this case is a coinlike object that has the insignia representing the branch of the soldier's service on one side, and the insignia for their separate company or squadron on the other. I couldn't believe what I was holding and what this serviceman was saying to me. I was pretty much speechless.

The second occasion took place that same week and was a

moment that left me touched, proud, and even bewildered at how far this simple comedy act had grown to affect others.

Once again Bruce told me there was someone he thought I should say hello to after the show. It was a woman this time; a mother of a soldier. I greeted her and she said, "My son is somewhere in the Middle East. He usually can't tell us exactly where he is, because he's in Special Forces and we don't get many details. He sent one of these home to me, and I thought you should have it. All the men in his squadron have them sewn onto their uniforms. . . ." She handed me an embroidered round patch, about the size of a drink coaster. It had a black background with white lettering around the edges. In the middle was stitched a very accurate representation of Achmed's face. Three or four sewn bullet holes seemingly riddled the patch, and the wording around the perimeter in bold lettering read, "SILENCE! WE KILLED HIM AND WE'LL KILL YOU."

It was now early December, and I tried to think of some sort of quick video we could shoot to put out on YouTube for the holiday season. I told Robert I thought we should do some sort of Christmas song with Achmed. "Jingle Bombs!" I said. All I had at this point was the title, but it sounded funny as hell to me, and I thought it could be something perfect for Achmed. "Rothpan and I can write some sort of goofy revision of "Jingle Bells" and Achmed can sing it. How about we tape it in the Chicago club next week? If it's good enough, we'll put it on YouTube."

"Sounds great," Robert said.

And then I added, "Let's just find some local piano player who can improvise. I'll kid around with him a little and see what happens."

That was the plan, so Rothpan and I sat down to write some Achmed lyrics to the tune of "Jingle Bells," a simple tune for any piano player. But the next day Robert called back and said he thought he had a better idea than a piano player, and the guy could double as my opening act as well. "He's a guitar player," Robert said.

"A guitar comic?" I replied.

"No, not a regular guitar," Robert said. "An *electric* guitar. He could literally add some rock and roll to your show."

"Oh, come on," I replied.

"Trust me!" he said back.

"Whatever," I replied.

Rothpan and I wrote a song that made us laugh, and we both met Brian Haner at the Chicago Improv for the first time that next Thursday afternoon. With Rothpan as opener and Brian as the middle act, we'd be doing two shows a night through Sunday. We had arrived barely in time on Thursday to set up and shovel down a quick dinner, thanks to typical snow and weather delays at O'Hare. As for rehearsing "Jingle Bombs," even though I didn't know a thing about singing, and had never even attempted any kind of music in my act, I told Brian I didn't want to bother with a rehearsal. "Who can't sing 'Jingle Bells'?" I said. I was just too tired to rehearse. I also knew that screwups onstage sometimes turn into comedy gold. And that's exactly what happened that first night.

While Rothpan was opening the show, Brian said to me, "At least sing the first couple of notes so I'll know what key to start in." I sang, "Dashing through the sand . . ."

"Okay. You're in E," Brian said. I had no idea what he was talking about.

Rothpan introduced Brian, and Robert was right—he put some rock and roll into the show. But the real test would be how "Jingle Bombs" came off. I did my stand-up, then Walter, then the first half of Achmed's routine. Brian then came out to help with the song—the video camera in the back of the showroom was rolling. We started in, and since I was completely out of my element, I couldn't have been more awkward or unsure of myself. But I did what I knew best. When Achmed messed it up, he'd turn and look at me with a knowing angry look, acknowledging what the audience knew, and that was of course, that everything bad happening was all *because of me.*

Walter: Now Achmed knows how I feel! But this time it wasn't booze; just stupidity.

The problem, as I didn't figure out for a few minutes, was that I was starting the song with the first verse lyrics, but I was using the chorus notes. So the words, "Dashing through the . . ." were being sung by Achmed with the notes from the chorus. Everyone in the room, including, of course, Brian, realized *how* I was screwing up and what I was doing wrong. . . . That is, everyone except *me.* We kept starting and stopping, and the audience was laughing their asses off because Achmed was getting angrier, and I was absolutely stumped as to what in the world I was doing wrong. Poor Brian didn't know what to do. We'd never worked together before, so he assumed I was doing this on purpose, simply for the laughs. Finally I think Brian figured out I really had no idea what was going on, maybe because flop sweat was starting to drip off my face. He sung in a whisper the correct words and notes, "Dashing through the sand . . ."

"OH YEAH!" I said, and then it was on with the song.

Dashing through the sand.
With a bomb strapped to my back.
I have a nasty plan,
For Christmas in Iraq . . .

And on it went . . .

Once again the next night, we didn't rehearse, and we had the video camera rolling. For comedy's sake, we repeated some of the same screwups, but did a perfect rendition of the song, then had it online in no time. Once again, the views were off the charts, and we had another YouTube hit on our hands. This would end up being just the warm-up for a very big special to come, one year from then. . . . But much was yet to happen before then.

As 2007 was coming to a close, I couldn't begin to count my blessings. It had been a whirlwind year of success, triumph, new friendships, and performances in the large-sized venues I had played in a distant fifteen years before. My kids were well and happy. Financially I was back on track. To reward the success and give the girls a little taste of the road, I decided to make a family trip out of the week of shows between Christmas and the New Year. Robin Tate had me booked for five dates at bigger venues with larger audiences than my family had ever seen before. Very purposefully, Robin and I had booked the south and southeast for this time because that's where my wife and her family are from and I knew it would be fun to have the girls and be with everyone for Christmas.

Beginning December 27, I played one theater each night in Charlotte, Mobile, Daytona, and Fort Pierce. Then finally on New Year's Eve, we ended 2007 with one of the largest venues I'd ever played up to that point: The Tampa Bay Performing Arts Center, in front of nearly four thousand people. I remember walking offstage at the end of my show to the incredible and *loud* ovation in that beautiful venue, with my wife standing and watching backstage. She was literally stunned at what she was hearing. As the applause rolled on, and with 2008 quickly approaching, I couldn't help but reflect on where my life's journey had brought me and how much I'd been given. I smiled and said, "Cool, huh?" Then I hugged my family. It was one of the highest, warmest, and most memorable moments of my life.

It's amazing how many times you hear the same story over and over of successful people's personal and professional lives simultaneously heading in opposite directions and in extremes, because little did I know that less than three weeks later, having been dealt an unbelievable blow, I would be in the middle of marriage counseling, and in the depths of a depression so low that I would be at the point of not caring if my life was over and ended.

I don't know how many people seriously think about suicide, but I'm pretty sure that most of us have taken the Jimmy Stewart *It's a Wonderful Life* journey in our own minds, and wondered what the world would be like without us. If we had never been, or if we were taken suddenly, *would it matter?* During the third week in January 2008 I was certainly at that point, and because of what I was now facing, for the first time in my life I started canceling shows. I couldn't find any way in my soul to walk onstage and make people laugh when I didn't care if I were alive or dead.

Show business, like many professions, presents an incredible number of pressures on a marriage. Some relationships are able to survive and withstand the stress, and some are not. Unfortunately, mine was one of those that did not. In late January, I knew deep down that my marriage was over. But, for the sake of our daughters, and through much turmoil and distress, we tried to keep the marriage together for many months. I went through the motions of, as our therapist described it, "Pretend *as if . . .*"

Despite the hard work, I finally made the most difficult and heart-wrenching decision of my life. I filed for separation in the fall of 2008 and moved out of my much-loved home . . . the first home I had truly called my own and where my beautiful girls had grown to be beautiful young ladies.

That evening, after having packed up my truck with a few changes of clothes, some important collectibles, and all my dummies, I drove to the Marriott in Sherman Oaks. Ironically this was the same hotel where the Sherman Oaks Improv had been, and where I had auditioned for Debra Sartell from the Improv nineteen years before.

During a session with our family therapist less than a week before, I told the girls that I was going to move out. As I remember back to those days, and now write these words, they are memories that I can barely face again now. The girls and I cried, but we also faced the uncertainty with as much optimism as possible. I had picked out a rental house a few miles away, and I was managing my work calendar so that I would have every other weekend home, something I had never done for their entire lives.

Something else we looked forward to was that in a few months I would let the girls help me pick a new house, one closer to their school with rooms that they could decorate themselves. Bree, my oldest, was now at school out of state, but she would have a room too. Though my career had been such a huge part of my life, and though I was out of town more than any of us would have liked, when I was home, I always tried to make sure that I was truly *there*. This would be even more so now, since I was now a single parent.

A broken family is rarely what any child wants, but there was no other choice for me. My parents have been married for fifty-four years now, and that is my example. I never imagined anything else for myself, and I had lived my family life and my marriage always with that intention. I like to think that I have remained the same person throughout all these years and that my values and morals haven't changed with success. I don't go to church as much as I used to, and the characters go a bit further with language and subject matter than they did when I was younger, but my core values and basic Christian beliefs remain the same. My girls have taken the good from both their parents, and I know they will grow into strong, smart women. I have tried to give them what I know best, and that is a sense of optimism and a sense of humor. I want them to be able to look at life and see first, the good in people and in humanity. I want them to dream and work hard for what they want, and I want them to never be satisfied with "good enough," but to push for greatness at whatever they choose in life and whatever path they take. I want them to be independent and never rely on another person for their happiness, but to also love and be loved so much that they can't imagine life without that other person. I want their hearts to be broken so that when they love again, they will know the beauty of love, and never take for granted sharing their soul with the person they choose to go through life with. I want them to be healthy and happy and to have their own children and experience all the joy that they have given me. I want them to fail and to succeed. I want them to fall and pick themselves up. Most of all, I want them to laugh.

Bree, Ashlyn, and Kenna . . . I'm sorry Mommy and Daddy didn't make it through the storms. I love you with all my heart . . . to the stars and back, times infinity.

CHAPTER TEN

Is This a Hockey Arena?

The purpose of this book is to tell you my journey, from beginning to current day, from childhood dreams to the current fruition. This is a journey full of accomplishments, failures, happiness, and heartbreak. We all, of course, live through this wide range of emotions and experiences, and hopefully for each of us, in the end the positive has outweighed the negative.

At the conclusion of the last chapter, in a few short paragraphs describing my personal life, I quickly took you through most of 2008: from my broken heart to moving out of my house and becoming a divorcing parent. It wasn't a quick ten months, however. It was rather drawn out, painfully, as if I were slowly pulling an arrow from my chest. My personal life was in ruins, and I hid it from my kids as best I could. But when children are part of the family and thus in the middle, the process is more difficult and confusing, as you must weigh what is best for everyone in the long run.

But this book is not about a broken heart. More than half of all marriages end in divorce these days, so I'm not relating anything that many of us haven't already been through. Also, I know that my marriage didn't end after fourteen years because of one issue. I accept plenty of blame, knowing that my wife and I didn't address and repair problems and disagreements that existed almost from the very beginning. The problems near the end weren't the cause of the marriage falling apart; they were the symptoms of a marriage that was already in serious trouble.

So while my personal life was taking a nosedive to depths I'd never imagined, my professional life was beginning an ascent on a trajectory that I'd never dreamed possible. It felt like the fabric of all

I had become was being torn in two different directions, with threads and strips still connecting the two, but with a tear that was becoming more obviously defined as time progressed.

After canceling five days of shows in late January, I forced myself back on the road to fulfill contracts and show up for performances that had been sold out for weeks. Deep down I knew that everyone has problems, and that mine were very small compared to people who were going through things that were much sadder and dealing with difficulties far more severe than anything that had been dished out to me. I knew that all of us have to push through obstacles in life the best way we know, learning, and living, and moving forward.

Additionally, besides the people that had already paid for tickets, there were also a great number of folks who relied on me for their own income: everyone from my agent to the guys who swept up after the shows. I kept reminding myself that I was living a dream and I had a great deal to be thankful for. At times, I was almost ashamed that I was allowing myself to wallow like this. So I forced myself onstage. In all honesty, my heart wasn't in it, but I was trying. Jeff Rothpan, my now good friend and opening act, was on the road with me for the first few weekends, and we simply *worked*.

I never truly knew how much all this affected me until not long ago when Kenna and Ashlyn and I were at Caesar's Palace during one of my weekends there. Kenna picked up the *What's Happening in Vegas* magazine from our hotel room table, and she and Ashlyn looked at my photo on the cover. "Dad, this was taken when you and Mom were splitting up, huh?" Kenna said and asked this, both at the same time. I looked at the cover. It took me a second to examine what I was wearing in the picture and to remember the photo shoot when that particular shot was taken. Sure enough, it was a photo from a shoot right after I knew the marriage would end. "How did you know that?" I asked. Ashlyn replied with Kenna, nodding, "You can see it in your face."

The size of the theaters we were now in was growing. In February of 2008, we were playing two-thousand- to four-thousand-seat houses regularly. We usually planned the tours in a way that made sense for easy travel. But now the ticket sales were big enough that we could build in a few typical touring amenities—which would eventually become necessities. The first was a tour bus.

I'd never seen inside a tour bus before. I really hadn't paid much attention or even cared, because who would ever think that a ventriloquist would be on an actual tour? But now we needed reliable and flexible transportation, so we picked out a brand-new one from a company in Nashville (where most U.S. tour buses call home) and had the interior completely customized. Of course we had bunks for me, Robin Tate, Guitar Guy (who was now my permanent opening act), and Jeff Rothpan. But I also needed some work space. And I don't mean office, though the bus had one of those as well. What I'm talking about was a workshop. Every so often the characters need maintenance, like a lever replaced or some paint touched up . . . also, I wanted the freedom to be able to build anything new for the act that I might need, so I e-mailed the tour bus company a list of required hand tools, power tools, supplies, and even correct lighting for painting, and a few weeks later, voilà! The bus company had removed eight of the twelve bunks and built me an entire mobile workshop. Next, they added an elliptical machine, a lounge in back, a kitchen and dining area in front with microwave, refrigerator and freezer, a pulldown TV in each of the four bunks, four big flat screen TVs, and even a couple of Xboxes and PlayStations. COOL. They also installed surround sound in both TV areas, plus another smaller flat screen and surround sound at my workbench. Good lord. This was awesome.

And yes, this was on-the-road opulence. This bus became my haven for more than half of every month.

Walter: I don't care if you make the bus look like a rolling palace, it's still a damn bus.

Jeff: But it's a *tour* bus!

Walter: We're driving around the country in a BUS. The only difference between us and the Beverly Hillbillies is that we forgot the chickens!

Bubba J.: Let's get chickens!

Walter: I quit.

Travel was pretty simple now. We would jump on a commercial flight, land at the first city of that particular run, find the bus, and be taken to the theater. Then after the show, we'd pack up the dummies, jump on the bus, and head overnight to the next town.

At first I thought this was going to be easy, with luxury and plenty of time to kick back and enjoy. What I didn't consider was that this schedule made *every* day a travel day. We *never* slowed down. While we were setting up for the show and then performing, the bus driver was at the hotel sleeping those six or seven hours. Then he'd wake up after we'd packed and take us to the next town. Honestly, I was working harder than I ever had. But, no complaints! On the contrary—the work had never been this rewarding, and the fans were awesome.

As many miles as we were putting on planes and on the bus, we were bound to have our share of unexpected moments and maybe some unwanted excitement. At the very opening of the book, I mentioned being rescued by a terrorist. Let me tell you exactly how *that* went . . .

Every so often our travel needs to get from gig to gig wouldn't match up with commercial flight schedules, so we'd have to rough it and get on a private jet. Not too shabby, but we were still subject to . . . well . . . fate.

One evening after a show in New York, Brian and I had to fly all the way back across the country to Medford, Oregon, for a show the next afternoon at an Indian casino. Well, after the six-hour flight, it was now about one a.m., and we were coming in for a landing at the Medford airport. In the last moments, our pilots decided to abort the landing due to heavy fog, and we had to divert. So we turned toward a place called Klamath Falls, Oregon. The pilots hadn't done much research on this particular destination, and upon landing at the not-so-large Klamath Falls airport, we taxied to a halt on the tarmac, and the pilots informed us that since the tower was closed, and no one was on the radio, they were going to pick a far corner of the airport next to the biggest hangar and just sit there until either the fog cleared in Medford, or we got ground transportation.

After parking the plane and as they were shutting down the engines, suddenly four military Humvees came roaring up and surrounded our plane. Flood lights ablaze, we then heard a very commanding voice over an incredibly loud PA announce, "ALL OCCUPANTS OF THE

AIRCRAFT: YOU MUST EXIT THE AIRCRAFT IMMEDI-ATELY WITH YOUR HANDS IN THE AIR, FIFTY METERS APART, ONE AT A TIME."

What the—? Honestly, my first thought was that we were being punked. I thought any minute, Ashton Kutcher was going to jump out of the bushes, laughing. Wrong. This was legit because as we looked down the aisle, our pilot was scrambling out of his seat, try-ing to get the door opened and the stairs down, all while shaking like a leaf. He then went down the stairs and outside with his hands up. . . . As he got there, I swear I could see him shaking *more* as he looked around. The copilot then made his way to the steps, and he too looked like he was about to cry.

Side note: Our captain, the first guy . . . he knew who I was, what I did for a living, and he knew the characters. The copilot? . . . *New* guy. Didn't know anything about me. Keep that in mind.

I then said good-bye to Brian and made my way down the steps, hands in the air. As I got outside, I then saw why there was even more panic on the pilots' faces. No joke: surrounding us, about twenty-five U.S. Marines, all with M4 rifles pointed straight at us.

I turned to look, and now Brian was gingerly making his way down the stairs. The difference was, while the pilots and I had our hands straight up in the air, Brian looked experienced at this, because he had his hands on the *back* of his *head*. The pilots and I looked like we were in a Western; Brian was on *Cops*.

Standing side by side, hands in the air, the guy got back on the horn and bellowed, "WHO'S IN COMMAND HERE?" The cap-tain of our plane went forward, and now it's just the three of us left standing there. As we stood there I thought, "This is just a horrible misunderstanding. . . . What can I do to get out of this quickly?" No joke. Without moving my lips, I whispered to Brian, "I'm going to try something." Then Brian started making unintelligible noises, without moving his lips, but he wasn't very good at it. All I heard was,

"Mmmmmmnnnnmmnnnnuhhhuhnmmnnn!" Then just to mock Brian, once again without moving my lips I said, "Ha ha, you can't do it!" Remember the copilot? He has NO IDEA what's going on. So now I'm thinking, okay, this *has* to work. . . . So I raised my voice pretty loudly and bellowed, "EXCUSE ME, GENTLEMEN?" A few more rifles suddenly came around, right in my direction, pretty much pointed at my head.

"Uh . . . DO YOU GUYS KNOW ACHMED THE TERROR-IST?" That's about the time the copilot pissed in his pants and Brian about fell over.

There were a few beats of silence, then one Marine yelled, "YEAH, WE WATCHED HIM ON TV LAST WEEK; HE'S FUNNIER THAN HELL."

I said, "You guys! . . . that's me!"

Another beat of silence, and then a second marine, "HEY! WE BAGGED ACHMED THE DEAD TERRORIST!" About then the copilot fainted, we all shook hands and took pictures with each other, and were off on our merry way.

 Achmed: You're welcome, infidels!

 Jeff: Thank you, Achmed.

 Walter: I thought this was comedy. It would have been funnier if they'd shot your ass.

Thanks to the success of "Jingle Bombs," we decided that a holiday special made a lot of sense. Again, the wheels of business started to turn. Comedy Central was on board, and I started working on Christmas material and a brand-new show.

The true genesis for the *Jeff Dunham's Very Special Christmas Special* came many years before, when a parent at our daughter's school invited the Dunham family to her annual (and fabulous) Christmas party. Jacquie Boggs had two sons, both near the ages of my kids, and with a few other school families, we became a pretty tight-knit group, taking trips and vacations together. But back in the very early years, when the girls were teeny tiny, Jacquie asked my wife if I could pull out one of the characters during the party and "do a little something" for everyone. Ugh. I'd always dreaded performing for friends and family, because they *know* you too well and it usually felt more like work than fun!

But I thought about it for a while on a long plane ride across the country. I recalled some discussions with my old friend David Erskine many years before regarding Bergen and Charlie reading a short piece of *The Night Before Christmas* together in one of their radio broadcasts. Erskine sent me an audiotape of the show, and I remembered Charlie messing up the story a bit to big laughs, and how funny that seemed to me, even fifty years later. So I thought, why not do the same thing with Peanut, but put a *really* twisted take on it with contemporary references and jokes? You hear of hit songs being written on cocktail napkins in a matter of minutes, and that's exactly what happened with my version of this Christmas classic. Twenty minutes after I'd started, I was pretty proud of what was later to become a big part of my act. It certainly wasn't a unique idea, as every holiday season, multiple TV shows, musical artists, and comics come up with a satirical take on that old story, but I made my own version, and it was vintage Peanut.

 Peanut: Everything I do is vintage Peanut. Even the new stuff.

When I started performing it, I realized how much cooler it would be if Brian the Guitar Guy came out and played a Christmas song on electric guitar while Peanut and I read. And, without any rehearsal, we did it onstage. Pretty soon it was a great bit.

We couldn't of course leave out Achmed and "Jingle Bombs," so that became a highlight in the show. Brian wrote "Roadkill Christmas" for Bubba J., and now the special was really coming together. Rothpan and I wrote Christmas and holiday jokes for all the characters, and every night, during every show, we began to turn my regular stage show into the Christmas special. Granted, this was the spring of 2008, and we were doing almost 90 percent Christmas material. But God bless the fans: They loved it. I've found over the years that audiences love being a part of the process, and if they know that they're getting a peek inside what few other people get to see, it makes the process almost a game. That's also one reason I don't mind screwups now and then. As a comic, if you can roll with a mistake or misspoken word, not let it throw you, and then acknowledge to the audience that you're okay playing the fool, the crowd loves it all the more. So every night I would tell the audience that we were practicing for our upcoming Comedy Central Christmas special, and they would go nuts.

It was now June of 2008. Yes, *June.* Granted, a strange time to be pretending it's Christmas, but that was the latest we could shoot to have the special ready to air by Thanksgiving *and* have the DVDs in stores at the same time. We were in Milwaukee, Wisconsin, at the Pabst Theatre . . . the *beautiful* Pabst Theatre. We were set to tape two shows that night as usual, but unbeknownst to the audience and me, a couple of big disturbances were heading our way.

Violent and threatening storms accompanied by tornadoes and

green skies had put Milwaukee under a blanket of heavy rain and lightning, plus tornado warnings. Thirty minutes before curtain, parts of the theater were flooding, and a critical electrical grid went out moments before cameras were to roll. I tried to push all those distractions and concerns out of my head and simply do my best to concentrate on doing the show that I'd done so many times the past few months. What was weighing on me much more heavily than weather and technical difficulties, however, was my precious family, which was in the midst of falling apart. And it wasn't as if that was a problem two thousand miles away that I could just put out of my mind for a couple hours. Quite the opposite.

Ever since I first performed *The Night Before Christmas* with Peanut at our friend Jacquie's party, my wife had encouraged me to put the bit on tape *somewhere* and sell it. I had resisted for many years, wanting to wait until there was a *true* demand for it. I thought it was too good to waste on a cheap production, to then be used as a small moneymaker, hawking the homemade DVDs at comedy clubs. I *knew* it could be big if I just waited for the right time and place. And now we were there.

My family had meant everything to me. I married my wife when I was thirty-two years old, and along with her came two-year-old Bree, her daughter from an earlier relationship. Bree became my daughter when I adopted her not long after the marriage, so my family started to grow very quickly. But as an adopted child myself, I had never known anyone who was related to me by blood, and the first time I held and looked into the eyes of Ashlyn and Kenna, I felt a lifelong isolation slip and melt away. The career was simply a dream and a driving force behind achievement . . . my three children and my wife were my *world*.

In my first three DVDs, you can hear all five of us woven throughout the material, especially in my stand-up. For the Christmas special taping that weekend, my wife and my two youngest were there. It had been decided almost at the last minute for all of them to be there, and I had agreed to it because Christmas had always been the biggest of all holidays for us as a family, and this taping was a significant part of our past because of the Peanut story.

As a marriage comes to an end, I think most couples go through the last throes of existence, trying to either sustain matrimonial life, or rid themselves of unwanted encumbrances. I also think that many of these moments can't be defined as to which type they are—is it a fight to push away or to pull together, or a confusion and convolution of both? While in Milwaukee, though we tried to hide them from the kids, a couple of the arguments were huge and heated. One was even in front of crew and some of the public.

I put my heart and soul into both my family and my professional life, and that night the two sides were pulling me apart again. But just like a sports team can win a game against an unpredictable opponent because of the relentless hours of practice they put in for so long before the game, it was having done the same show over and over throughout the preceding weeks that got me through that night.

Whoever was there for the early show knows that I took a while to find my stride. I started into my stand-up, and very uncharacteristically forgot my lines and my story a mere two minutes into the show. I had to start and stop a couple of times, but finally the adrenaline and the "muscle memory" of having done it so many times kicked in, and twisted Christmas magic began to happen.

We slapped the PC thing in the face right off the bat when Walter came out and I wished him "Happy Holidays." He snapped back with, "Screw you! It's MERRY CHRISTMAS!" to a huge round of applause and even a hoot from the crowd. The funniest part to me about *that* joke was that many of the main players in my career at that time were Jewish, including Rick my agent, Stu our executive producer, Rothpan my head writer, and a few other guys, and they all thought that joke was funny as hell. In fact, if I remember correctly, Rothpan *wrote* that joke! Oy vey!

Achmed altered his own greeting to, "MERRY CHRISTMAS—I KEEL YOU!" and while I read the lovely and traditional *Night Before Christmas*, Peanut managed to demolish it with this kind of banter:

Jeff: And now I will read *The Night Before Christmas*.

Peanut: This would be a good time for the Muslims to go to the bathroom.

Jeff: Peanut, enough. 'Twas the night before Christmas . . .

Peanut: And all the Jews were at the movies.

Jeff: Peanut . . .

Peanut: . . . Eating Chinese food.

Jeff: . . .

Peanut: Sorry. Just trying to include everybody.

Jeff: 'Twas—

Peanut: Hold it!

Jeff: WHAT?

Peanut: Who says 'Twas?

Jeff: It's in the story!

Peanut: It's old and stupid.

Jeff: It's a tradition!

Peanut: 'Tis it?

Later we got to the part about hanging stockings:

Peanut: Seriously, how did *that* tradition start? . . .

Jeff: What?

Peanut: Hanging up dirty laundry hoping Santa would fill it with goodies? "I'd like to suck on this candy cane but it smells like Dad's FEET."

Jeff: . . .

Peanut: Good thing the tradition wasn't a jockstrap. "Sally, what's in yours?" "Nuts."

Jeff: You are RUINING the story!

Peanut: You're the one eating out of your underwear! PERVERT!

Along with all the Christmas and holiday jokes, Achmed sang "Jingle Bombs" and Bubba J. sang "Roadkill Christmas" and Brian of course came out to play along with Bubba J.'s crooning.

Bubba J.: I like to sing in the shower too.

Walter: How about washing, have you thought of doing that while in the shower?

Bubba J.: Huh?

The results of our Christmas in June couldn't have been merrier. When the special finally aired in late November, it drew 6.6 million total viewers, making it Comedy Central's most watched telecast *ever*. The special even surpassed the classic *South Park* episode, "Cartman's Mom Is Still a Dirty Slut," which pulled in 6.2 million viewers in 1998. Proud company to keep, I must say.

Walter: And I was worried about your mother reading *shit happens*. Good lord.

The summer and fall of 2008 included the second of those three surprises I referred to before. The first surprise had been the international acclaim. The second came when ticket sales in theaters in the United States began to exceed the saturation point, and talk of arena shows started. I said, "Do *what*? What do you mean an *arena*?" I had no idea that we would even attempt anything larger than a big theater with three thousand or so people. But now,

Robin and Robert were talking about doing basketball and hockey arenas.

Soon we were filling arenas that sat between five thousand and sixteen thousand people per show. We had huge videos screens as tall as thirty and fifty feet that made it possible for everyone to see the action up close with a view unrivaled by even the front few rows at a small comedy club. "Backstage" was no longer a Green Room with a couch. Now it was subterranean parking with two busses, plus two semis filled with giant packing cases full of lights, sound equipment, and video components. We had our own eleven-member crew with guys that had names like "Psycho" and "Chovy." All hardworking and tireless, they would travel by bus at night, show up at a venue at seven a.m., then spend the entire day rigging and setting up. That night they'd run the two-hour show, then tear everything down, pack it back into the big rigs, and be on the road again at one a.m. and on to the next arena to do it all again.

So without a doubt, we had taken that next crazy step: We'd gone from theaters to the big time. And trust me, I wasn't taking any of this for granted. Every time I'd walk into one of these arenas, I'd look around and just shake my head and think, "How in the *world* did *this* happen?" It was a rock tour, plain and simple.

One of my favorite things to do when we showed up at an arena was to ask the venue's manager what act had been there the night or weekend before us. We'd get answers like Nine Inch Nails, Bon Jovi, George Strait, or the Monster Trucks. I'd usually get a laugh when I'd then say, "And now you have a puppet show."

Sometimes I get the question of what my worst moment onstage was. Well, the scariest *ever* happened in November of 2008 at The Comedy Festival in Las Vegas. I was one of five headliners who would perform solo at the Colosseum at Caesar's, each on a different night. The other comics were Katt Williams, Ellen DeGeneres, Chris Rock, and some guy named Jerry Seinfeld. To be in that venue, on a list with those names, was truly something I didn't take for granted. This was the theater that had been built for Céline Dion many years before. It seated 4,200 people, and I was booked for the Saturday night of the festival. Not only was this an important gig because it was in front of so many industry people, but it was a huge opportunity with Caesar's too: If I did well, there could be a future with them with more bookings, possibly multiple weekends a year. Even a show in an arena with ten thousand people didn't matter as much as this one gig. This could be one of the rare career makers.

The Colosseum was packed, and the applause was thunderous when I walked onstage that night. This was one of those rare times when not only I was enjoying the moment, but so were all the folks around me who had worked long and hard to get me and my little guys on this stage and in this venue. But this night meant more to me than most people realized.

My parents had brought me to Las Vegas when I was twelve years old. We drove around town, looked through a few casinos, and then saw the taping of a very early Siegfried and Roy television special. I remember walking through Caesar's, even back then thinking it had to be the greatest casino on the entire strip. And for twenty years since moving to Los Angeles, I had been visiting the city, playing smaller Vegas rooms that were makeshift comedy clubs, always walking or driving by Caesar's and wondering what it would be like to be on a big stage there with my name up in lights.

Then in September of 1978, Edgar Bergen announced his retirement and that he would be doing his final shows, opening for Andy Williams in Las Vegas. After his performance with Charlie and Mortimer on that last night, his closing words were these:

"Every vaudeville act must have an opening and a closing, so I'll

pack my jokes and my little friends . . . and say . . . good-bye." Edgar
Bergen, the man who had inspired me in my life's work, died in his
sleep that night, having done his final performance at Caesar's Palace.
The irony and the poignancy of this first performance for me at Caesar's was almost too much to add to the evening.

Those closest to me in the audience that night claim they never
knew anything went wrong. Maybe I had done it so many times that
I pulled it off without any noticeable stress. But unlike the Christmas
performance, there was no starting over after a screwup. There was no
kicking it into gear and shaking off cobwebs. It was do or *die*.

I hadn't been onstage for a couple of weeks . . . and I hadn't really
gone over my set before the curtain went up. I just figured it would
all fall into place like usual. Good lord, how many times had I done
this show?

After Brian did his set, then the video intro ran, I came out, did
my stand-up, then got Walter out first, as usual. But about three minutes into Walter's segment, my mind started to wander. There was
nothing unusual about that. Sometimes I'll find myself in the middle
of a performance thinking about where I wanted to have dinner, or
if the Cowboys were doing well this season, or if I'd left the lights on
in the kitchen . . . that night, however, my mind began to wander to
a not-so-safe place. I started thinking about where I was and what I
was doing and who was watching. Then suddenly, WAY out of left
field, some kind of weird panic attack hit me and both sides of my
brain jumped the tracks and everything came to a grinding halt. I had
absolutely no idea what came next. I didn't even know what joke Walter had just told, yet I was hearing the laughter die down in typical
timing, but there was nothing next. Nothing. I didn't know what was
supposed to be said and by whom, nor could I even remember any
other joke or bit of Walter's that I could jump to while I figured out
where I'd left off. And THEN, for the first time in my life onstage, I
started getting light-headed. The room started to swim and I could

just begin to hear that buzzing sound. I suddenly felt clammy, sweat formed on my brow, and I felt my knees go weak. The laugh was now finished and silence had enveloped the Colosseum. And just as I was about to falter and either faint or admit to the audience that I was lost, some instinct of fight-or-flight must have kicked in, because the next joke exploded in front of me and Walter was talking again. As he spoke, I had to consciously regain composure and force myself not to think about anything other than performing, plus not fall over or drop Walter. I just had to do my act.

I have no idea how long that moment lasted. Everyone told me that there was never a single pause or hiccup in the show. I could have sworn it was obvious to everyone, and that I must have looked like a zombie for at least a few seconds. You'd think I'd look back at that story as a funny one . . . but I don't! It was just too dang scary. Kind of like *almost* being run over by a bus. I've never looked back at that tape, and I really don't want to. I don't remember where exactly in Walter's routine it happened, and I don't care. All that mattered was, Caesar's keeps having us back, but I won't go onstage there ever again without cheat notes in my back pocket!

Early 2009 was spent much like the previous year, doing arenas and traveling the country. But after the ratings from the Christmas special, Comedy Central was now willing to do a lot more with us. As the press called it, we made a full 360-degree deal with CC, which included promises of a fourth special and DVD, a television show, a touring sponsorship, and extensive merchandise development and sales.

Next on the agenda was my first European tour. When they brought the idea to me, I thought for certain we were talking about just England and Ireland . . . you know, where *English* is spoken most of the time. I was mistaken. The YouTube clips and Comedy Central specials had made Achmed and company superstars in some incredibly unexpected parts of globe. So on this first jaunt, we played sold-out arena gigs in not only London, England, but also in the Scandinavian cities of Stockholm, Copenhagen, Helsinki, and Oslo. You'd think that these would have been difficult gigs at the very least, and that the translation of language, not to mention the translation of the sense of humor would have been tough as well. Honestly, exactly the opposite happened. Those crowds of between four thousand and eight thousand people each ate up almost every joke each night. *Boy* did they know the characters.

Spark of Insanity and the Christmas special DVDs had been released in Europe, but not my first one, *Arguing*. So since Bubba J. was only in *Arguing* and hadn't yet been introduced into the marketplace, no way would any of the Europeans know who he was. I was in for a big surprise.

The opening show of the tour was in London at the Apollo Hammersmith, a beautiful and historic venue where everyone from Mr. Bean to the Beatles had played. I'd brought Bubba J. along, but had left him at the hotel that afternoon, simply because I knew I wouldn't need him, since no one knew who he was. Well, the video opening that we'd brought with us to start the show included a quick appearance of Bubba J. As each character came on screen, the audience would hoot and holler for their favorites. As we got close to the Bubba J. clip, Brian and I were standing backstage listening to the crowd, and I said, "Oops . . . forgot about Bubba J. These guys are going to be clueless. Should have cut him out of the video here."

I was dumbfounded when little white trash Bubba came on screen talking about Budweiser and Walmart, and the crowd went nuts. What the HELL? Needless to say, Bubba J. made it into the shows on the rest of the tour, and was somehow a highlight. Go figure.

The audiences in Europe loved the show, and later in 2009, we made another international trek, heading down under to Australia, playing Melbourne and Sydney for two shows in each city. Equally enthusiastic as the Europeans, the Aussies made it obvious that we'd be returning for more shows there sometime soon.

The Jeff Dunham Show was a television project that many great people put all their efforts into, although it wasn't exactly the concept I had envisioned and sought all those years: For almost two decades, I had imagined doing nothing but a sitcom. However, Comedy Central just didn't *do* traditional sitcoms, so we had to come up with something that made sense for the network, but also fit the characters and me. We decided to create a television show that showed the characters interacting with the real world. We would put them in real-life situations and with ordinary people. Sometimes I would be in the segments, and sometimes I would not. It made perfect sense to all of us *and* the network.

Writers wrote and the wheels turned. We taped and edited for many months and then shot the live studio pieces with studio audiences, introducing the taped segments. It turned out to be an incredibly expensive production, almost double the typical Comedy Central budget. But the live audiences in studio *loved* it. Everyone backstage *knew* we had a hit on our hands.

When the series finally premiered in late 2009, ratings were off the charts, but we knew not to get too excited, because in television, rarely do ratings for subsequent airings stay as high as a premiere. We also didn't mind some of the show's critics, because those people weren't our audience. There were plenty of other successful shows on the air that were far more offensive than what we were doing, so we let that stuff roll off our backs. If someone was screaming about what they didn't like on our show, that would make other people tune in because they thought *that* part was the funniest.

After a few weeks, the ratings finally settled down to what normally would have been good numbers for Comedy Central. We were coming in just below their number one program, *South Park*. The problem was, because our show was so much more expensive than anything else they had on the air, it was beginning to look like it would be a nonprofit venture. Comedy Central didn't cancel the series, as they kept airing and repeating the episodes. They did, however, choose not to renew the series.

In the end, it didn't surprise me, and I tried not to view it as a failure, but more as a learning experience. In Bergen's movies from the 1940s, there were scenes with Charlie by himself or interacting with other actors in the films, without Bergen. We utilized the same formula in our television show, with my characters being independent of me now and then. We thought those pieces worked and were really funny, but what we found in research in the following months was that *those* were the segments that audiences really *didn't* like. In other words, people most wanted to see the guys and me *together*. What we didn't realize until too late was that for the viewing audience, this is when the magic truly happens; it isn't just the characters coming to life—it's the relationship between us that makes the best comedy. Also, when I was alongside the characters, it helped knock the wind out of some of the outlandish things the little guys would say. That's how it works onstage too. If one of the characters tells a joke that's offensive, I'm always right there to counter it and argue with their sometimes callous sensibilities. It's a comedy team. I'm the Abbott to the Costello, the Penn to the Teller. Those individuals are funniest working *together*, and so it was with me and the guys.

Peanut: We learned a valuable lesson that day . . . that there is no *i* in *team*.

Bubba J.: But there is in *ice cream*.

In the end, we could easily point to the segments that were audience favorites, and to those that didn't work as well. The exception to this line of thinking was my favorite piece: Achmed and the U.S. Marines. I say it was my favorite, because I couldn't believe we were actually where we were, doing what we were doing. It was also, however, one of the most difficult segments to tape, mainly because I had to put myself and Achmed in incredibly unnatural positions that kept me sore for days afterward. But on shoot day, when we landed by helicopter at Camp Pendleton, the actual marine training base just north of San Diego, I was stoked. Here we were, working with actual U.S. Marines, who all said they loved Achmed, and who wanted their picture taken with him. I was like a proud dad . . . in a weirdly twisted kind of way.

In addition to the real one, we also had a few stunt Achmeds that we blew up and had run over by giant military vehicles. Plus, Achmed got screamed at pretty brutally by a few of the training officers, and *that* made *me* laugh. To see Achmed on screen trying to do push-ups with these guys in his face like he was a real recruit was just too darned funny.

Another segment that involved Achmed gave me the heebie jeebies for a few weeks afterward. The setup was that the little terrorist had never had a proper funeral, so now he wanted one. We went to an actual mortuary and Achmed took the tour. What made the episode not so fun for me was when he had to sit up from inside a coffin he was trying out, to talk to the funeral director. There was only one way to be able to make this work: We had the top half of the coffin opened so Achmed could lie down, then sit up. But to operate him, I had to get *inside* the casket and then ball up into the fetal position in the lower portion of the casket with that half of the lid *shut*. I had a flashlight to see my notes, and could hear the muffled sounds of everyone talking . . . but no actual contact with the living world. *THAT* was creepy. And by the way, I know what it feels like to lie in a real coffin now. (Lots of springs and not much back support.) Sheesh.

Also scattered through 2009 were a good number of notable national television appearances as well as some big-time articles on me and the guys. Bonnie Hunt and Carson Daly welcomed us, as did Leno and David Letterman again. . . .

Oh yeah . . . Letterman . . . now *that's* a difficult one to even *remember what happened* . . .

The next showbiz tale I'd like to relate is probably the absolute closest I've ever come to a crashing and burning on national television. It has a happy ending, but it was close . . . oh, so very close.

We had just flown back from our first European tour and I took basically a nap at home in Los Angeles, before then jumping on another plane and heading out for a full weekend of shows in Northern California. No rest for the weary. After the Sunday night show, I then hopped a red-eye across the country to New York City, where we landed at about eight a.m. I backtracked three days in my head, and realized that the miserable cold I now had, I must have picked up on that long, stuffy, international flight from Europe. A guy in front of me was sneezing and sniffling and hacking the whole time, and I was run down as could be. I was now suffering the consequences with *his* cold.

 Achmed: There is nothing worse than you getting a cold.

 Jeff: Why do you say that?

 Achmed: I haven't exactly figured it out, but if *you* get a cold, the rest of us sound like crap.

I took a long and laborious cab ride to a hotel in Manhattan for a three-hour nap, because I then had to get over to the Ed Sullivan Theater to appear on *Letterman* . . . again. (Remember, they tape in the afternoon, not at night.) I was constantly making sure I kept the postnasal drip to a minimum, because *that's* what would take my voice away. I had tea, honey, throat lozenges, plus day- and nighttime cold medicine. As my alarm blared around noon, I went into the bathroom and downed what was to be a well-timed daytime, very powerful and effective cold medicine. I'd planned for exactly when the best time to take it would be for the most relief at the most opportune time for performing, and that was right then. As I threw away the now-empty cardboard box of Alka-Seltzer Plus Daytime Cold Medicine, I turned to walk out of the bathroom. Then I stopped.

"Wait a minute," I thought, "I don't *have* any more daytime cold medicine. I was going to buy some more. Oh shit!" I ran back to the trash can and yanked out the box. "Ohhhh . . . shit!" I yelled again. Then a few *more* colorful words came flying out of my mouth too.

I hadn't taken any daytime cold medicine because I didn't have any more. In my stupor, I had downed two Alka-Seltzer Plus *Nighttime* tablets. HOLY CRAP.

I'm a lightweight when it comes to medicine. I rarely take any, so when I *do* ingest them, *they work*.

Rehearsal was in an hour and the actual show began taping in three hours. "HOLY CRAP," I thought again. Everything went through my mind in a second. I had never made myself throw up before, plus I figured the stuff was already in my system since it was in liquid form . . . "Crap, crap, holy crap . . ."

 Peanut: I couldn't stop laughing.

Jeff: It wasn't funny.

 Peanut: That's why it was soooo funny.

Big shows and these national television spots are always performances I prepare and *over*prepare for. I try to work like an athlete— eating and drinking just the right things, exercising, and rehearsing just the right amount in the right timing to make sure the body and mind are in the best shape to do the best performance possible. I had no idea what to do about *this* screwup. It threw off *everything*.

I got my clothes and Peanut together and headed over to the set. Robin was there since he'd been with me for the weekend run, and I told him what happened. "Go get a carton of Red Bull!" I pleaded. "That's the only thing I can think of!" I always drink one small Red Bull before every show, but this time it was going to be *a lot more*. "SUGAR FREE!" I yelled after him as he ran down the steps.

I was starting to feel heaviness behind my eyes. "Good god," I thought. The memories of those moments are a little blurry now, but I know I made my way downstairs and to the stage. Waiting for me were a couple of producers, plus all the stage guys, Paul and the band, and *everyone* important. I figured I would be able to push through the rehearsal with just a little haziness from the meds.

Almost every story and every moment in my life that I've written about in this book I can recall in great detail, no matter how long ago it was . . . except for *this* one. It's all very fuzzy. I remember that I got a few lines into a very simple four-minute routine and then stopped . . . I repeated a joke I'd just done, then hit a roadblock. The medicine was now hitting me full force and I was doing everything

I could just to hold my eyes open and keep Peanut from falling over. Keep in mind that *everyone* was watching me, including possibly Letterman, who was probably at a monitor somewhere thinking he was being punked. I started and stopped a couple more times, then had to ask what the last joke I'd just told was.

The guys back in the control room as well the director and producers were probably looking at each other, thinking "Is he drunk? What's wrong with him? Can we even use him?"

I remember that I stopped and asked for someone to print out the jokes that I had e-mailed to the show a few days before. I knew I could do it by looking at that sheet. I then explained very truthfully what had happened, apologized, and reassured them wholeheartedly that I would be fine for the actual show. Honestly, I don't remember much more than that, other than downing about four Red Bulls minutes before I hit the stage.

Adrenaline, a little extra time, and energy drinks were my friends that day. The spot went great and I was certainly happier with it than the time before, when I was censored and edited. My team and I all laughed about it later, and it's become a great story, but I've also tried to learn something meaningful from the experience, and I think it's this: DON'T FORGET THE RED BULL.

Bubba J.: You shoulda had a beer.

Jeff: Beer would have made it worse.

Bubba J.: Yeah, but you wouldn't have cared.

I got my first big break with *The Tonight Show*, and since then, NBC has always been very good to me. I'm a big admirer of Jay Leno, because for thirtysomething years now, he has been one of the hardest working stand-ups in the business, constantly traveling coast to coast, performing in every venue imaginable. He is tireless and committed, and when it comes to hosting *The Tonight Show*, no one can argue with his numbers. After an almost ten-year hiatus from being on with Jay, however, I made up for lost time and appeared three times on *The Tonight Show* in 2009. The third appearance that year took me and my people, as well as Leno and the producers, by surprise. In December, I was booked on the show to promote my Comedy Central show. The plan was for me to have a brief chat with Jay by myself, telling a quick story, then pull Peanut out for a few jokes. They asked me to have two or three stories ready for my solo part of the interview, with questions given to Jay in advance to lead me into the tales. Well, my first story, which was a true one about tricking Rothpan into going to a Miley Cyrus concert with me and my girls, went so well that Jay decided to forgo the dummy part of things, and just let me tell another story without a dummy. My entire appearance on *The Tonight Show* that night, unlike any other time or on any other show, was only *me*. Peanut never made it out of the suitcase. For the first time ever on television, I was just *me*.

 Peanut: Congratulations on that solo appearance.

 Jeff: Thanks, Peanut.

Peanut: It only took thirty-eight years for you to be funny without me.

After my segment, I walked back to my dressing room, and there waiting for me all stone-faced, waiting for my reaction, was my little entourage of management, agents, and publicists. Since I never got to do my thing with Peanut, they didn't know if I was going to be happy or ticked off. I was doing everything short of a jig. This had been a *big* deal.

As 2009 was coming to a close, there were articles on me and the guys in *USA Today*, *Time* magazine, the *Los Angeles Times*, and *The New York Times*. It seemed like we were all over the place, and I was in the middle of a whirlwind career, like I'd never known before.

Now in this tale of my life comes the third of those big surprises that I've been talking about. This also happens to be the *most* important one, and that's why I saved it for last. It's a dream come true and something that I never, EVER thought could possibly happen. Ready? Here it is: I have actually become *cool* to my teenage daughters.

I don't know exactly how it happened, or exactly what I did. (Is it all simply because of Comedy Central and YouTube?) I will qualify it by saying that maybe it's just my imagination, but it *seems* that I have become one of those few, very lucky parents who have the honor of seemingly *not* being an embarrassment to their children. Honestly, my daughters don't seem to mind when I hang around, or take them and their friends to dinner. Also, I THINK they like hanging out with friends at my house, even though I'm pretty strict. ("NO BOYS UPSTAIRS" . . . that kind of thing.) Granted, it could be that I just have incredibly kind and loving daughters who don't want to hurt my feelings, or (and I do mean *or . . .*) I just *might* be funny *even to them.* . . . But that seems like a long shot.

Walter: Long shot.

Peanut: Long shot.

Achmed: Long shot.

Bubba J.: My tooth is loose.

Thank you, my loving and beautiful daughters! You don't ever need to buy me another present; just keep letting me hang. Oh, and please keep downloading songs on my iPhone. Thanks to you, I seem hip to friends when they look at my playlists.

The year 2009 ended with me playing a part in the Steve Carell–Paul Rudd movie *Dinner for Schmucks.* Though I had a small part, it was my first feature film, and I introduced a new character that I created just for the movie. Diane was the only dummy I've ever built that is . . . well . . . anatomically correct, at least from the waist up! Besides her head, I also sculpted her upper torso, and she has some darned impressive boobs, I must say. It was one of the few times that my daughters steered clear of my workshop at all costs, but I thought the body was very tastefully cre- ated *art.* Well, it was art up until the point that the movie's paint guys got a hold of the body. It quickly went from art to pornography. In full color her breasts were even *more* impressive, I must say.

One of the coolest parts about being in that movie was where we were on location to shoot the exterior scene of the mansion burning down: It was the original Wayne Manor! Bruce Wayne's mansion from the original 1960s Batman television series! But alas, no Bat Cave: I checked thoroughly.

Besides the sound of laughter, one of the most rewarding parts of all that has happened in the past few years has been the ability and opportunity to give back to people in need. Beginning in 2009, I decided to take a dollar from every ticket sold in the arena and theater dates and put the money aside for charity. When a significant amount has amassed, my business manager and I decide where to distribute the funds. Most of the time, we've given to food banks in cities that have unemployment rates greater than ten percent. It's been a truly great experience for everyone involved. I present the check onstage at the end of a show to a representative from the local food bank, and the audience is able to see what *they* helped to do.

Of all the times and places we've been able to give, my hands-down favorite was at the American Airlines Center in Dallas, where I was performing for thirteen thousand people. It felt like a homecoming show of sorts. We gave $50,000 to the Dallas Food Bank, and $50,000 to the Salvation Army where my mother still volunteers. I had Mom walk out onstage and help give the check. Then all thirteen thousand people sang "Happy Birthday" to my eighty-year-old sweet mom. Dad was having a little trouble with steps at the time, so he got to watch and listen just offstage on a monitor. It was a magical time for all three of us.

Also that night, I gave $10,000 to a representative from the

Dallas Public Library for an overdue fine. In 1972 I checked out the book *Fun with Ventriloquism* by Alexander Van Rensselaer and never returned it. I pulled out the exact book and showed it to her and the laughing crowd. I then handed her the check, but wouldn't let her touch the book. I of course still have it.

 Walter: Ten grand? Holy crap!

 Jeff: Pretty cool, huh?

 Walter: No, I still have a library book from 1966!

As is pretty obvious, I love this quirky little art of ventriloquism. I consider myself to be one of those lucky people who happened to have found something at a very early age that I had a passion for. I've worked very hard to achieve some lofty goals, but I've always been supported by family and friends, plus I've been blessed by my Maker, and along the way I've had a lot of help from a handful of some very significant and great people. There's also the fact that my parents pray for me constantly, and I'm pretty sure that's a big part of why things have gone so well for so long. Until I decide to call it quits, I hope this all keeps going and growing, because right now I simply can't think of anything I'd rather be doing.

As I type these final thoughts, I'm sitting on a plane, flying back to the United States from our second tour of Europe. This time we did shows all over England, Ireland, and Holland, repeating one city from our first tour, where I was delighted, amazed, and honored to have played a second time in London, but this time at the 02 Arena in

front of twelve thousand laughing Brits. In a few months we're heading to South Africa for some shows, and there's even talk of China.
"How the *heck*—?"

       Bubba J.: China! Cool.

       Jeff: What do you want to see in China if we go?

       Bubba J.: USA town.

       Walter: Please, PLEASE will someone just put a bag over
his head?

       Bubba J.: That was my Halloween costume last year!

The loves of my life, my daughters, Bree, Ashlyn, and Kenna, are all
doing great, and I couldn't be a more proud father. As for my time
spent offstage, I continue to fly helicopters, and I'm just now beginning to build my fourth kit. It will probably take a couple of years to
complete, but I'm pretty sure this one will have Achmed painted on
the side!

I love American Muscle Cars both old and new, and as I have since
the first Macintosh was introduced in 1984, I love all things Apple. As

for new horizons, both Peanut and Walter have an old subject to kid me about, because I'm dating again. . . .

When I first met Audrey, she had no idea who I was or what I did for living. She'd never heard of me or Peanut or Achmed, nor any kind of pepper on a stick. You might think that would have tromped on my ego a bit. On the contrary, it was refreshing. There were no preconceived expectations or suppositions, and never once during any of our first dates did she ask me to make something talk!

 Walter: I'm still not sure she knows what you do for a living.

Audrey just knew me as the guy who asked her out for a cup of coffee one day after being attracted to her by nothing more than her smile. As sappy as it sounds, the very first time I saw her, she was a sunshine that warmed me from the inside out . . . birds tweeted, butterflies flew around . . .

 Walter: Please stop!

 Peanut: I'm going to puke.

As a certified nutritionist and personal trainer, Audrey continuously has a handful of clients, and she also competes in bodybuilding competitions herself. She comes out on the road with Robin and Brian and me and the rest of the crew, encouraging all of us to eat more healthfully and exercise regularly.

Bubba J: She tells me to limit my kegs.

Most importantly, however, Audrey brought a peace and happiness into my life that I hadn't known for a very long time. John, Robert, Robin, Brian, and Judi had helped me through my darkest days as the best of friends do. And now after so long, I feel and share unconditional love with someone very special.

The biggest vote of acceptance of Audrey into my life came from the people whose perspective I cared about the most: my parents. The first time they met her, we all had lunch at the café in Nordstrom in University Park, which is a few miles north of downtown Dallas. It had been a long time since I'd watched anyone meet my parents for the first time. Through Audrey's eyes, I got to see two of the most wonderful people I've ever known. I'd forgotten how charming and engaging and *funny* both my parents actually are. I think that sometimes we forget about the best traits of those we love the most because we start to take who they are for granted. We grow to overlook the best parts of people we're closest to. I saw my mother and father through fresh, genuine, kind, and loving eyes. And just as important, my parents adored Audrey from their first meeting.

Understandably, the acceptance of someone new in my life has taken more time for my daughters. Even now, a day doesn't go by that I'm not saddened at what happened to my marriage and our family. So much happened in the subsequent days after January of 2008, that even the family therapist has said many times that there is no going back. So . . . we move on. Life is short and precious, and I learned from my parents, and then later on my own, that laughter is not only an elixir, but a sustenance to life. And as Audrey has taught me, happiness is a *choice*. Onward and upward . . .

Walter: Good book.

Peanut: Sweet ending.

Achmed: Don't tell anyone I had a tear!

Bubba J.: I love endings.

José: Too bad it's over, señor.

Jeff: Well, thanks guys. Actually, there's still
an afterword—

Walter: Aw, hell!

Achmed: It's endless!

José: My eyes hurt.

Peanut: Is this more romantic crap?

AFTERWORD

One of my favorite lines from the Christmas special was when Achmed said, "Killing folks is easy. Being politically correct is a pain in the ass."

I've tried to figure out exactly what it is that has made Achmed and the characters popular and gain notoriety within so many walks of life and in so many diverse cultures throughout the United States and around the world. I think that if a critic bashes me, he's wagging his or her finger at exactly what most other people like and what has taken my career to where it is: I don't care about being politically correct and I think it's funny *not* to be. I also think that's what a comic does: He pushes buttons. After that, it boils down to taste. Either you like it or you don't. No one is forcing you to eat a particular food. If you don't like it, leave it alone. So if you don't like my comedy, change the channel and please, whatever you do, don't buy and watch the DVD. But if you *do* like it, the oven is hot and I'll be dishing out some more. The little guys in my trunk and I hope to see you at one of our shows very soon. We really do.

Jeff Dunham
June 14, 2010

ACKNOWLEDGMENTS

"Who did I leave out?" That was the question that started banging around in my head a few weeks ago when this book project was nearing the finish line. There have been countless people throughout the years whose stories you still haven't heard, and some of whose names I'll leave out even in this acknowledgments section. There are just too darned many people to thank throughout this forty-year pursuit. So to those friends, family members, and business associates whose names aren't in these pages, I offer my sincere apologies, but thank you universally.

 Walter: He really hates you.

 Jeff: No, I don't.

 Walter: Whatever.

And as for the very few of you throughout the years with whom there has been any type of friction or disagreement . . .

 Achmed: We will KEEL you!

 Jeff: No we won't.

 Achmed: Then *I* will!

Jeff: Nope.

 Achmed: DARN!

Although it is often easier said than done, I try my best to forgive and forget, and I hope the same can be applied to me, if and when I have been the offender.

 Walter: You're full of crap.

 Jeff: Thank you.

There are a few names, however, that I simply can't leave out, and I'll start with the ventriloquist world. Some of my oldest friends I met in 1975 at the very first ventriloquist convention, and we've been together almost every summer since, sharing laughs and experiences and biscuits and gravy at two a.m. in Chaucer's at the Drawbridge. Al Semok, Mark Wade, Al Getler, Pete Michaels, Bob Rumba, Lynn Trefzger-Joy, Clinton Detweiler, Jimmy Nelson, Dale Brown, Liz VonSeggen, Bob Isaacson, Ken Groves, Jerry Layne, Gary Owen, Lee Cornell, Nacho Estrada, Phillip Jones, Bob Hamill, Brook Brooking, Harold Crocker, and Bill DeMar.

And to Annie Roberts and Lisa Sweasy, both former curators of the Vent Haven Museum, as well as our newest curator, Jen Dawson, thank you for your continued support of our art and for your tireless work to make and keep the museum alive and growing. (I actually hope the smell in building 2 never goes away.)

And, finally, Mr. Tom Ladshaw . . . Tom is a fellow vent, but he is also one of my favorite people in the whole world to hang out with. . . . Not just because he knows seemingly everything there is to know about ventriloquism and its history, but mainly because he's one of the kindest and warmest souls I've ever met. As for helping me on this book, I would phone Tom at the weirdest hours of night and day while I was writing, checking facts and making sure I got all historic things regarding "vent" correct. If there is anything in this book having to do with ventriloquism that I've misquoted or is incorrect, it's only because I forgot to ask Tom about it. Tom, thank you for your unending help on this book, but most of all, a very special thanks to you and Leslye for your friendship and support these past couple of years. I always look forward to being with you guys, anywhere, anytime.

And now, my managers and closest business associates, Robert Hartmann, Judi Brown Marmel, John Power, and Stu Schreiberg. Thank you for your teamwork and unending dedication and friendship, and helping build my career to what it is today.

Robert, the days in the late eighties and early nineties at the old Irvine Improv seem very long ago, when you were merely a club manager and I was a struggling middle act trying to prove myself. Thank you for so much support, and for staying with me on this long road, fighting to book me when others didn't believe I would sell tickets.

Judi, you saw the vision with me long before it happened, so thank you for your faith and determination and tireless work. When no one else got it, you did and you wouldn't give up. Thank you.

John, you've been not only my business manager and accountant, but along with Robert and Judi, you too are one of my closest friends, and have been, throughout the good and the bad, the past decade. Thank you for the sound business advice and guidance, but mainly for the camaraderie and friendship. One of the most fun times of my life was the three days we spent in Corvettes at the Bob Bondurant's Grand Prix Racing School a few months ago, and the memories of slamming on the brakes at 115 mph with you only a few feet behind still makes me laugh. We'll do it again soon.

And Stu, thank you for your creativity and skills and enthusiasm when putting what I do on tape, and helping build the catalog of work that has kept things moving for us for so long and so well.

To my agent, Matt Blake, as well as all the other guys at CAA who explore countless ways to push my career forward, Jason Heyman, Martin Lesak, Jon Levin, and Steve Smooke. Thank you for your accomplishments and continued pursuits on my behalf.

Thanks also to my agent of many years, Rick Greenstein. Rick, I followed you from William Morris and then to Gersh, and we had well over a decade of working together, and I thank you for the big part you played in all this for so long.

Kelly Asbury: Thank you for your friendship and the laughs and the advice, both in business and personally. Our love for ventriloquism and then the paralleling of our careers have made me proud to call you one of my very best friends. Can't wait for more sunshine and drinks on a beach somewhere with you and Jacquie. . . . Also, congratulations on your future life together.

David Erskine: We have been friends since the days you took snapshots of me on the steps of the Southern Palace at Six Flags over Texas. Thank you for many years of advice, knowledge, and wisdom regarding all things vent and Bergen.

To Debbie Keller, my longtime friend and publicist. . . . Thank you for your vision and belief in what this all could become and for being such a huge part of making it happen. You're the best, Debbie!

To Elaine Shock, my *other* publicist and friend. Though you haven't been in this camp as long as Debbie, your work has also been invaluable and I can't wait to see what lies ahead. . . . Thank you.

To Mary Ann Taylor, who has taken up where Verna left off. Thank you for keeping Peanut alive and fresh and looking great for so many to love.

To Marnell White and Steve Quinn and our eleven crew guys who work tirelessly on the road with Robin Tate, making all our crazy live arena shows run so smoothly, thank you.

To Tom Burrington, our bus driver, who has a steady hand at the wheel and has always managed to keep the shiny side up and the dirty side down. . . . Thank you, Tom.

And though I already talked about them in the book, my heartfelt thanks and big man-hugs to my good friends Robin Tate and Brian "Guitar Guy" Haner, with whom I have shared so many experiences and countless hours on the road in every corner of North America, and now beyond. . . . Thank you for the warmth of friendship and the sweat of making those gigs kick ass . . . and we're nowhere near finished.

To my longtime friend and a guy who makes me laugh more than anyone, Jeff Rothpan. Thanks, buddy, for your hard work and welcomed, twisted sense of humor. Some of my favorite moments in life have been on the bus with you, Robin, Brian, and Audrey, laughing until we almost passed out. Don't stop, my friend.

To Jimmy Nelson: Thank you, sir, for teaching me this art.

To Carrie Thornton, my editor; Peter McGuigan, my book agent; and all the folks at Dutton who have made this project a possibility and now a reality, thank you.

To the countless others who have represented me and worked so very hard, or who have simply been great support and encouragement along the way: Gary Brightwell, Randy Chalawsky, Matt McNeil, Jim Ricker, Derek Van Pelt, Reg Tigerman, Darrin McAfee, Dave Harrison, John Bravakis, Steve Kroopnick, Myra Byrne, Stacy Hashimoto, Stefani Schmacker, Mike Carano, Max Smith, Kevin Moshier, Steve Marmel, Dave Bernath, Brooke Isbell, Susan Egan, Dawn Able, Bruce Ryan, Tammy Dorman, Mike Lacey, Bill Blumenreich, Jimmy Finn, Tommy Williams, Bruce Ayers, Janet George, Les and Pam McCurdy, Rebecca O'Sullivan Schulte, Brenda Garcia, Bob Foster, Barry Gordon, Richard Buchalter, Garrett Lee, Diana Flaherty, Sandy Terranova, Melanie Mandles, Katherine Sellwood, Andrew Dorfman, Brian Dorfman, Steve Twersky, Beth Rakow, Anna Derparseghian, Jason Brown, Alex Kraemer, Michael Gasser, Barbara Tron, Tsoler Kojan, Angelica Vasquez, Jack Sinoryan, Brian Poor, Gary and Carmen Busk, Tom and Isa Brown, Jeff Endlich, Marty Singer, Joseph Bon Jovi, Anthony "Chovy" Bell, Michael Korpi, Corey Carbonara, Lisa Dent, Skip Mahaffey, Dan and Gerri Abrahamsen, and Paul and Beth Moore, as well as the late Eric Azarcon, thanks to all of you.

And finally, once again, thanks to my mom and dad for a lifetime of love and support. To my daughters, whom I love more than I could ever express: Kenna, Ashlyn, and Bree, thanks for loving me and for making me so proud and happy to be your father. To Audrey, who has been a precious gift, and has brightened my life in the darkest of times, growing into someone I love and cherish beyond measure. Oh . . . and speaking of love . . . I can't leave out Bill, my golden retriever and best buddy, and who was the only other male in my houseful of women for more than twelve years. Just last night, as I was finishing these final words, he died quietly in his sleep. I'll miss you, boy. I hope someday we'll be playing together again. . . .

jd

Jeff Dunham is a comedian and ventriloquist whose record-breaking specials on Comedy Central launched a global phenomenon of sold-out live concerts, DVD sales, and consumer products. A frequent guest on *The Tonight Show* and *Late Show with David Letterman*, he remains the only person to ever win the prestigious Ventriloquist of the Year award twice. In 2009 and 2010 he was named the top-grossing live comedy act in the world by *Pollstar*, and *Time* magazine called him the most popular comedian in the United States. Dunham regularly plays to sold-out arenas in North America, Europe, the UK, South Africa, and Australia. He has three beautiful daughters and lives in Los Angeles.